What leaders are saying about Go

"If you are looking for a 'quick fix, read at the beach' leadership book, ***Good King / Bad King*** is not for you. However, if you are serious about your leadership and want to lead at the highest level God has equipped you for, ***Good King / Bad King*** is for you. It is easy to read, comprehensive, inspiring and practical. I highly recommend this book; it can change the trajectory of your life and leadership."

Dick Wells
CEO (ret.), The Aerostructures Corporation

"***Good King / Bad King*** is the summation of 30+ years of real world leadership experience grounded in a biblical foundation. By implementing the principles explained in this book, we were able to inspire the employees of a 74-year-old company to achieve more. Anyone wanting to lead and inspire his or her organization or group needs to learn from Leon's exceptional career and life spent learning. This book is that opportunity."

Eddie Lunn, III
President, Boiler Supply Company, Inc.

"There are many rules and laws of leadership that fill the pages of books in the leadership section of my personal library, and now there is a *must read* book by Leon Drennan that distills all of them down to the ***Good King / Bad King*** for those who want to lead with their heart and head for the Lord. A masterfully scripted dance of leadership principles rooted in biblical foundation jumps off the pages and into business and life applications in this fascinating and memorable approach to organizational and personal success. Definitely one of the top five leadership books in my personal library."

Mark Rainey
Founder and President, Rainey Consulting Group, LLC

"When I read Leon Drennan's book, ***Good King / Bad King***, I realized that I would have profited so much from these principles by following them. Mr. Drennan has taken the principles taught by God and applied them to our secular needs. I would hope that every person in a position of responsible leadership will read and follow these wise teachings. The author has written from the platform of many years of experience and relates the lessons he learned from what works, and what does not work, to produce success in the marketplace."

Gerald Stow
Retired Pastor and Children's Home Executive Administrator

GOOD KING
BAD KING

WHICH ONE ARE YOU?

THE 5 ESSENTIALS FOR
ORGANIZATIONAL AND PERSONAL SUCCESS

Leon Drennan

Vision Leadership Foundation
Brentwood, TN

Published by Vision Leadership Foundation, Brentwood, TN 37027

ISBN 978-0-9904033-0-2

Scripture quoted in this book comes from one of the three sources noted below:

Scripture taken from KING JAMES VERSION, public domain.

Scripture taken from the NEW AMERICAN STANDARD BIBLE®, Copyright © 1960 1962,1963,1968,1971,1972,1973,1975,1977,1995 by The Lockman Foundation. Used by permission.

Scripture taken from THE HOLY BIBLE, NEW INTERNATIONAL VERSION®, NIV® Copyright © 1973, 1978, 1984, 2011 by Biblica, Inc.® Used by permission. All rights reserved worldwide.

The contents of this book are based on my recollection and understanding of Scripture as inspired by the Spirit, a lifetime of leadership experience in a large complex organization, as well as the observation of others in leadership roles. My thoughts were influenced by some great books and Christian authors as referenced in this book. Any perceived similarities to leadership or management materials in the marketplace are coincidental except those which I have specifically cited. — Leon Drennan, Vision Leadership Foundation.

For more information about Vision Leadership Foundation, please visit:

www.Vision-Leadership.com

or, contact Leon Drennan at leon@vision-leadership.com

Dedication

This book is dedicated in loving memory of my mom and dad who taught me to work hard, persevere and pursue God. Also, to my children Scott, Allyson, and Kelsey—in birth order. They bring me great joy and gave me three good reasons to persevere. Finally, and most importantly, to my wife Debbie who has loved me unconditionally for thirty-six years and who has persevered with me. She is my greatest single joy on this earth. She was the first one to know for sure that God wanted me to write this book.

Acknowledgments

I appreciate the Frist family and all the leaders at HCA, too many to mention by name, who allowed me to serve and learn in a great organization for thirty-one years. I thank Diana Rush, my executive assistant of many years and trusted friend, who worked a full time job and helped in her spare time with formatting and graphics in this book. Thanks to Jim Baker, Brian Ball, Debbie Drennan, Tom Hall, Louis Joseph, Billy King, Prentis McGoldrick, Jim Patton, Mark Rainey, Joe Steakley, Gerald Stow, Jim Tyson, and Vail Willis who read this and gave me such valuable feedback. Finally, I thank all my past colleagues, employees, peers and associates for the fun we had together, what I learned from them, what we accomplished together and, most importantly, for their friendship. Thank you, Teresa DeMonico for your diligence in editing this manuscript. Also, a big thank you to Scott Drennan and Darrel Girardier for your inspiring work and design of the book cover. A special thanks goes to Fred MacKrell at AuthorTrack.com, who guided me in every major phase of this project. Thanks also for adding your creativity to the graphics and layout of the book.

Table of Contents

Handwritten margin notes (top left):

p. 131
- Clear Purpose
- Right People
- Clear Priorities
- Empowered People
- Clear Progress

p. 195 - My Job
  "The Dream"
p. 197 - Authority - "guiding people with goals to Freedom"
p. 208 - Sacrifice
p. 231 - Delegation
p. 274 - Vision Def.
p. 281... - Start Small + Move Slow
Ch. 25

Handwritten margin notes (top right):

p. 6 - Viktor Frankel ref. - Purpose

p. 14 - Better than "find people to accomplish your vision" - "Find people with visions that can harmonize with yours"

p. 39-40 - The Consulting Process

ch. 7 answers worries about valuing people in ch. 3

ch. 9 - Good challenge to finding those who fit the work I need done

PREFACE

I've always been fascinated with people, leadership, and organizations. I learned about these growing up on the family farm, hauling hay as a teenager, working in a factory, working in a rock quarry in my college years, over thirty-five years in business, church and non-profit organizations, through studying the leadership of kings in the Old Testament and through studying the life of Jesus, the King of Kings.

I realized as a young man that my calling and passion was to develop leaders and help improve organizations. I worked for thirty-one years at Hospital Corporation of America (HCA), the largest for-profit hospital company in the world. I was blessed with the opportunity to lead in a variety of executive roles which allowed me to lead auditors, construction and engineering professionals, nurses, doctors and others. I had the opportunity to serve in my last twelve years as President of HCA Physician Services.

My calling and passion never changed though I wore many different hats and worked with people in many different professions in my career. I loved developing people and building, redefining, and improving organizations.

In my last ten years at HCA, I began to develop a strong sense that God would lead me to a different platform for service. In 2001, while still working at HCA, I was asked to assume the role of Executive Pastor at a mega-church on a volunteer basis for three years. I thought that might be the beginning of a transition into some ministry role. While a lot was accomplished during those three years that still serve the church today, it became clear that was not my ultimate calling in life. I continued to work hard at HCA and assumed I would never leave until traditional retirement.

Although my division was maturing and growing fast, I started sensing God leading me to make a move. I swallowed hard and, in faith, started making plans to leave the company where I had spent most of my adult life. It was one of the hardest things I've ever done. My transition took a couple of years before I left HCA and was ready for the next phase of life.

I formed Vision Leadership Foundation where my goal is to train, coach, and mentor leaders and consult with organizations using what God has taught me through many years and varied experiences. This phase involves developing leaders and helping organizations function better in the business, non-profit, and ministry sectors. The goal is to help leaders: ***Get more done in less time and with less frustration and stress.***

- Have more time for their spouses, children, churches, communities, friends, and enjoyment of life.

- Create healthy organizational cultures to benefit their employees versus bringing difficulty and stress into their lives.

- Create more profitability, if they are business owners, so they have more financial resources to contribute to ministries and charities.

I have a growing desire to be able to give more to ministries and charities. I believe through helping others that more can be done for ministries and charities than I would have ever been able to do myself.

In my first few months after leaving HCA, I had plenty to do but was not engaged at the level I had expected. I was beginning to feel a little bit frustrated. One morning my wife told me she sensed God telling her that I should write a book. The thought had crossed my mind, but it was not something I had ever set a goal to do. This direction was clearly confirmed for me in a couple of other ways. So I started writing.

After I completed the dictation of the first draft, I finally understood the reason for the book. I never thought the book would sell in large numbers. Then, I began to realize if I only distribute fifty copies a year for the rest of my life it could be used by God to have a significant impact. There is no possible way I could share this much information with fifty different people on a one-on-one basis every year. The more I thought about that, the more grateful I became for the opportunity to do this.

I'm writing this so that you have what it took me many years to learn. I learned a lot through trial and error and from hundreds of leaders. I saw great successes, failures, and good and poor examples of leadership and organizational effectiveness.

My prayer is that you learn more quickly what it took me over thirty-five years to figure out so you can have more time to be a better spouse, parent, church member and civic leader. I hope you avoid causing some pain and frustration in other people's lives by learning from my mistakes.

INTRODUCTION

Leaders find themselves in a variety of situations today. And the situations you encounter change as your career progresses. Many of the situations below may resonate with your experience if you've been a leader for a long time. What is your situation?

- Has your organization been fine for a long time, but you sense a need to change because of the changing environment? You're just not comfortable with how to best do that?

- Do you have great people that you love working with, but sense the environment is changing and will require changing some of your team?

- Are you frustrated with your team? Do you know you don't have the right people for the future, but don't know how to go about getting the right team in place?

- Have you changed your team constantly over the years, but always seem to be frustrated with the shortcomings of your people?

- Have you lost focus on the future and all sense of priorities other than dealing with the next crisis or the next quarterly financial reporting?

- Have you empowered enough of the right people so that your organization can continue to grow and you can have more sense of freedom?

- Do you know how to lead progress consistently to minimize the risks to your organization and increase the satisfaction and enjoyment of your team?

- Are your organization and your life messed up and you know it? Do you want to change, but don't know where to start?

- Are things going well, but you know you can do better? You're just not quite sure how?

Regardless of your situation, there is hope for better days ahead. In this book, I will attempt to take the very complicated issues of leadership and make them much simpler by focusing attention on the five essentials of a healthy organization, career, or life.

A lot of leaders are like me. They want to change the world and change their organization, but they don't want to change themselves. It seems like many people are looking for the silver bullet which would give them success. It took me many years to realize that success comes only from God. It's a process. Even with God's help, it's hard and takes time. There are five essential transformations that you, your career, or your organization must go through to realize your potential.

The five essentials are the same regardless of your vocation. They work in business, non-profit organizations, churches, and ministries. They work in small or large organizations. They can also be applied to your individual life and your family life.

This book is organized in five major sections related to each of the five essentials and the transformation required:

1. **Purpose**

2. **People**

3. **Priorities**

4. **Power**

5. **Progress**

These are discussed in more detail on the pages that follow.

1. **Purpose**   From pursuing your plans for your life, career, and organization to God's calling and purpose for you, your career, and your organization. God created you for a purpose and has significant plans for you.

"For I know the plans I have for you, plans to prosper you not to harm you."

Jeremiah 29:11

"Your eyes have seen my unformed substance; and in your book were written all the days that were dreamed for me, when as yet there was not one of them."

Psalm 139:16

"For you have been called for this purpose ..."

1 Peter 2:21

2. **People**   From using people to understanding them and partnering with them to achieve God's plans.

"Before I formed you in your

mother's womb I knew you."

Jeremiah 6:3

"I knew you before you were even conceived."

Jeremiah 1:4-5

3. **Priorities**   From trying to have and do it all to realizing what is important.

"The way is narrow that leads to life."

Matthew 7:14

"I came that you might have life,

and have it abundantly."

John 10:10

4. **Power**   From trying to grab more power for yourself to empowering others to achieve their calling in life.

"Do not look out merely for your own interests.
Look out for the interests of others."
Philippians 2:4

"For even the Son of Man did not
come to be served, but to serve,
and to give his life a ransom for many."
Mark 10:45

"But the greatest among you shall
be your servant."

Matthew 23:11

"Have this attitude in yourselves which also was
also in Christ Jesus, who, although He existed in
the form of God, did not regard equality with God
a thing to be grasped, but emptied himself taking
the form of a bond-servant..."
Philippians 2:6-7

5. **Progress**   From "firefighting" and playing the "blame game" to realizing and sharing steady progress.

"A faithful man will abound with blessings,
but he who makes haste to be rich
will not go unpunished."
Proverbs 28:20

"Immediately the one who had received the five
talents went and traded them, and gained five
more."

Matthew 25::16

A starting point for the leaders guiding the organization with these five essentials is to understand why they are in a position of leadership.

THE LEADER'S CALLING AND PURPOSE

"...for there is no authority except from God,
and those which exist are established by God."
Romans 13:1

God places people in positions of leadership. Some leaders are reluctant, like Moses. Some are willing, like David. Some are rebellious and proud like Nebuchadnezzar, who didn't initially acknowledge that God had given him his place of leadership (Daniel 4:28-37). But, regardless of vocation, leaders are called to the role. So, for what purpose are they called? David was known as one of the greatest kings in the Old Testament. Here is what he learned:

> *"And David perceived that the Lord has established*
> *him as king over Israel and that he exalted*
> *his kingdom for his people Israel's sake..."*
> *2 Samuel 5:12*

God's blessings are not just for us. We are to bless all the people in our sphere of influence. How do we do that? Is it by having Bible studies and prayer meetings at work? Is it simply by loving our neighbors as ourselves? Does that ensure people are happy, productive, and blessed? The story of Moses helps answer this question. First, let us define blessing. To bless people is to bring wholeness into their lives. Wholeness has many elements. One is purpose so they know they are making the difference in this world that God created them for. One is vision so that they have hope for the future. The others are contentment and joy in what they are doing. Blessing includes all of these elements plus more. When people are blessed, they have the life that Jesus spoke of when he said, "I have come that you might have life and have it to the full." I am not talking about the "prosperity gospel" here. The life Jesus was speaking of included a right relationship with God and others and sufficient resources in all other areas of life to live out their purpose and calling on their lives.

MOSES – GREAT MAN! GREAT LEADER?

No one questions Moses' spiritual depth. After all, he gave up the luxuries of Egypt to identify with God's people. He prayed for the rebellious Israelites to the point of asking God to blot him out of the book of life to spare the Israelites. Moses was a great guy, great spiritual man, and had great love for his people. Yet, did loving people and being deeply spiritual make Moses a good leader? Not according to his father-in-law, Jethro, early in his ministry.

Jethro visited the family while the Israelites were in the wilderness. He observed how Moses was leading and said, "The thing you are doing is not good. You will wear yourself out, both yourself and these people who are with you, for the task is too heavy for you; you cannot do it alone." Exodus 18:17-18.

> **You'll wear yourself out and your people! Is this not a perfect description of many organizations—maybe your own?**

Jethro gave Moses practical advice about delegation and organization. He told Moses to select dependable leaders and share the workload. He gave Moses the criteria for selecting good leaders. He told him to train the people in the laws of God and empower other leaders to make decisions. Finally, he talked to Moses about management by exception. He told Moses to hear only the major disputes (Exodus 18:19-22).

THE SPIRITUAL AND NATURAL WORK TOGETHER

In this example, we see how the spiritual and natural work together for effective leadership. In separating the spiritual from the natural or practical, much harm is done to organizations and the people in them. Though Moses had a good heart and was working himself to death to hear the disputes of the people, he wasn't blessing them. They were standing in long lines wasting their days in the hot desert waiting on Moses. But then, Moses actually blessed them by organizing, delegating, and training.

Leading only with the head can be cold and harsh. Many kings of the Old Testament proved that. But leading with the heart without the head can be very dysfunctional. Moses certainly proved that. Good leadership takes both.

When we refer to the head, we mean the rational, analytical, and problem-solving portion of the leader. The heart refers to the emotional and spiritual aspects of the leader. Jethro observed Moses' approach to leadership with his head (rational and problem-solving ability) and gave Moses good organizational advice. Moses looked at the Israelites with his heart (spirit and emotions) and asked God to spare them.

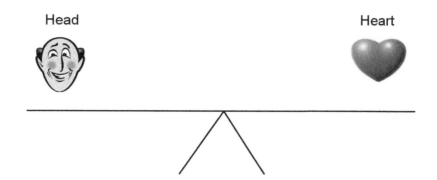

Leadership Requires a Balance of Head and Heart

Head · Heart

A balance or a Conversation? Taking Turns or Working Together? (interdependent?)

Think of people you know who are all head. What kind of culture exists in their organization? Think of someone you know who is all heart. What is the culture of their organization? Think of someone who has a good balance of both head and heart. What is their organization like? Think about where you are on the scale. Are you where you want to be? If not, what would you have to change to be there?

I'm thinking of three leaders. One was a founder. One got fired. One failed. Where do you think each was positioned on the balance beam above?

The founder was in the middle. He founded and led a highly successful corporation for many years. He had an excellent balance of heart for people and head for organizational life and business. He disciplined himself to think of ideas regularly to improve the lives of employees but is one of the smartest, shrewdest, business people that I know.

The persons who got fired were positioned on the left and closer to the head. They were nice people. But, they were not well-balanced. Under pressure, they went purely for the results and watched out more for themselves than for other people. They got fired. I've observed many that fit this category and ended with the same fate over time.

The person who failed was a leader in a non-profit organization. He led mostly with heart. He really cared about people but did not understand organizations, did not understand priorities, and did not stay focused on the mission. Because he could not stay focused and follow through on commitments and be held accountable, his organization imploded.

BLESSING PEOPLE IN PRACTICAL WAYS — USING YOUR HEAD

In this book, we integrate biblical principles with practical actions that will make life better for you and the people in your sphere of influence. How are people blessed when leaders make sure these are in place and how are they hurt when they are not?

People are energized by clear **purpose and vision**. They get confused without it. People I led always wanted to know two key things: Why am I here? (Purpose), and where are we going? (Vision).

People are most productive in a job that fits their talents, passions, and "calling." It's a grind when they are "working against the grain."

It sharpens the focus of the team if leaders make **priorities** clear. If priorities are constantly changing or are unclear, it causes stress and anxiety for people.

Leaders who **empower** their teams add to their sense of self-esteem, value and freedom. When leaders hold all the power, they diminish the self-worth, freedom, and, ultimately, productivity of the team.

Leaders benefit people through enabling **progress.** They do this through prayer, planning, leading change, providing training and documentation, implementing enabling control systems that guide and protect people, and finally by sharing meaningful measures so people know where they stand and how much progress they are making.[1]

LEADING WITH HEART

I remember a story of a relatively young man. He was washing his bright red sports car at the public car wash. He attracted the attention of a nine-year-old boy. The young lad peppered him with questions such as, "Mister, you must work a lot of hours to own a car like that" to which the young man replied, "No, I don't work a lot of hours."

The boy said, "Then, you must have a really high paying job to own a car like that." The young man replied, "No, son, I don't have a high-paying job."

The boy scratched his head, thought, and said, "Well then, you must own the company to be able to own a car like that" to which the young man replied, "No, son, I don't own the company."

To avoid further questioning he said, "Look, son, I don't work a lot of hours, I don't make a lot of money, I don't have a big job, and, in fact, I don't even have a job. The truth is my big brother bought me this car."

The little boy looked down and kind of pawed at the ground with his foot. He stuttered and said, "Mister, I wish, I wish, I wish." The young man, sure he knew what the young boy would say, was going to go ahead and finish the sentence for him. Something along the lines of "I know, you wish you had a big brother like that." Before he got it out, the boy finished his sentence and said, "Gee, mister, I would sure like to be a big brother like that." The young man was stunned but carried that with him the rest of his life.

I hope you carry this thought with you as well. If you don't truly have in your heart the desire to be like a big brother, to do something extraordinary for somebody else, please get out of the business of trying to be a leader! *Be a big brother*

LEADERS SERVE THROUGH TRAINING

From my earliest days with HCA, I traveled throughout the company and had the good fortune to observe and learn from some of the best and brightest leaders. I also learned the difference between leaders and managers by observing the most skilled managers and leaders. Also, through the process of acquisitions, I observed and learned from some weak leaders and managers. The company made a number of training opportunities available to me throughout my career for which I'm grateful.

I want to be clear about the purpose and focus of this book. It is written to Christian leaders who want to bless people and their organization by leading based on biblical principles. *Thesis*

There is much that managers and supervisors need to know to be most effective in organizational life. If you want a comprehensive management development course for your team, I recommend you consider *Model-Netics* from Main Event Management. This book will not meet that need. The *Model-Netics* course can be taught to people at every level of the organization. The use of models makes the material memorable and easier to use among a team that has had the training. Operating managers teach the course to their people so that it applies to their circumstances. Harold Hook and his team at Main Event Management are very good in the field of management training.

LEADERSHIP VERSUS MANAGEMENT

Before we jump in, let's make the distinction between leadership and management crystal clear. In my very simple view based on what I have observed and experienced, leadership is about who you are—your character, values, and vision that others are attracted to. Leaders inspire and guide others toward a shared vision that they are passionate about. Management is more about what you do daily to keep things going on a certain path. Vision is about what the business (organization) wants to become.[2] The leader casts vision and draws people to it. The manager executes

Leaders: Heart
Managers: Head

strategies to achieve the vision. Managers tend to be more about controlling people to get things done whether the people are passionate about the work or not. This book is about how godly leaders should lead their people in order to bless them. It is not about how to control them. Let's look at how a visionary leader sees the world. The first part of my career, I thought and acted like a manager. The last few years of my career, I thought and acted more like a leader, although I never reached the level of leadership I would have liked.

VISIONARY LEADERS SEE THE BIG PICTURE

I actually had a dream about this. In the dream, God told me that I would soon see a small waterfall and to stare at it to see what I could see. A few days later, I was in the mountains and did indeed see a small waterfall. I thought about it and prayed about it for an extended period of time. The analogy that follows came from this time of prayer and reflection. The theme is used throughout the book.

Organizational life reminds me of nature. Imagine in your mind's eye a waterfall. What do you see? Some people see the white mist at the bottom and to the side of the fall. Others see individual drops or streams at the side. Still others see the continuous blue water in the middle of the fall.

Visionary leaders don't just see the current situation. They see what formed it and the potential for where it can lead and the hazards along the way.

What do visionary leaders see? They don't just see a waterfall. They are able to see that the waterfall is neither the beginning nor the end. They understand there was a rain shower first. Individual raindrops ran together to form small streams. Streams ran into creeks. The creeks ran into rivers. They understand the individual raindrops are united with the river. They see the river has banks, which cause the water to flow together in a wide channel. They understand the banks don't control the individual drops but rather guide the flow. They twist and turn but continue in the same general direction. They don't force their way through big obstacles. They follow the path of least resistance that moves them in a continuous general direction. Often banks narrow leading up to a great waterfall. The channel deepens. There is a great tipping point where the water runs over the fall.

They notice a solid blue stream of water in the center of the waterfall representing the oneness of the individual drops. They also notice the drops and spray at the outer edge which reminds them that the river is made up of millions of individual contributions. They see the power, force, grandeur, and beauty of it all.

They understand that it doesn't end at the fall. They see the stream with rocks and rapids. They notice the potential for fun and the potential for danger from the rocks below. They notice the twists and turns of the mountain stream, but they also notice that it continues in the same general direction.

So what does this have to do with organizations? Many things in nature make a good analogy for what we see in organizations. The raindrops could represent individual people, tasks, or activities. As these flow together, you have a process. As processes flow together, you have a department or function just like streams form creeks.

As these flow together, you have an organization. Individuals in an organization are unique but flow with the organization. In a good organization, individuals do not lose their distinctiveness. But, there is a oneness where people and processes come together.

Just as a river has banks, creating boundaries and giving direction, so does an organization. The organization gets boundaries from its values, policies, training, and accountability systems. It gets direction from its vision and priorities. Through these, people retain their uniqueness and are given guidance without being micromanaged. Good organizations flow in a steady direction but have some twists and turns as they work around barriers and pursue unforeseen opportunities. The leader knows to watch out for people who are like beavers. They are very active people who only use the organization for their purposes. They are not really part of the organization and can stop the flow of progress if allowed.

A clear set of priorities around major initiatives will create a great inflection point similar to a waterfall. Things move much faster with much greater power. There is a force and beauty to it all. As this happens, the leader knows that much happened beforehand to reach this inflection point. They understand this is made up of contributions of many individuals, processes, and activities. The spray at the bottom of the waterfall reminds leaders that many small contributions are all part of making the organization great.

After the inflection point in an organization, there continues to be a flow. The leader knows there will be obstacles in the way. They know there's danger coupled with the potential for great excitement, adventure, and fun. The leader knows that the river, the waterfall, and stream all serve a purpose. God made rivers for a reason. Visionary leaders see the purpose of their organization and how it all works together.

Most importantly, they help people see the big picture. They help people see where they fit into the flow and add to the power in accomplishing the vision of the organization. They help people feel connected. They help them feel more alive. They help people feel good about the connection and contribution because they see where they fit in. They help people see the beauty and power of it all. The most important part is they help them feel good about being part of it.

> **"Truly great organizations are crystal clear about where they are going."[3]**

If you want to bless the people in your organization or who are joining your organization, you need to be clear about where you're going, where they fit in, and the values you will operate upon. This gives people a feeling of meaning and belonging. It improves morale and productivity. And since people are generally one of the greatest assets and costs of any organization, that makes you a better steward of the organization's resources.

LEADERSHIP – JOY OR PAIN?

I've seen firsthand the great joy and good that comes from organizational life when there is effective leadership. I'm also aware of the stress, pain, and misery that can exist in organizations under bad leadership. I acknowledge that my leadership brought some of both. I'm excited about your journey and pray that God blesses you through the words in this book.

THE NEED FOR A MAP

When I visited London, I walked across Hyde Park, five hundred acres, to get to my hotel in South Kensington. I had a map in my pocket, but I instead chose to ask people along the way for directions. I asked the first person, and he pointed me in one direction. The next person told me to go in a different direction, and so on. I finally got to South Kensington but realized I had zigzagged across the park to get there. I'd spent twice the time and energy making this trip as would have been necessary if I had just had the common sense to look at the map. For some strange reason, I thought the people who lived there and were in the park would give me a better set of instructions. Yet, logic dictates that whoever made the map had seen it from a broader view and knew everything about the area. If I had only followed the map, I would have saved myself a lot of time and energy.

This experience makes me think of this book. I know a lot of people in leadership and management roles who are lost, stumbling around and asking other people on the journey what to do next, believing that those people know. Some of them do, but many of them don't. What I'm offering you is a map. I worked in the business world for over thirty-four years in hands-on roles. I worked in executive roles in a multi-billion dollar complex organization for over twenty-five years. I saw hundreds of executives function, many that were great and some who made a lot of mistakes. In my journey, I made most of the mistakes a leader can make. I learned some things quickly and others it took me repeated attempts to finally see how things should work. Having traveled the journey and being able to look at it from a broader perspective, what I'm offering you is similar to a map so that you don't have to wander around and make the same number of mistakes that I did. Use it like a map. Look at the Table of Contents and if you have a particular issue that one of the thirty chapters speaks to, simply go there and get some direction. At a minimum, you may learn what not to do, based on the mistakes I made. I hope you enjoy your journey.

How to Use this Book

This book is written so that you may read it from beginning to end. It is also written somewhat like a reference manual. Everyone who wants to benefit from the contents should read the preface, introduction, and first section on purpose. These sections will give needed context for the rest of the book. After that, you could read the Table of Contents to pick chapters that will speak to your questions or issues. Also, each of the applications at the end of each chapter can be completed from the perspective of your organization, career, or personal life.

I. Purpose

God created you for a specific purpose . . .

Be transformed from pursuing your plans for your life, career, and organization to God's calling and purpose for you, your career, and your organization.

"For you have been called for this purpose..."

1 Peter 2:21

"Now Solomon proposed to build a temple for the name of the Lord."

2 Chronicles 2:1

"I came that you might have life and have it to the full."

John 10: 10

*"Your eyes have seen my unformed substance;
and in your book were written all the days that
were dreamed for me, when is yet there was not one of them."*

Psalm 139:16

Questions to Ponder

- Do you have a clear sense of why God has placed you where you are? The job you are in? The family you belong to? The place where you live?

- Are you clear about the purpose He created you to serve in this world?

- Do you have a clear vision of where your organization is going? Where your life is going?

Issues Covered in this Section

- Why people need purpose and vision.

- How to make the purpose and vision of your organization clear to your team.

- How to connect them to the purpose and vision of the organization.

- What a functional and dysfunctional organization looks like.

- How to change the direction of your organization.

- Determining your purpose as a leader.

Chapter 1

Definition of Vision ?

PEOPLE NEED
PURPOSE AND DIRECTION

Thought:
How much stronger would your organization be if everyone
on the team believed in the mission, were committed to it,
had a clear understanding of their role in it, and were willing
to help achieve the vision and were as excited about it as you are?

"Where there is no vision, the people perish."
Proverbs 29:18

Everyone has his own vocation or mission in life; everyone must carry out a concrete assignment that demands fulfillment. Therein he cannot be replaced, nor can his life be repeated, thus everyone's task is as unique as is his specific opportunity to implement it. [4]
—*Viktor Frankl*

"God has a purpose for each life He creates, and each purpose is as unique as the individual's fingerprint."[5] God created everything on purpose and for a purpose. Things that don't serve a purpose should not exist. This is like the preface and introduction of the book that many people skip over. They serve a purpose. Or at least they serve an important one in this book. Some things won't make as much sense later on if you don't read them. So if you happened to skip them, please go back now and read them before you start this first chapter.

"I want my life to count" — the deep desire I heard people express in organizations.

"Where are we going?" — the most common question people asked me in organizations.

The two phrases above are my attempt to capture the heart cry I heard from people in many years of leadership experience and my own personal experiences. "I want to make a difference." That's the most frequent statement I've heard in thirty-five years of my professional career. In interviews, people say, "I want to make a difference, I want to have an impact, and I want my life to count." There are many other ways they say it, but it all means the same thing. They want to matter—to have meaning and purpose. They say it in organizational meetings, in annual reviews, and in everyday life in the hallways. I've literally heard it hundreds of times.

People have a deep seated need to know their life counts.

Purpose is to people's souls like oxygen is to their lungs.

IT HURTS WHEN WE DON'T FEEL LIKE WE MATTER

I was just a kid the first time I ever saw Daddy cry. Dad was a dairy farmer. He was emotionally and physically tough. I had seen him cut himself with a chainsaw and only flinch. I had seen the flesh on his hand gape open to the bone. But I had never seen him cry. One day he slipped and broke his foot. He couldn't go to the barn and milk his cows for about two weeks. I'll never forget seeing him sitting on the couch crying. It wasn't the pain of the broken foot. As he sobbed he said, "I'm just no good for anything." ✓

Of course that wasn't true. He was a dad, husband, and played many roles in life other than farming. But, like most people, he linked much of his self-worth and purpose to his work. When he couldn't work, he did not feel he was achieving his purpose.

ON THE FARM I KNEW WHAT I ACCOMPLISHED
AND WHY IT MATTERED

I didn't like being out in the cold in the winter. But there were many things I <u>did</u> like about growing up on a farm. I could look behind the tractor after I plowed a field and see what I had accomplished. I could look at the milk can and see the milk after I milked the cow. I could see a full barn after I hauled hay all day.

People need to know why their work matters.

I knew the purpose of plowing the field, milking the cow, and hauling the hay. And I felt a connection to that purpose and a sense of accomplishment. I felt like what I did counted—that I mattered that day.

Crucial phenomenon

Contrast that to work in organizational life. <u>It's so easy to work a day or even a week and often feel like you're further behind than when you started.</u> That zaps a person's energy and zeal for the job. The reason is because people need to feel like they're contributing to some purpose that matters. If we cannot see how we contribute, we don't feel like we matter. To be optimistic and highly productive, people need a clear vision of a better future and how they impact it meaningfully. Otherwise, they die a slow, painful death in our 21st century organizations.

Working in an effective organization is like time on the farm. At the end of the day, week or year, you accomplish something, know the purpose for it and feel a strong connection to that purpose. When the individual's purpose is aligned with the organization's purpose, there is very high morale and low turnover. Working in a weak organization feels the opposite—no feeling of accomplishment, purpose, or connection to what matters.

WE DIE EARLIER AND EASIER WITHOUT PURPOSE

Exert in Brewer's "Retrieval of Ethics"

God made us to serve a purpose in his world. Why wouldn't we have a strong need for meaning and purpose? Viktor Frankl, in *Man's Search for Meaning*, made the point that people in concentration camps that found a purpose for living, a reason why their life counted, survived while those without purpose died much more quickly.[6] When they created a purpose for survival, which was always associated with helping others who were weaker and sicker, they lived much longer than others. There is a reason why Rick Warren's *The Purpose Driven Life* sold over thirty million copies.[7] People are genuinely interested in their purpose.

What's that got to do with life in corporate America, churches, ministries, and non-profit organizations? I've seen enough in all those organizations to be convinced people are slowly dying emotionally and physically from their impact. It's just so slow and common it's not viewed as a crime. The impact I'm talking about is people working really hard without clear direction and purpose. They don't have a clear understanding of what God designed them to do in this world, how what they do has a meaningful impact on the organization or the betterment of other people.

PEOPLE DON'T WORK JUST FOR MONEY WITHOUT PURPOSE

Is Lower Pay possible for more Meaningful work? What is the real obstacle to heightening More people - Trust + Cooperation

I remember a study about meaningful work. The going rate for ditch diggers was $10 per hour at the time. People were hired and paid $12 per hour. Needless to say, this attracted a lot of attention. People were paid $12 per hour the first day for digging a ditch. The next day, they filled in the ditch and were paid again. This was the routine. Dig a ditch one day and fill it in the next for

$12 per hour. After a few days, the workers began to lose interest. They lost half the workforce. They raised the pay to $15 an hour, 50% above the market for ditch diggers. After a few days of the same routine, half that workforce left. This continued until the pay for digging and filling in a ditch was $25 per hour, two and half times the going rate. Finally, no one was willing to work even at this rate. Why? When the workers were interviewed, it was discovered the extra money wasn't worth it because they lost all meaning in their work. Digging a ditch only to fill it in again served no useful purpose. And the workers weren't willing to do it.

PEOPLE WILL COMMIT THEIR LIVES TO A GREAT PURPOSE

> *A man can bear any what if he has a big enough why.*
> —Nietzsche, the German philosopher

The *why* Nietzsche refers to is really meaning or purpose in life. Purpose matters! I have seen firsthand in business and many ministries that people will give their lives to achieve a meaningful purpose. Some are willing to die for a great cause—purpose. People are willing to work only so hard in a job, but they will give their all for a great purpose. According to Dan Miller in *Wisdom Meets Passion*, this is especially highlighted in the generations of our children and grandchildren. They are especially attuned to what they perceive matters in life versus career and money.

So what about a job chokes out purpose?

> *We are never really happy unless, and until, we are moving*
> *toward the accomplishments of something that is important to us.*
>
> — Brian Tracy

History has shown us that some people are willing to kill for money. But, people will only be willing to die themselves or make great sacrifices for a significant purpose. The highest motivation is what people are willing to die for or commit their lives to. Jesus said, "He who loses his life will save it, and he who saves his life will lose it." We understand the difference that purpose makes.

Do you have an organization people kill for or Die for? Competition ↓ Culture

MAKING A DIFFERENCE

I saw Mark a few weeks ago. He was really tired. After he told me about his schedule, I understood why. He was putting in a lot of hours and hard work. I was curious as to why he didn't do something else. He is very qualified and can make a good living with other companies without the long hours and intense schedules. I asked him why he was doing this. Actually, he was setting the pace and putting the expectations on himself, not the company. The reason he was working so hard was because he saw a window of opportunity to really make a difference in the lives of people through his project. He believed it would improve the quality of healthcare for patients and make a difference for the company. When the discussion was over, it all boiled down to one thing. He genuinely wanted to make a difference.

I'm also reminded of Janine. She's not a high level executive in a healthcare company like Mark. She is a lower-level employee with a company that helps dry out buildings after floods or any kind of water damage. She came to my house on the Saturday following the great flood of Nashville in May 2010 when she was supposed to have the day off. She had worked two weeks without taking even a day off. I had some flooding in the basement, and she remembered something that she wanted to check. She came to my house, not for the money, not to further a career, and not for the recognition. She came because she cared about people and their lives and wanted to make a difference. And sure enough, she found an area of mold which had been overlooked. She did make a difference!

Application

As a leader, what difference did you make in someone's life last week, last month and last year?

_____

_____

_____

_____

_____

For each of your key team members, do they know what difference they made in someone's life last week, last month, and last year? Have you talked to them about the difference they're making to your organization and to other people? If not, what will you do to help them see the difference they make? Write it here.

_____

_____

_____

_____

Notes

Chapter 2

PURPOSE – THE BIBLICAL BASIS

> **Thought:**
> Have you asked yourself the age old questions
> "Who am I? Why am I here? Where do I fit?
> Why does it matter?"
> —Chuck Swindoll

Definition of purpose?

PURPOSE

It is clear from the previous chapter that people have a deep need for meaning, or purpose. Besides my dad and biblical teachings, Viktor Frankl's *Man's Search for Meaning* was the earliest significant influence on my thinking in this direction when I was in my mid 20's.[8] Another significant impact on my thinking was Rick Warren's *The Purpose Driven Life*.[9] This is so central to man's basic need, there's no wonder it sold over thirty million copies.

So, where does our need for purpose come from? There are numerous articles available on the subject, and the issue is raised in some secular seminars. None of these secular sources deal with where the need comes from and why it exists. The best answers are in the Bible or come from Christian authors. Chuck Swindoll says it well in *Living the Psalms*. "All of us need to be needed. We want to be wanted. God created us with the desire to know we can contribute something valuable and have a significant impact on the lives of others. In years past, great men and women

That's False

wanted to leave their mark on the world, to create a legacy that would continue after they passed away." [10]

In a speech at the Dallas Theological Seminary, Howard Hendricks said, "Much of our religious activity today is nothing more than a cheap anesthetic to deaden the pain of an empty life." [11] Hendricks' statement is the flipside of the same coin that Swindoll speaks about. It highlights the need for meaning or purpose in our lives and the pain that is caused when we can't find it. Rather than turning to God for the answers, some people take extreme, and often harmful, measures to deal with the pain of an empty life.

GOD CREATED YOU FOR A PURPOSE

A search of the Scripture makes it clear that God is a God of purpose. He made everything and everyone with a clear purpose in mind. The fact that God has a purpose and carries out His purposes is very clear in the Scripture.

"Declaring the end from the beginning,
and from ancient times the things which have not been done, saying,
'My purpose will be established, and I will accomplish
all my good pleasure.'"
Isaiah 46:10

"I know that you can do all things, and that no purpose
of yours can be thwarted."
Job 42:2

"Calling a bird of prey from the east, the man of
my purpose from a far country.
Clearly I have spoken; I will bring it to pass.
I have planned it, surely I would do it."
Isaiah 46:11

God had a unique purpose for His son, Jesus. "But he said to them, 'I must preach the kingdom of God to the other cities also, for I was sent for this purpose'"(Luke 4:42-44). In the Garden of Gethsemane, Jesus said, "But for this purpose, I came to this hour" (John 12:27). Jesus was crystal clear about the purpose for which God had sent him, and all of his life was about achieving that purpose. Even when family and friends would have deterred him, he stayed focused on the purpose God the Father had for him.

God also had a special purpose for David, the great king of Israel. "For David, after he had served the purpose of God in his own generation, fell asleep, and was laid among his fathers and underwent decay" (Acts 13:36). Even though David made many mistakes throughout his life, God called him "a man after his own heart." His mistakes were not what characterized his life but rather his constant desire to seek God. As a result, Scripture says he served the purpose of God in his own generation. That causes us to stop and ask, "Will God be able to say of us that we served His purpose during our time on this Earth?"

YOUR UNIQUE PURPOSE

"God has a purpose for each life he creates, and the purpose is as unique as the individual's fingerprint." Unfortunately, "some people seem to drift aimlessly through life, with no specific direction."[12] Scripture says:

"Your eyes have seen my unformed substance;

and in your book were written all the days that were

dreamed for me, when as yet there was not one of them."

Psalm 139:16

"For you have been called for this purpose ..."

1 Peter 2:21

God had a plan for your life before He ever created anything. His plan for you is a good plan (Jeremiah 29:11). It's a unique plan, created especially for you. Nobody ever has or ever will be created to occupy your specific time, place, and plan in the course of human history. As Psalms 139:16 above says, God knew every detail of our life before He made us. God forms our days so that they are exactly the kind of days we should have to become the kind of person He wants us to be.[13]

The question before each one of us is if we will discover His plan for us, which is best because of His infinite wisdom and love. Or, will we create and follow our own plan?

(handwritten margin notes, top left)
① Problems:
- Define Vision
- Define People
- Describe how people redirect or contribute to vision (i.e., their relationship) "Come First?"
- How does vision "come first?"

YOUR ORGANIZATION'S PURPOSE

Ever since I started leading people, I believed that purpose and vision came first and then people. Then, Jim Collins' book *Good to Great* made me question my view of this priority.[14]

(handwritten margin note, left) Vision rides on the People →

He contends that in great organizations, the CEO picks a great team of people first and then, in essence, figures out the vision. I can certainly see where a CEO with a group of strong, well-rounded, flexible leaders would figure out a better vision than a CEO with a group of less talented, less balanced, and inflexible leaders.

(handwritten margin note, left) ① Oversimplified. Does vision not come through a person, if even God?

I finally settled this in my mind by looking at what the Bible teaches in this regard. God didn't create people and then come up with His purpose and vision for them. Purpose came first and then people. Jesus, the ultimate example of a leader, didn't pick a group of people and then say now let us figure out what we should do. Instead, he was clear about his mission (purpose), why he was on this earth, from the very beginning. He said, "For this purpose I have come to offer my life a ransom for many."

Next, Jesus had a vision. His vision was the New Testament church which was his way of reaching the world. Remember, in the Old Testament, Israelites were God's chosen people and were given the call to take up the mission and given the vision to reach other nations for God. They refused to take up the call and, therefore, the mission was given to the New Testament church, and the vision was given to Jesus' disciples.

Jesus' mission was to reach the world for God's kingdom, and his vision was to do it through the church. Then, he called his disciples, after a season of prayer, for the role each one would play. He selected Peter to be spokesman of the group. He selected Judas, knowing that he would be the one that betrayed him. He selected John, knowing that he would be a loyal friend and that he would leave the care of his own mother to him after his death. With Jesus, it was purpose and vision first and then the selection of his team.

I see this pattern throughout Scripture. Let's go early in the Old Testament to the story of Moses. He was living his life quite content on the backside of the desert raising a family. God did not say to him, "Moses, pick some good leaders and then figure out what you would like to do with the rest of your life." God had a mission for Moses. It was to free the Israelite people. He had a vision for the Israelites. It was the Promised Land—the land of Canaan flowing with milk and honey.

(handwritten margin note, left) Right

We should pause at this point and talk about where vision comes from in the life of a godly leader. Many leaders come up with their own visions. Or, as suggested by Collins, they get a good team of people who come up with a vision. For God's leader, vision is really a revelation of God's plan. Scripture says that God shares His plans with His trusted people. God had a plan, a vision, and

He shared it with Moses. Later, God had a plan to rebuild the walls of Jerusalem, and He shared it with Nehemiah. The examples are numerous.

Christian leaders should get God's revelation in prayer for what their life and organization is to be about—its destiny. This should be the vision. Sometimes, God gives revelation to an individual, and sometimes He gives it to the group of people. Engaging your leadership team in the discernment of God's revelation or vision for your organization is both inclusive from a practical standpoint and healthy from an organizational view.

The bottom line is when I look at this issue from a biblical perspective, I see a pattern. God envisioned, revealed the vision to His people, and then selected the team based on the vision. For example, God's vision was to reach the world and draw people back into relationship with Him. Peter had a unique background which allowed him to do that with the Jewish people and was called to that task. By contrast, the Apostle Paul was prepared to reach the Gentile people and was called to that task.

On the basis of Scripture, I have concluded that mission (purpose) and vision come first and then the selection of people. Therefore, I have organized this book accordingly.

Since God has a purpose for you, your life has a direction and a destiny. We see this in Scripture at the national level with the children of Israel. God had a purpose, direction, and destiny for the children of Israel. If you are leader, God has a direction, a destiny, and purpose for the organization you lead. How often do we think about our daily lives and how we are serving God's purpose? As a leader, how often do you think about why God put you in a leadership role, the purpose He wants you to serve in that role, the purpose He has for the individuals in your organization, and the purpose He has for the individuals your organization touches? We tend to compartmentalize life. We often think and act as though we live on an island. But, everything we do touches others, who in turn touch others. God has a grand purpose for it all. How aware are you of God's purpose for your life, your leadership, and the direction of your organization?

UNDERSTANDING GOD'S OVERALL PLAN

I wasn't very old before I began to understand there are physical laws that govern the universe. For example, I understood the law of gravity. I knew that if I jumped from something high, I could fall and hurt myself. I knew if I touched a hot stove, I would burn myself.

It took a number of years and much study of the Scripture before I began to recognize God's spiritual laws at work around me. These laws are just as obvious and are just as consistent and dependable once you learn how to recognize them. I realize there are many people who don't believe in God's spiritual laws. That's fine. They still work just like the physical laws whether people believe in them or not.

I have realized through Scripture study and experience that life works much better if we are aware of God's plan, His purposes, and His spiritual laws, and if we cooperate with them.

Before our world was ever created, God had a plan for creation. He had a purpose in creation which was to reveal His glory and to have a relationship with His creation. In Genesis, we see that God called a person, Abraham, to help accomplish His purpose, and then He called a people, the children of Israel, to help accomplish His purpose on this earth. Before we go further, let's be clear about something. God did not need anybody's help to accomplish His purposes. Out of love and to bless His people, He gave them roles to serve in His great purpose for their benefit, not for His.

Oversimplified? [handwritten margin note]

God gave people priorities as expressed in His instructions to Adam and Eve in the Garden of Eden as well as through the Ten Commandments later.

We see He empowered His people. He gave Adam and Eve dominion over His creation in Genesis. He gave power to the church to carry out its calling and work in the book of Acts at the time of Pentecost.

And finally we see that God expected progress. The parable of the talents is a good example of how God entrusts resources and opportunities to people and expects people to do something with them.

Therefore, if we are going to have a successful life, career, or organization, we need to be aligned with God. What does this look like? First, we would be aligned with His purpose, plan and ways—spiritual laws—for our life, career, and organization. Next, we would discover our calling related to this purpose. In other words, we would find our place in the world to serve to carry out His purposes. Then, we would follow his priorities explained in the Bible for how we live our lives. Also, we would not abuse the power He gives us but rather use it for doing good and share power with others like He has empowered us. Finally, we would realize progress in all areas of life and be good stewards of resources and opportunities that He gives us.

What does cooperating with God in organizational life look like?

Application

1. Do you know your purpose? Why God put you here?

_____

_____

_____

2. Have you connected your personal purpose to your purpose as a leader?

_____

_____

_____

3. Do you see the connection between the direction and purpose for your life as a leader and how it impacts your organization? The people in it?

_____

_____

_____

4. Are you leading your organization for your purposes or with a constant awareness of God's?

_____

_____

_____

Chapter 3

ARE YOUR ORGANIZATION'S MISSION AND VISION CLEAR?

Thought:
How much easier would it be to lead and guide your organization if
everyone agreed with the mission and were excited about the vision?
Do your people even know the mission and vision of your organization?

"Come, let us build the wall of Jerusalem..."

Nehemiah 2:17

People need to feel connected to a purpose larger than themselves. "Hire people who are mission driven. This is why Steve Jobs was so successful."[15] That's one of many reasons why so many people wanted to work for HCA. They felt they were part of something really significant. The leader needs to help them see their purpose in the organization. People need to understand where they fit in and how they impact the organization. They also want to know where the organization is going. The most common questions I was asked in interviews or organizational meetings revolve around "Where are we going?"

[handwritten margin note: What about whether they are replaceable? P.58 P.59]

[handwritten margin note: [7.]]

[handwritten margin note: But how clear can you get if vision is not static. What if it's Dialectic?]

> **"Truly great organizations are crystal clear about where they are going."[16]**

How do you know if the purpose and vision of your organization is clear? How do you know if you've done enough to rightly connect people to the organization's mission and vision?

Each time I think of this I'm reminded of Jim Collins' analogy of having the right person in the right seat on the bus. If that's important, having people on the right bus is even more critical. Bill Hybels, Pastor of Willow Creek Church, says, "If your vision is not clear enough to upset some people, it's not clear enough." Sometimes, organizations act as if it's more important to have a seat filled than to have the right people on the right bus in the right seat. I've seen this many times throughout my career in working with new assignments.

Let's consider the analogy of traveling. I traveled a lot in my early years. What gives you a sense of confidence that you're getting on the right plane, subway or bus? For me, it's really good signs! I was in London over thirty years ago on a business trip. I was on the public transit system wanting to see a particular portion of London. I had a great time with the team that day. I saw good portions of London and enjoyed the trip, but I never saw the portion that I started out to see. One reason may have been because I was a country boy fairly fresh off the farm. But, maybe one reason was the signage. After all, there were smart people with me that were just as lost as I was. That's the key, isn't it? Whether we are at the airport, subway or bus station, we need clear signs to know where we're going. It's not a pleasant trip if we get lost along the way.

Consider this hypothetical example. Assume you go to the Nashville bus station and one line runs to Memphis and the other to Chattanooga. What if the signs are confusing and you, a Chattanooga passenger, get on a bus to Memphis?

An hour into the ride, you expect to start seeing mountainous terrain. Instead, it starts getting flatter. You ask questions to those around you who are trying to sleep, work, or think. You discover the bus is going to Memphis. Now you are upset.

You start complaining about going to Memphis. You start explaining why you preferred Chattanooga over Memphis. You may even go out of your way to explain why you don't like Memphis. You complain and contrast the virtues of Chattanooga to Memphis the whole trip.

So what is this like for the rest of the passengers? The four to five people sitting closest, at the very minimum, are getting annoyed at the distractions and the ranting over how good Chattanooga is versus Memphis. Some of the Memphis passengers might start wishing they'd chosen Chattanooga based on how good it sounds. Some may be confused about which city is the best to visit or do business in.

The bottom line is, by the time you get to Memphis, you as the Chattanooga passenger are extremely upset, and the four or five people sitting around you are either annoyed, distracted, confused, or upset about being in Memphis.

Assume the signage was so poor that there was at least one Chattanooga passenger for every four or five Memphis passengers. In that scenario, you have a bus full of people most of whom didn't have a good trip. They're unhappy.

So what's the point of the story? This is what happens in many organizations. People join organizations without a clear understanding of its mission or vision. Once they find out where they're going, they are miserable and become a distraction or morale barrier to the people closest to them in the organization. Get enough of those in the organization and the morale and productivity of the whole group will be impacted.

CREATING THE SIGNS?

As you do your strategic planning, there are a few things that need to be communicated clearly. Some believe that setting direction is a matter of "defining the organizational mission, vision and values."[17] I have a different view as I will explain later. The triangle below is a picture of what I'm talking about.[18] The red arrow is the "plumb line." It shows alignment needed for an effective organization.

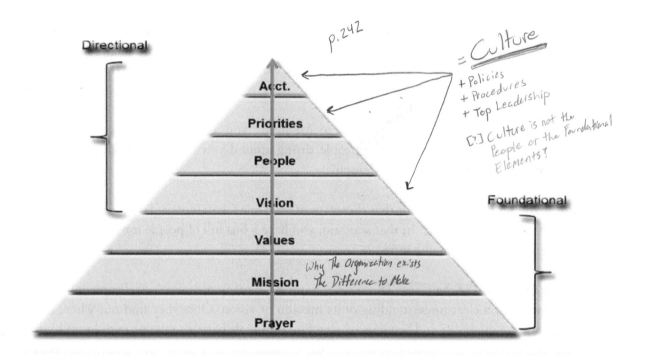

p. 242

= Culture
+ Policies
+ Procedures
+ Top Leadership

[?] Culture is not the People or the Foundational Elements?

Why The Organization exists
The Difference to Make

I. Prayer

Is prayer Collaboratively Discerned?

Everybody prays at some point. I've read testimonies of even some of the most devout atheists praying on their death beds. So it isn't a matter of *if* we pray, but when and how we pray. Leaders have a tendency to make their own plans and then ask God to bless them. Some leaders rush ahead with their plans and start praying when they run into trouble. The biblical approach is to pray upfront to discern God's plan. This is what Jesus did throughout his ministry. He prayed before choosing his disciples—one of the most important decisions he would make in his ministry. We see the same pattern from Nehemiah before rebuilding the wall in Jerusalem. King David also led by this pattern in praying before major potential battles to discern God's plans for him. If prayer is not the foundation of your planning process, you are likely "building on sand, not the rock" (Matthew 7:24-27).

II. Mission *The Difference to Make*

Peter Drucker and others have written about the concept of mission over the years, but it has its basis in Scripture. In Genesis, it becomes clear that God had a mission for Abraham as the father of His people when He sent him to Canaan. He had a mission for the children of Israel which was to carry His message of redemption to the world. He had a mission for Moses which was to lead His people out of the captivity of the Egyptians. And He has a mission for you and for your organization.

Def. Mission

In organizational life, the mission describes why the organization exists.[19] It deals with questions like "Why are we here," "Why do we exist," and "Why do we get up each day and do what we do?"[20] Without clarity of mission, the organization seems to serve no purpose. Without a meaningful mission, the organization would not receive funding, support, volunteers, or employees. Mission is about purpose, and it draws people who want to align with that purpose.[21] It is foundational to the existence of the organization. Once clearly established, the mission of the organization rarely changes. Do you know your God-given mission for your life, your career, or your organization?

One reason why mission is so critical to a functional organization is seen in the encounter Jesus had with the Herodians and Pharisees. They teamed up to question Jesus about his view of taxes in order to trick him. If he said he was against taxes, he would be viewed as a revolutionary by the government. If he said he was in favor of taxes, his own people would be against him because they hated being taxed by the Roman government. He did not fall for the trick but responded by saying, "Render to Caesar what is Caesar's and to God what is God's." The Herodians and Pharisees failed because of Jesus' superior wisdom. They did not fail because they did not give it their best effort to work together. What is most interesting is that they were natural enemies. The Herodians favored the government and thought everyone should pay taxes. The Pharisees were the leaders of the Israelite Nation and hated the tax burden the Roman government put on them. Yet, both groups put their differences aside to work together because they had a common mission. Many organizations spend money on teambuilding exercises and tools. These are often very fine things to do. However, they will be of little effect unless people are clearly aligned around the mission and vision of the organization.

One of the first things I did when I started leading the audit function for HCA was to be clear about our mission. We existed to help the company's leaders in their responsibilities to have sound internal control systems, not to be the corporate cops or the "Gottcha" function as some people liked to play the role. I detested that view of the role. It wasn't the real reason the function existed. I did the same thing in other leadership roles I assumed. It's amazing to me how many people and functions are not really clear about why they exist.

III. Values

Driving Concepts

Really?

(Jesus had a clear set of values) that he lived by such as sacrifice, unity, forgiveness, and humility. These values made some people furious but drew many people to him 2000 years ago and today.

Values clarify what you stand for and believe in.[22] Values are guiding principles that influence both "who and what fit in around here."[23] Values need to be clearly stated. But, most importantly, they have to be lived out in day-to-day life by the leader. The true values of the organization are established by the attitudes and behaviors of the leaders. To focus on stated values different than the behavior of the leadership team is actually destructive. I've seen the power of positive values lived out and the destructive nature of stated values not lived out. Studies have shown that people stay with organizations for less money and other perks if their values are aligned. I have seen this play out many times. People are either drawn to the values of an organization or leave because of them. Values are also foundational to the organization and once established should not change over time. Some people teach and write about values as though they are directional. I see values as more foundational. They are something you can build an organization on or something that can cause one to crumble. Even though many organizations talk about mission and vision first, the underlying basis for both is values.[24] Core values are the principles and standards at the very center of our character.[25]

How so?

IV. Vision

Strategy?

Proverbs 29:13 says, "Without vision the people perish." Without vision, there is no hope for the future or sense of direction. When people lose hope, there are no goals or dreams. I recently heard a speech by a gentleman from Homeland Security. He made the point that before people go on shooting rampages, they reach a significant level of despair. In that state, they have no vision for the future, and they have lost a sense of hope.

Same?

"While mission is a statement of what is, a vision is a statement of what or how you would like things to be—a picture of the future you're working to create. Nothing was ever created without vision."[26]

"A vision statement is the other side of the coin of a mission statement. It is a picture of a mission fulfilled. Whereas mission speaks to the head for decision, vision speaks to the heart for inspiration. 'Can you imagine if…'"[27]

> **Goals can be energizing-when you win.
> But a vision is more powerful than a goal.
> A vision is enlivening, it's spirit-giving,
> it's the guiding force behind all great
> human endeavors.
> Vision is about shared energy, a sense of awe,
> a sense of possibility.** [28]
>
> **BENJAMIN ZANDER, CONDUCTOR,
> BOSTON PHILHARMONIC ORCHESTRA**

We need to distinguish here between vision as the world understands it, which is a compelling future created in the minds of leaders. This stands in contrast to vision as taught in Scripture. Scripture shows that vision is actually God's revelation of His future plans to His chosen servants. We should bear in mind Jeremiah 29:11 which says, "I know the plans I have for you, plans to prosper you not to harm you." God's plans for you, the people you lead, and the organization you're part of, are always for good. People will ultimately be blessed under your leadership when you are leading toward God's revelation of His plans versus dreaming up your own. Vision is directional for the organization.

Andy Stanley in *Visioneering* writes, "A vision makes you an important link between current reality and the future. Suddenly you matter. You matter a lot."[29]

He goes on to make the point that God-ordained visions eventually feel like a moral imperative and will be in line with what God is up to in the world.[30]

The logo of Vision Leadership Foundation is a "V" with a river flowing through it. The reason is because everything flows from your vision—for your organization, your career and your life.

V. People

A leader who can't or doesn't pick the right people for the organization is not a good leader. Jesus spent all night in prayer before he picked his team. We should do the same. Picking and keeping the right people is so important that I devoted an entire section of this book to it. Staffing an organization with people who agree with the mission, believe in the values, are excited about the vision, understand the priorities, and accept accountability are critical to a successful organization. What is expected of them and their ability to work with the team are critical components to success. Individuals must accept and be accountable for goals that will help the organization achieve its mission and vision.

VI. Priorities

Priorities help an organization focus. They save time and resources while building momentum and strength. They are expressed through strategies, tactics, goals and objectives. Peter Drucker says, "Objectives must be derived from what our business (organization) is, what it will be, and what it should be." They are the action commitments through which the mission of a business (organization) is to be carried out and the standards against which performance is measured. Objectives, in other words, represent the fundamental strategy of the business. Objectives are statements of what we plan to achieve over the next one to three years. Objectives are then achieved by creating strategies, tactics, goals, and action plans.[31]

VII. Accountability

When God created the world, He gave people great freedom but with accountability. Adam and Eve were given dominion over every living thing with only one restriction—Genesis 2:15-17. But there was a consequence associated with violating that one restriction which they unfortunately realized. The Bible has much to say about accountability. It is a twofold concept including the potential for reward and discipline which Jesus spoke of many times. This is also illustrated many times in the lives of God's people in the Old Testament. Deuteronomy chapter 28 outlines a passage illustrating the blessings of God for following Him and the curses for ignoring Him. Accountability is often thought of in a negative sense. However, biblical accountability should generally be thought of in a positive sense. God told Cain, "If you do well, will not your countenance be lifted up?"(Genesis 4:7). The restrictions are for your benefit, and any discipline you receive is to bring you back on the right path. For example, King David said in Psalms 119:71, "It is good for me that I was afflicted, that I may learn your statutes." Scripture says that those whom God loves He rebukes and chastens as a father who loves His son (Proverbs 3:11-12; Hebrews 12:3-11).

The book *Good to Great* points out that one distinguishing point of great organizations is their internal discipline. From my experience, I believe this exists only in organizations with the right understanding of accountability. Those organizations which focus too much on disciplining mistakes rather than treating them as learning opportunities create cultures of fear. Those organizations that focus only on bonus programs and perks tend to create cultures where people cross the lines chasing the dollars and perks they seek.

Summary

1. **Prayer** grounds people in God's good and gracious plans for them and their organization.

2. **Mission** gives people a **purpose**.

3. **Values** give them a foundation to depend on and a framework to operate within for their behavior.

4. **Vision** gives hope and direction.

5. **Priorities** give focus and feeling of importance.

6. **People** attracted to the mission and vision can be trusted with a piece of the vision.

7. **Accountability** gives them encouragement to do their best.

HOW CAN YOU TELL IF THEY AGREE?

When being interviewed, people should be able to discern their level of agreement broadly for each of the above. If agreement is not reasonably high for everything, they're not going to be happy or productive.

The same is true for people already in the organization. It's not uncommon for people to join an organization and be reasonably happy. Then, things change, and they're less contented. Sometimes, this is because the organization has taken a directional turn that doesn't match them anymore. But, often times it is simply because the signs in the organization have become outdated, blurry, and simply not clear.

The challenge in organizational life is that these things are generally clear to the leadership. But if you go to the base of the triangle in the organization, it becomes less clear and gets blurry over time.

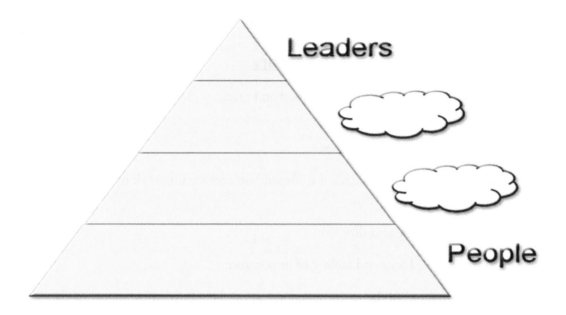

Imagine if you were going from Nashville to Tampa, Florida. What if you are five degrees off? I'm not an engineer, but I'm not sure you would even hit the state of Florida. The same is true with organizational direction. The top leaders may know where they're going. But assume the rank-and-file employees don't. If there's even a five percent variation in a really large organization, by the time you get to the base of the pyramid, people are confused about where the organization is going. This causes dysfunction, disorientation, loss of morale, and lost productivity. Though less pronounced, the same is true in small organizations.

HOW DO YOU CONNECT PEOPLE TO THE PURPOSE?

The team being connected to the purpose of the organization is key. So what is the practical thing we must do regularly for leaders to create that sense of connection? Perhaps this is best illustrated in the story of the cathedral. I've heard this story two times in different sermons but don't remember the name of the pastor who told the story. I later discovered that this story is three hundred years old and has been told many times.[32]

A man noticed three brick layers. They appeared to be doing exactly the same thing. He walked up to the first one and said, "May I ask what you are doing?" The man replied, "I am a brick layer. I lay bricks on top of each other all day long and get paid $15 an hour to feed my family. It's hard work."

The gentleman asked the second man the same question. He replied, "I'm a builder. I love building. And, it lets me feed my family."

The gentleman went to the third man with the same question. The man replied, "Oh sir, I'm building a great cathedral. I love building. But this building is special. It will be grand and beautiful. Many people will gather here to worship. Their spiritual lives and destinies will be changed in this mighty cathedral. I'm so blessed to have the opportunity to be part of this project. Can you believe it? I get to participate in something so special and actually be paid for it."

Note: My rendition of this story doesn't exactly match the book but is more like I remember it from the sermon I first heard it in.

CONNECTING PEOPLE TO PURPOSE

I'm a brick layer.	I'm a builder.	I'm building a great cathedral.
• Making a living	• Making a life/career	• Making a difference
• Pursuing money	• Pursuing a passion	• Pursuing a calling
• Using muscle–gutting it out	• Using a talent	• Using passion and talent
• It's a hard task.	• This is who I am and what I like to do.	• This is what I was called to do, what God made me for, and I can't believe I get paid for doing this!

The point is that all three men were performing the same activity, on the same project, and for the same pay. But they had radically different perspectives.

The first one could only see the task he performed as a duty because of what he and his family got out of it. It felt like labor and drudgery to him. He is like those individuals in the organization who are given a task to do with no explanation or connection to how it fits into what the organization is doing.

The second man had a broader perspective. He saw himself as a builder. He enjoyed his work and was thankful that he got paid. Unlike the other person, he was exercising his natural talents and passion in his work. He is like those individuals who enjoy being part of the organization they are with, but they are not connected mentally and emotionally to the mission and vision of the organization.

The third man saw the uniqueness of what he was building and felt truly fortunate to be part of it. He was grateful that he could be part of something so grand and, on top of that, get paid to support his family. This man was connected to the mission and vision of what he was doing. He saw the work as a privilege of being part of something bigger than himself. He is like those individuals who are committed to the mission and vision of an organization. They are using their natural talents. The mission and vision resonates with their passions. They sense they are fulfilling their destiny or calling in life. If they didn't need money to live, they would do the same thing and work just as hard at it.

Isn't this what we see in all kinds of organizations, regardless of the type of work performed? Some see their job as only the task, the labor, and the drudgery for what they get paid. Some see their work as what they do, enjoy it, and are glad they get paid. Some see their work as part of something great and feel privileged to be part of it. And at times, they are amazed they get paid for doing something so wonderful.

What are the key differences? One is people doing what they are most talented at and having passion and sense of purpose for doing it. The other is having more information and a broader perspective of what they are part of. The leader impacts both of these by:

- Putting people in roles they have the talent, passion, and a "calling" for;

- Empowering them to do it;

- Supporting them when they need help; and

- Sharing information and perspective about how what they do fits with the mission and vision of the organization in a meaningful way. This requires ongoing communication with the team.

THE EXECUTIVE ASSISTANT

I know a person who is a great executive assistant. She worked for a pretty demanding executive for several years. After he left his role, I thought she would be relieved because he was so demanding and she worked so hard. After a few months, but before his position was filled, I asked her if she was happier. She said, "No, not at all." I asked her, "Aren't you working less?" She replied, "Yes." I asked, "Then, why aren't you happier?"

She said, "I did work really hard when he was here. But, he would tell me what we were doing and why. I felt like I was contributing in a meaningful way to what was happening in the company. Now I feel like I'm pushing paper, taking calls, and scheduling." In other words, she was really saying she went from feeling like a cathedral builder to feeling like a brick layer. Unfortunately, organizations do this to people frequently.

This discussion really struck me. It's how we explain people's jobs/roles to them and share information that connects them to the mission and vision of what we're doing that changes their perspective. It's like the difference between a brick layer and a person building a great cathedral. This sharing of information and perspective is something that should happen all the time in a healthy organization.

APPLICATION TO NON-PROFIT ORGANIZATIONS

Because the apex of the triangle illustrating an effective organization is "accountability," we tend to think this doesn't apply to non-profit organizations. (Remember, accountability includes the potential for both reward and discipline.) We shouldn't be so quick to make that assumption. Scripture says, "A workman is worthy of his hire." Also, Peter told Jesus that he had left everything to follow him. He asked about his reward. Jesus did not rebuke him for asking the question. Instead, he told him he would be rewarded handsomely in this life and also would receive eternal life.

Given that the missions of non-profit organizations are for the betterment of mankind and absent the profit motive, it seemed less acceptable to me for non-profit organizations not to operate at the height of efficiency and effectiveness, thus having the potential for reward and discipline like any other entity in society. Think of it this way. If a for-profit organization can operate at mediocre levels of effectiveness and efficiencies but still produce a good or service and provide an acceptable rate of return to their shareholders, who is being shorted? If customers are getting value for the goods or services they buy in a competitive market, have they been wronged? Have shareholders been wronged if they believe the return on investment is adequate and have other competitive opportunities to invest their funds?

Conversely, much of the funding for some non-profit organizations and, indeed, all the funding for many other non-profit organizations come from donors who give money they worked hard for, trusting that the mission of the non-profit organization will be carried out effectively and efficiently. If this is not the case, the leadership of the non-profit organizations has not properly stewarded the gifts of their donors and should be held to as high or even higher standards of stewardship as their for-profit counterparts.

Application

Assess the key people in your organization. List below in three columns the ones who approach their jobs like bricklayers, builders, and cathedral builders.

Bricklayers	Builders	Cathedral Builders

What will you do to change the perception of those who feel like bricklayers?

_____

_____

_____

— 34 —

_____

_____

_____

_____

_____

Chapter 4

IS YOUR ORGANIZATION FUNCTIONAL OR DYSFUNCTIONAL?

> Thought:
> How much more could your organization accomplish
> if you could eliminate the dysfunction that exists?

Good

"Let all things be done decently and in order."

1 Corinthians 14:40

Our God is a God of order, not of chaos. If God gives us a leadership role in an organization, it should have a sense of order, not of chaos. The diagram below shows a very broad perspective of a functional organization.[33]

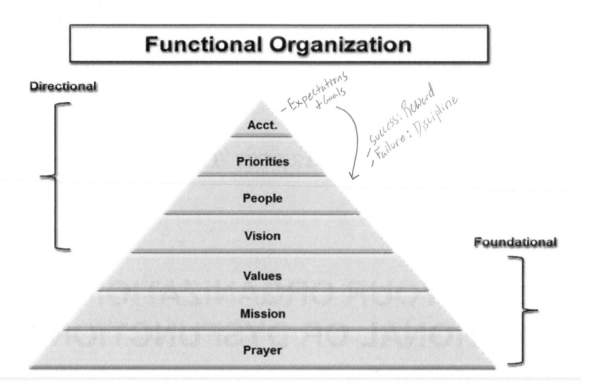

Prayer aligns us with God so that the mission is about His purposes and not just our own. The mission indicates why the organization exists. In other words, what purpose does it serve in society? The values support the mission and give people a sense of security. The mission and values are foundational for all the organization does in the future. The vision needs to be clear and shared by the team. Priorities are set to achieve the vision. These are supported by strategies, tactics, and goals. These are converted to expectations or goals for the people on the team. Finally, there is an accountability that individuals face for their part the in organization's success or failure. This accountability can include either rewards or discipline which can be both financial and non-financial.

The mission and values are foundational elements of the organization. The vision, priorities, and accountability all determine the direction of the organization.

By contrast, the diagram below shows a picture of a dysfunctional organization.

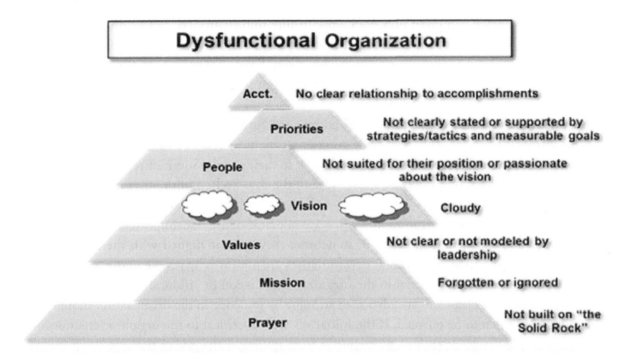

Organizations not founded on **prayer** are not founded on the "solid rock" and will eventually crumble (Matthew 7:24-26).

Mission creep or mission amnesia is something organizations often experience. Mission creep is when the organization starts operating outside the scope of its mission. Mission amnesia is simply when the true mission of the founder is usually forgotten and not focused upon. Some major universities are good examples. They started as seminaries and strayed from the mission of their founders. Non-profit organizations, especially churches, are particularly at risk of mission creep. They have benevolent goals and often accomplish much through volunteers. When individuals have a good idea that helps people, they will tend to take it on if they have resources to do so whether it truly fits their mission or not.

More dysfunction is created when **values** are not clear. They should be written, displayed, and modeled by all leaders in the organization. The worst dysfunction is when there are documented value statements that get some attention but are not modeled by the leadership. In other words, leaders don't "walk the talk."

HCA had a strong values statement dealing with treating everyone with dignity and respect. I'm proud to say that the senior leaders took this seriously and lived it out in their leadership style.

However, there was one senior vice president who did not agree with it nor live out the value of treating others with dignity and respect. I remember thinking it was hypocritical of the executive leadership of the company to keep this person in place. Then, I realized that on my team I had a leader who was not living out one of the key values I talked about a lot— teamwork. I had counseled this person and given him every opportunity to turn around, but he did not. I finally released him. Then, I pulled my team together and apologized for allowing someone at the senior level to work against the values we were to be living out. From that point forward, the team grew stronger and the results got better because we all lived out the values we talked about.

Sometimes, leaders are so confused with the current and future environment that they don't have a clear **vision** themselves. They are trying to get past the next crisis or next quarter. Since they don't have a clear sense of direction, they can't give it to their people. Some entrepreneurial founders are true visionaries, but others are more "idea of the day, week, month, or year" type people.

Priorities in dysfunctional organizations often are not clear or are not supported by good strategies, tactics, and measurable goals. Also, sometimes they are not aligned with the mission and vision of the organization. Sometimes, new initiatives are put forth by people in the organization that are good ideas but not central to the organization's mission or vision. The fact that they are good, well-intended ideas, and are advocated strongly by someone in the organization should not be enough for them to be pursued. If the initiatives are not critical to the organization's mission and vision, they detract attention and resources from initiatives that are critical.

People are not passionate about the mission and vision in dysfunctional organizations. They may not agree with the values or priorities. They may not be best suited for their jobs. They are not clearly aligned with their accountabilities in dysfunctional organizations. A lot of organizations fall down in this area of having clear goals to which people are held accountable. This seems to be especially true for non-profit organizations. They quite often do not have good accountability systems for their people.

Accountability is not clearly established in dysfunctional organizations. There is not a clear alignment of the rewards or discipline to the actions or results of the individual. People don't see a clear correlation between what they do and contribute to how they are recognized or disciplined financially and otherwise. This seems to be particularly problematic in non-profit organizations. Often, people are rewarded or recognized for not rocking the boat and for their longevity in the role. In fact, systems are often set up based solely on longevity versus being rewarded for helping achieve specific goals. This is especially true in the area of government service. Don't get me wrong. There are very good, hard-working public service employees in our nation. Yet, the organizational structures are not established to clearly distinguish performance and reward people for providing superior service versus mediocre service. In the parable of the talents, the man who worked hard and doubled his five talents to ten was also given the talent of the bad steward who buried his one talent and did not produce anything with it.

I am a proponent of using consultants under the right circumstances. However, organizations often waste substantial money and time having consultants review internal processes or functions, evaluating and trying to strengthen teams, improving teamwork, and so on. But often the issues are structural. When people are pitted against each other structurally based on unaligned goals and incentives, teams aren't ultimately going to work well together. When misaligned, organizations and their processes and functions aren't going to work well, and people are not likely to come together to resolve internal issues.

My consulting approach focuses on evaluating the areas of dysfunction in an organization from a "100,000 foot view" and dealing with those issues. This takes much less time and money and can be a much bigger lever for the organization improving itself. Other consultants can come in with specialized areas of expertise and help get other improvements when the organization is properly aligned.

CHANGING DIRECTIONS

Look at the preceding diagram and think about how you would change the direction of an organization if needed. HCA gave me a number of opportunities to lead organizations perceived to be going in the wrong direction. I used a common approach each time to change the direction. Changing direction requires changing the organization's vision and priorities. I followed these steps:

Step # 1

We engaged key leaders in the process. We used facilitated brainstorming sessions to clearly establish the mission and values which would be the foundation for the organization.

Step # 2

We had facilitated brainstorming sessions to establish direction. I led the team in a SWOT analysis. This is where we brainstormed the strengths, weaknesses, opportunities, and threats of the organization. Generally, I would engage many layers of the organization and summarize the results. Then, I worked with the leadership team to reach concurrence on the highest priority strengths, weaknesses, opportunities, and threats.

Step # 3

Based on these, we would create a vision of the change needed to build on the strengths, fix or avoid the weaknesses, avoid the threats, and capitalize on the opportunities.

Step # 4

I led the teams through the process of writing a clear vision statement. We established three to five, but never more than seven, clear priorities for the next year.

Step # 5

Then I worked with key leaders to break the priorities into goals for them and their direct reports.

Step # 6

We tied the incentive compensation into the expectations and goals of each team member.

Step # 7

Each quarter, I met with direct reports to go over the progress toward their goals. And I required that they do the same for their direct reports. Each quarter, and sometimes more frequently, the entire leadership team and I would look at the progress toward our vision and priorities. We also would revisit our mission and values to make sure we were being true to both.

Using this process, it was possible to make significant changes in organizations in relatively short periods of time.

Application

Complete the following for your organization.

Mission statement:

_____

_____

_____

_____

Values statement:

_____

_____

_____

_____

Vision statement:

_____

_____

_____

_____

Priorities for the next year:

_____

_____

_____

_____

Summary expectations of your leadership team:

_____

_____

_____

_____

Accountability for how your leadership team is compensated or disciplined, financial and non-financial:

_____

_____

_____

_____

The principles discussed in this chapter can be applied to any type of organization of any size. They can also be applied on an individual basis, especially to the leader. Just like an organization needs to be clear about its purpose and direction, individuals—especially leaders—need to be clear about theirs. If theirs are foggy, the organization is significantly affected.

Apply this to your personal life. Does it look functional or dysfunctional?

Chapter 5

WHAT IS YOUR PURPOSE AS A LEADER?

Thought:
If you are not clear about your purpose as a leader,
how clear do you think your team
will be about their purpose?

"Do not look out merely for your own interests.

Look out for the interests of others."

Philippians 2:4

The leader needs to answer the question, "Why am I here?" They need to be clear about their own personal mission in life, their vision of where their life is going, their personal values, what they expect of themselves, and the rewards they are seeking to reap.

 Good Heart Check

The mission, whether spoken or not, for some leaders is to exercise power, to control, to make money, and to receive perks. This doesn't match with King David's understanding of leadership. Nor does it match the biblical instruction to be interested in others and not just yourself. So here's the first real question for you personally. Are you in your place of leadership with the mindset you are there to serve and support others? The world gives one answer and Scripture another. This matters, even from a very practical standpoint. The life of King David is a good example.

King David sometimes forgot his purpose of blessing people. He did quite well by anyone's standards for a leader when he was focused on the good of the people. It was the times he focused solely on himself that he got into trouble.

The first example is his affair with Bathsheba. Here's one that hasn't changed in thousands of years—leaders using their position for sex. Then, there was the denial and cover-up where he had her husband, Uriah, killed in battle. This hasn't changed either. He used his power for the cover-up.

Then there was the time when he became prideful and had his armies counted to show how powerful he was. The result was a plague on the people because of David's pride. How often do leaders create great damage to their organizations and people through taking pride in what they can count versus counting the difference they're making in people's lives daily?

Last, but not least, was David ignoring his family. He did not pay attention to his children or discipline them as he should. As a result, Amnon raped a half-sister. Then, his half-brother, Absalom, killed Amnon.

In the end, David was considered a good and great king. God said, "He's a man after my own heart." That was because he repented, changed directions when he was wrong, and lived most of his life focused on God. But just think about how much better life would have been for David, his family, and his people if David's focus had stayed constantly on others versus being self-centered at times.

Misstep: Selfless vs. Selfish

The dynamics and focus in organizations with selfless leaders is really different than organizations where the leader is self-focused. And the outcomes are radically different.

SELFLESS LEADERS

Really...?

In healthy organizations, leaders are not selfish, but rather selfless.[34] They guide the team and empower them to create the best product or service for their customers or constituents.

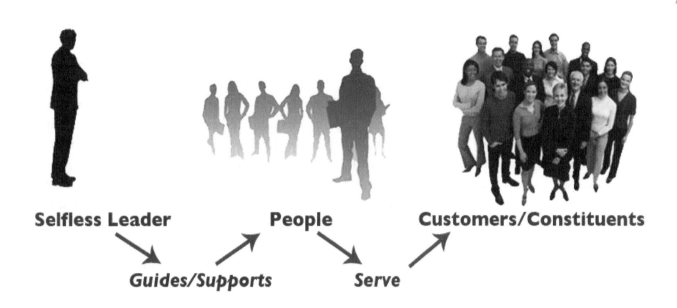

Selfless Leader → **People** → **Customers/Constituents**

Guides/Supports   **Serve**

In this organization, all the people and activities are focused on providing a good or service to others. They look to the leader for purpose, vision, and support, but their daily focus is on providing a quality product or service.

Here's a picture of an unhealthy organization.

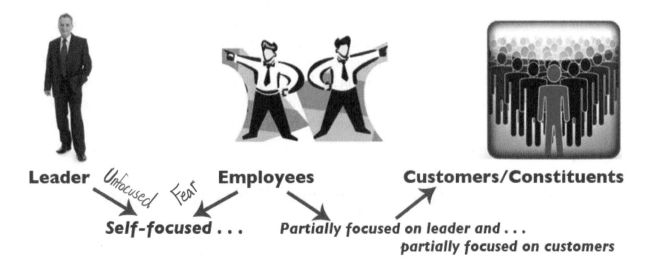

Leader *Unfocused* *Fear* **Employees** → **Customers/Constituents**

Self-focused . . .   **Partially focused on leader and . . .**
                          partially focused on customers

In this organization, the leader is self-focused. Therefore, the people's first priority is determining how to please the boss versus serving others or producing the highest quality product.

The bottom line is this. If we are self-focused, we will cause others to be focused more on us than on who they're supposed to be serving. But if we serve and support our team and focus them on the mission, vision, and goals of a quality service or product, we will have a better organization.

I know people who are very servant-oriented when they go to church or take on community projects. Then, it seems when they go to work, they flip the switch. Rather than being servants, they see themselves as being better than others. They violate the Scripture that tells masters not to "lord it over" their people. In other words, Scripture says don't be heavy-handed with those who work for you. Yet, many do not see the duplicity between being good servants at church and in the community and being oppressive at work. I'm acquainted with some people who have great relationships in every area of their lives other than work. And it's because they see themselves differently at work than anywhere else. They see themselves as servants in other roles but not servant leaders at work. They don't realize that if they lead well and support their team well, their customers are served better, the business prospers, they prosper, and there is opportunity for the employees to prosper. And the leader can receive respect and esteem from their team.

TRANSFORMATION

Leaders start out early in life with zeal and passion. We want to lead great organizations. We want to change the world. We want to grow organizations. We want to transform them into something better. We want them to be great. And many of us, and I especially, start with the idea that we can transform an organization without first being transformed personally, that we can grow an organization without growing personally, and that we can somehow create a great organization without becoming more than we already are. We want to be the fixers and the changers of organizations. We want to act like doctors to the organization that's not quite as healthy as it should be or maybe that's sick and broken, without being healed and fixed ourselves. Jesus told us to get the logs out of our own eyes before we try to get the splinter out of our brother's eye. What a great command. We would all make much better progress if we were healed ourselves before trying to fix an organization.

WHERE ARE YOU IN ANSWERING THESE QUESTIONS?

Are you clear about why God put you where you are? Are you clear about your direction in life? Are you a beginner like I once was where my vision was about what promoted and prospered me versus the impact on other people?

Are you clear about your values? Have you determined how you will live your life before the people you're leading? Have you determined what will be the basis of important and sometimes pressure-oriented decisions? Are you going to consider other people more important than yourself like Scripture says? Have you come to realize that, regardless of your stated values, the true values and impact to the culture in your organization are those you live out?

Are you clear about what you expect out of yourself? Are you willing to work as hard as you expect others to work? Conversely, are you willing to draw a line on the hours you work to be a good example to others? Or are you one of those leaders who will sacrifice your family for the organization? Do you expect more of yourself than you do of others?

[handwritten margin note: willing to be selfish?]

Sometimes, entrepreneurial leaders work really hard for a long time and then have a breakthrough to real financial success. They start flaunting their material rewards in front of the workforce and start playing more and turning the work over the others. It's fine to benefit from the fruit of your labors, and it's fine to empower and train others to do the work so that you can delegate more. But when leaders are perceived as flaunting their resources and playing while expecting the rest of the team to keep grinding, it almost always results in dissension, poor morale, and lesser commitment to the organization. Look at what happened when King David didn't go with his armies into battle.

If owners/leaders are going to be involved in the organization, they need to be viewed as working as hard as the rest of the team.

How do you determine what your reward is for your leadership? Leaders who want their rewards to be primarily financial, perks, and privileges will never be great leaders. Leaders who find rewards in the relationships they form, the positive impact they have on the lives of others, how much they are able to share financially with others in the organization, and how much they will be able give away because of their work will be better leaders and create more productive cultures for their employees.

Application

What about you? Is being a leader all about your power, pay, and perks? Do you have a strong sense of mission and vision for why God has you where you are?

Write your personal mission statement:

_____

_____

_____

_____

Write out the values you will live in front of your people:

_____

_____

_____

_____

Write your vision of the impact your life will have over the next five years:

_____

_____

_____

_____

What are the expectations you have of yourself this year? What will you specifically do to make the team more successful?

_____

_____

_____

_____

How will you measure rewards you receive for your leadership?

_____

_____

_____

Chapter 6

MY JOURNEY TOWARDS DISCOVERING PURPOSE

> Thought:
> Have you discovered your purpose for leading?

"for you have been called for this purpose . . ."

1 Peter 2:21

How I understood my purpose for being in HCA changed significantly from when I joined the organization when I was twenty-three years old versus ten years later. It was all about me when I started. My goal was to be a vice president, and I worked my heart out to achieve it. I was like the young lion, Simba, in the movie *The Lion King*, "I just can't wait to be king."

Along the way, my perspective began to change. I realized being there served more purpose than simply letting me be in charge. I began to see that I could impact that culture through a leadership role. I saw the opportunity to train, encourage, and guide young people toward their true potential.

The relationship our department had with operations was not good either. It was antagonistic and combative at times. I saw the opportunity to change the way we related to the rest of the organization and add more value.

Within nine years, my goal of being a vice president was a reality. I felt great for about a week, and then I was empty. I was thirty-two years old, a vice president, and had no hope or goal of ever running the company. So what was I going to do—just sit there and run the department year after year for the rest of my life?

I already had begun to understand that I could make life better for others through a leadership role. I had an epiphany and realized the rest of my life could be about training and developing people and seeing how many others I could help get promoted to other areas of the company over the course of my career.

I realized there were two things I did best—bring order to chaos and develop people. So, developing people through training, coaching, and mentoring and helping with organizational improvement became my mission. My vision related to helping certain numbers of other people over five-year spans be promoted. That was the focus to the rest of my career regardless of the platform I had for service. And it is still my mission and vision today.

One other thing still needed to change. That was my purpose. Being clear about whether I was doing this for me, for others, or for God was the key. When I came to understand that my purpose for being in HCA was a platform for serving God and thereby helping others, the dynamics changed. I must quickly admit sometimes I forgot or ignored my purpose by noon on many days. Some days, I didn't even make it to ten o'clock. But when I stayed focused on my purpose of serving God and helping others, it changed how I viewed everything.

When my purpose changed, it did not put me at odds with the organization. In fact, I served the company and its interest better when I changed. If my purpose had been at odds with the company and its leadership such that I was undermining its objectives, I would have been in the situation that I should have left. However, that was never the case.

MISSION

My mission statement is <u>"To invest my life training, coaching and mentoring leaders for the benefit of everyone they touch and to grow God's kingdom."</u>

VISION

My vision is to help at least three hundred leaders over the next five years improve their leadership styles to:

- Get more done in less time and with less frustration and stress;

- Have more time for their spouses, children, churches, communities, and friends and to enjoy life;

- Create healthy organizational cultures to benefit their employees versus bringing difficulty and stress into their lives; and

- Create more profitability, if they are business owners, so they have more financial resources to contribute to ministries and charities.

To make the kind of changes necessary in my approach, I knew that I needed to change. And not just a little bit. I needed to change radically from the inside out. This wasn't something that I could do on my own. I had to ask Jesus to help me. I wasn't able to do it all on my own and still can't. Some people are easy to love and some aren't. Some people are easy to care about and others aren't. I need Jesus helping me to love and care about others and putting them first versus me. This is still a daily challenge for me.

I realize as I look back at this that I may have made discovering your purpose sound easier than it really is. This was a struggle for me over many years with a number of setbacks, fears, and confusion before it started to become clear. And it's still an ongoing journey for me. I just hope I can help make yours quicker and easier.

Notes

II. PEOPLE

God created people to serve a purpose in His plan . . .

Be transformed from using people to understanding them and partnering with them to achieve God's plans.

"Before you were formed in the womb,

I knew you . . . "

Jeremiah 1:5

"Do not look out merely for your own interests.

Look out for the interests of others."

Philippians 2:4

". . . Give preference to one another in honor."

Romans 12:10

Questions to Ponder

- Can the people in your organization live out their purpose and calling in life and contribute directly to the purpose of your organization?

- Are people your greatest asset or biggest problem? Or are they both?

- Do you have the right people in place?

- Do you have the wrong people in place but don't know what to do?

- Do you love your people but know things have changed and they don't fit their roles anymore?

- Do you really understand your leadership style, including your strengths and weaknesses?

- Do you understand the personality profiles of your leadership team and key team members?

- Do you understand how they complement your style?

Issues Covered in this Section

- Understanding the whole person.

- Understanding yourself and your people better using personality profiles.

- Choosing the right team.

- Dealing with people who don't fit their roles.

- Knowing the best way to remove a person from a job or the organization.

Chapter 7

UNDERSTANDING
THE WHOLE PERSON

Thought!
Have you ever thought about how strong your organization would be
if people there clearly understood their calling (purpose) and their
unique talents, and they could contribute directly to the mission/vision
of the organization by pursuing their calling and using their unique talents?

"For I know the plans that I have for you, declares the Lord,
plans for welfare and not for calamity
to give you a future and hope."
Jeremiah 29:11

God has great plans for us. If we cooperate with Him, He carries out these plans in our lives because He knows us better than we know ourselves. God put trout in mountain streams because that's where they fit. He put marlin in the ocean because that's where they belong. Not all fish are the same. They do not prosper and survive in just any environment. Likewise, individuals don't just prosper and survive anywhere. They do best in the environment they were created for.

A lawyer once asked Jesus to sum up all of the teachings of Scripture up to that point. Jesus told the lawyer, in essence, to love God with all his being and his neighbor as himself. When you lead an organization, how do you love your neighbor as yourself when you're hiring people or making assignments? If you're going to bless people through your organization, there are five things you have to be aware of in hiring and in ongoing delegation:

- **Purpose**, which I refer to as people's callings. What did God create them to do and accomplish?

- **Personality profile**, which is their hardwiring and unique personality traits.

- **Passion**, which is what they care about deeply.

- **Preparation**, which includes their education, work experience, and other life experiences.

- **Potential**, which includes their ability to grow with the job and organization.

There is a difference between pursuing a calling versus just having a job. Having the ability to do something is not enough. The word vocation comes from the Latin word, "to call." It suggests you are listening for something that is calling out to you, listening for God's voice—something that is particular to you. A calling is something you have to listen for—a connection to something larger than yourself.[1]

Stephen Covey says we all want "to live, to love, to learn and to leave a legacy." There's no better way to leave a legacy than by following our calling.

God called me to work with leaders who would grow His kingdom. The balance all of us as leaders must maintain is how do we influence each situation for the good of the organization and for increase in the kingdom of God?

It is easy to assume that because people have similar personality profiles—hardwiring—that they are the same. There will be some similarities, habits, and approaches to work, but that doesn't mean they're the same.

Our talents are different. People with similar profiles can have different talents. There are a lot of people with profiles similar to mine that are a lot smarter than I am. Scripture says God gave one man one talent, another man two talents, and another man five talents. We are accountable to use our talents, but we all have different talents. *What is a talent?*

Our experiences differ. I led the internal audit department in a big corporation for a number of years. My personality profile may be very similar to others in the company with similar roles. But, I grew up on a very small dairy farm in western Kentucky, and the work experiences I had are significantly different than others. They had and always will have an impact on my mind, emotions, and spirit. I may respond very differently in certain situations than anybody else would.

Our passions differ. Joyce is a nurse. She is very talented, like most nurses. She has a similar profile to many nurses and a lot of the same type experiences. But Joyce has a passion for patient advocacy above and beyond most of her nursing peers. Many people with my talent, personality profile, and work experience are interested in leadership development. But, I have a passion for investing my life in leaders that goes beyond many of my peers.

I believe people are unique. In our culture, we like to rate people as average, above average, or below average. This starts in grade school with the bell-shaped curve for grading people and continues throughout our life. People may be average, above average, or below average in the use of their talents, but they are unique. The combination of their personality profiles, talents, experiences, passions, and calling makes them different from anyone else ever created. Scientists tell us no two snowflakes are identical. Do you think God ran out of ideas on people?

MISTAKES

I always made mistakes when I only looked at a person through a limited lens. Businesses tend to look primarily at preparation and experience while ministries tend to look more at calling and educational preparation. Let's look at these in more detail.

LOOKING ONLY AT PREPARATION AND EXPERIENCE

Let's understand how these interrelate and identify common mistakes leaders make in this very important area. In most businesses, there is an over concentration in one of these areas: preparation. Employers want to know that people have the skill and experience to do the job. They also want people who want a job, but they often are not careful to assess whether these people have passion for the job or they just need and want the job for the income.

Most managers (vs. leaders) hire and assign work based on talent and experience only. I believe every person was created for a unique purpose in the universe, and in God's kingdom, that purpose is one only *they* can fulfill. The mentality in many organizations is that "if you can't get it done, I will find somebody that will." The truth is, if a job is not getting done, a change very well may be in order. But all individuals are unique and if they are the right people for the job, nobody else can do it exactly like they can, and they should be treated as such.

[handwritten margin note: The irreplaceability of Persons 7.9.20]

As a Christian leader, if your main concern is finding somebody that has the skill and experience to do a job, but doing it is not consistent with their God given "calling," or they do not have great passion for the job, you're simply using that person and their skills for your purposes. If, however, the job you give a person is consistent with their calling, personality profile, passions, and preparation, you have a situation where neither is using the other. Rather, the organization has meaningful work that needs to be done to serve society and engages people to do it who can live out their calling in that role, express their passion through it in a way that is consistent with their personality profile, and uses how God has prepared them up to this point. There is not only great harmony in this arrangement, there's less conflict. And, the leader is a much better steward of the organization's resources because this creates a much more productive environment and much higher morale for the entire team.

[handwritten margin note: Very Kantian but good]

IGNORING PERSONALITY PROFILES – EXPECTING TOO MUCH

I'm thinking of at least two different people now in leadership roles. Over time, I have seen them get extremely frustrated and angry at some of their key people. As they talked out with me their frustrations and anger over the performance of their people, I began to understand the personality profiles of the people. It became very clear to me that the problem was not with the people. They were really good, hard-working people, well qualified for their primary role. The frustration and anger came in when the employers asked them to do things that they did not have the personality profile for. The employers made the assumption because they were excellent at certain things that they should be able to do the other things they wanted them to do. That just wasn't the case.

One example in particular stands out. Jim was constantly irritated with the performance of Joe. I asked why he didn't just release him and be done with the aggravation. He said that Joe is really good at certain things. I asked what Joe was good at and Jim explained. Jim also explained those things he needed, but Joe was never good at. We ran a personality profile which indicated that Joe was hardwired to be good at those things where he had been successful but had no aptitude for the other list of things that Jim wanted. I asked Jim about just delegating those things to Joe he was good at and doing the rest himself or finding someone else for the other work he needed done. He did, and they have had a successful working relationship for a number of years. I must acknowledge, however, the difficulty that a person in a smaller organization with limited staff has in this area. There is always the temptation to want someone to do something beyond an individual skill set and personality profile. I had this temptation many times even in a large organization.

[handwritten margin note: No X; when you get the right person for it, you're a good steward of what you have.]

IGNORING PASSION

[handwritten note: So people p.20 before Vision?]

There are a number of business employers and some ministries and non-profits that use personality profiles in their selection process. I believe this adds to their success rate in finding people who fit the job. However, you can still have someone who has the right personality profile and the necessary preparation to do the job that still doesn't have a calling and passion for it. I know a young man trained as an accountant. He does a very effective job where he works, and his boss would be distraught if he lost him. However, the young man has no real passion for accounting, even though he's good at it. His real passion is cars. He knows everything about cars and loves working on them. He can do incredible things better than most mechanics. In the role he's in, he's being used by an employer as an accountant, but I believe his true calling and passion would have him serving people by doing a good honest job of repairing their cars. He has both the personality profile for that, as well as adequate preparation. If he followed his calling and passion, all the dots would connect for him. He makes a good living at what he's doing, but he would have a better life doing what he is called to. And, in this circumstance, this individual would likely have a higher standard of living and more independence.

It is sometimes surprising how far off base we are in the assumptions we make about people. I remember a guy recently in a meeting saying that he had two good gentlemen who worked for him for many years. He made an assumption that one of the guys preferred certain types of projects, which he always gave to him. One day, it occurred to him to ask the guy what he really liked to do. To the employer's surprise, the work this employee most enjoyed doing was work being given to the other gentleman and vice versa. We get in such a hurry trying to do things that it is often truly amazing how little we really know about the preferences and dreams of our team.

OVER RELIANCE ON CALLING AND PREPARATION

In some churches and ministries, the focus is often almost exclusively on people's understanding of their calling and education. It's rare that personality profiles are used to make sure individuals are suited for the exact role and situation they are being placed in. In some positions in churches, there is high turnover because individuals are put in roles where the expectations don't match their personality profiles. I made reference to people's understanding of their calling, which in many cases may be different from their real calling. I have friends in the life coaching profession who tell me stories about people in ministry with no real passion for ministry and with often poor or mediocre results. There is one I think of in particular that was gifted as an artist but pastored a church because he thought that's what he ought to do. When he left the church and pursued his real calling and passion, he was met with great joy and success which continues to this day.[2]

I understand it's not my role to question people's callings. I'm reminded of a statement by Chuck Swindoll in one of his books where he said, "If you can do anything else, don't go into the ministry." Based on the context in the book, my understanding was that he was saying that unless your passion for ministry and sense of calling is so great that you can't bring yourself to do something else, you are well suited for ministry. The turnover rate among people who go to seminaries and go into some form of ministry is very high. Some of that is likely the spiritual battles fought and lost. But much of it may be very practical. In other words, it's possible a number of these people were not really called in the ministry, don't have the passion for it, may or may not have the personality profile for it. But, they get the preparation and experience and then wonder why it doesn't work.

Using people versus engaging as partners

Do you know why many leaders don't consider the whole person in making hiring or delegation decisions? I'll use my own experience as the example. Frankly, many times I was so interested in getting the job done that I used people to accomplish the task versus looking at the world from their perspective. I wasn't trying to make sure that what I was asking them to do matched their hardwiring, talents, experiences, passions, and calling. I'm going to make an admission here. Over my career, I hired hundreds and likely well over a thousand individuals. I made thousands of job assignments. To be honest, most of the time I had in mind what I needed done and would help reach the objectives that I needed to make for the organization. If I had understood what God has made painfully clear to me now, I would have put even more time in the interview process and thought process before delegating and making assignments, and I would have had an even more effective organization. I would have been a better steward of what God had entrusted to me.

The most effective organization I can imagine is one where people are hired or join the organization that has a very clear sense of their calling in life. If they can clearly live out their calling and contribute directly to the mission of the organization, you have an ideal fit. In this environment, people do what they do because they simply feel like that's what they were created to do. There's no forcing them. While money is important because they need to make a living and provide for their family, more money won't necessarily cause them to work harder if they are there living out their calling. They will work harder, be more committed, be very hesitant to ever leave the organization, and look out for the best interests of the organization if they can achieve the vision of the organization by living out their calling. In this type culture, problems and friction are avoided. Morale and productivity are high. Customer service improves and so does profitability.

How about you? When you are hiring or making job assignments, do you consider:

- The calling of your people?

- What they are really passionate about?

- Their personality profile? Do you really think about how the job or assignment fits how they're hardwired? Or, is it just something you think they should be able to do?

- Their preparation? Do you know them well enough to know what they are truly capable of so that you'll give them work to do they're not going to fail at?

- Their potential to grow in the job and with the organization?

Application

Do you really know your people? For the three people on your team that you think you know the best, can you be specific about their unique talents? Do you know the significant experiences, personal and professional, that have shaped their lives? Do you know what they are really passionate about? Have you ever asked them what they would do with their time if money were no object and failure not a possibility? Have you ever talked to them about their calling and purpose in life? What is it that they feel like they were just created to do?

	Name	Name	Name
1. Unique talents	_____	_____	_____
2. Significant life changing experience	_____	_____	_____
3. Passions	_____	_____	_____
4. What they would do if money were no issue.	_____	_____	_____
5. What they feel called to do	_____	_____	_____

Now, do this for yourself.

_____

_____

_____

_____

_____

_____

Chapter 8

UNDERSTANDING PEOPLE'S PERSONALITIES — THEIR HARDWIRING

Thought:
Have you ever wondered how much more productive and fun
your work could be if you really understood
what "makes your people tick?"

*"For you formed my inward parts: you knitted me together
in my mother's womb... intricately woven."*
Psalms 139:13-15

There is an old joke about a man who heroically saved some people's lives. To reward him, God offered to do anything for him that he asked. The man said, "I've always wanted to go to China, but I don't like to fly. Would you create a bridge so that I can drive to China?" God said, "That's not a difficult thing for me to do. But that seems rather self-centered. I was hoping you would ask for something that would benefit many others as well." The man thought for a few moments and said, "I want you to help me understand women. I want to understand why they laugh, what makes them cry, and what makes them mad at men. That would help all men and make life better for women, too." The man was rather pleased with his request, but now God seemed perplexed. After a moment, God said, "Now about that bridge, did you want it to be two lanes or four lanes?"

I don't tell that joke to be chauvinistic. The truth is men often do not understand women, women often do not understand men, parents do not understand children, children do not understand parents, people do not understand people, and very often we don't even understand ourselves.

More than once in my career, I've closed my door, sat at my desk, and banged my head on the top of my desk saying, "What were you thinking?" The truth is I was really confused about what I was thinking and why I had just taken a certain action. I don't know if you've ever banged your head on your desk, but I strongly suspect you've had the same feeling as I had at some point in your life.

The truth is many leaders do not know themselves well, nor do they understand other people. What's the solution? We need to understand how we and others are made—our hardwiring or personality profile.

We seem to be schizophrenic in organizational life about our people. Most successful organizations have some value statement affirming the worth of its people, such as "people are our greatest asset." Yet some leaders complain about their teams saying things like "my job would be fun if it weren't for the people." The truth is your people can bring great joy to your life and value to the organization. Or they can bring great pain, problems, and destruction in organizational life. So how do we understand ourselves and others better? One piece of this is by understanding personality profiles.

God knows us, and He knows us intimately. He knows the purpose He created us for. He knows everything we need to live out our destiny. As leaders, one of our goals should be to help our people discern their uniqueness and live out their unique God-given purpose.

WHEN GOD GIVES US A JOB, HE GIVES US THE TOOLS TO DO IT WITH

Every mechanic has a toolbox. Good mechanics know what every tool is to be used for and how to use it. Imagine a mechanic who did not know the difference between a 5/8 inch socket wrench, a 1 inch open-end wrench, or a monkey wrench. Do you think they could make a living? Would you want them working on your car? Of course not!

You couldn't make a living being a mechanic if you didn't understand the difference in your various tools.

Electricians have a lot of knowledge about wiring. In fact, they are required to have a license showing their knowledge of wiring. If they do not know what they're doing, they could electrocute themselves. They could do a faulty job and burn a building down. If this happened, other people could be hurt or killed.

Assume a building contractor allowed an unlicensed electrician to work on his job. The electrician does faulty wiring, the building burns, and people are killed. What happens to the building contractor? He is sued for damages to the building. He is likely sued by family members for the cause of death or injury to people. It's possible he could even face criminal charges. In other words, there's great accountability for letting people deal with the wiring in the building where they don't have sufficient knowledge.

How does this apply to leadership? The height of God's creation in value, worth, and complexity is a human being. In addition to the other resources God gives leaders to work with, the most important is people. These people have a unique personality—hardwiring—that God gave them. We refer to these as personality profiles. What do most leaders understand about personality profiles in general and specifically the personality profiles of the people they are impacting? Very little! I shudder to think how little I understood about the personality profiles of people when I began leading.

You can't be an electrician without training and a license showing you know about wiring. Why are people allowed to lead others when they don't understand their "wiring" or Personality Profile?

Owners of businesses and leaders of other organizations often give people management responsibility with significant influence over the lives of people who have very little understanding of the personality profiles. When you're dealing with people "hardwired" a specific way, with little understanding of that hardwiring, it's likely that over time you're going to fry their mind, emotions, motivations, passions, and spirit. No licenses are required for leaders and managers to understand the hardwiring of people, and there's no accountability of the owner when bad things happen.

So, how can we understand the hardwiring of our people? God knows us intimately because He made us. Jeremiah 29:6 says, "Before you were formed in your mother's womb, I knew you." We can begin to understand how people are designed better by understanding and using personality profiles in our work.

UNDERSTANDING PEOPLE'S PERSONALITIES

Have you ever seen a trout in the mountain stream? They are actually hard to see. They seem to just blend with the stream. Unless the sunlight hits them just right or they make a sudden movement, they're hard to see. They tend to flow with the stream. It all seems rather effortless. They just seem to fit that mountain stream, don't they? But not every fish fits a mountain stream. There are salmon that swim upstream and die after laying their eggs. The marlins don't fit a mountain stream at all. They belong in an ocean.

I remember a conversation with a guy at a key point in his career. He was trying to determine if he would take the CEO job in a big company or the CEO job in a small start-up company. After listening to him for a while, I told him that he wasn't meant, at that point in his life, to be a big fish in a small pond but rather a big fish in the ocean. That statement immediately resonated with him. How God made us determines where and what we are suited for. Understanding our unique personality profile is one step toward understanding how God made us.

There are a great number of good systems on the market. For purposes of this discussion, we will refer to one of the oldest and most basic—the **DISC**. I use it because it is one of the easiest to understand and communicate to other people. Also, it provides great context for any other system I use that is more complicated. I am able to explain those other complexities using the DISC model.

In the DISC system,

The "D" stands for <u>dominant</u>. These people are driven to get results.

The "I" stands for <u>influencer</u>. These people are very social. They tend to be the life of the party. They never meet a stranger.

The "S" stands for <u>steady</u>. These people tend to stay calm when others panic. They are very team oriented.

The "C" stands for <u>competent</u>. These people are analytical, intuitive, and very detail oriented. The chart below gives more details about the characteristics of each.[3]

DISC

C = Competence	D = Dominant
• Conscientious authority	• Driving achiever
• Analytical	• Makes quick decisions
• Sensitive	• Takes action
• Factual	• Is forceful
• Diplomatic	• Is time conscious
S = Steady	**I = Influencing**
• Steady worker	• Influential personality
• Loyal	• Helpful
• Patient	• Persuasive
• Specialist	• Emotional
• Team member	• Trusting

Your unique personality impacts:

- Your marriage — how you relate to your spouse

- Your parenting — how you parent your children

- Your work — what you do best and enjoy the most

- How you communicate

- How you deal with stress and the related impact on your health

- Your approach to delegation

- How you're motivated and try to impact the motivation of others

I will discuss each of these to help you understand personality profiles better. My goal in this chapter is to give you a working knowledge of personality profiles that you can use in real time and to acquaint you with tools you can use. I am not trying to make you an expert in this material. I will begin with your personal life that you can relate to the easiest and then I will discuss organizational life.

Marriage relationship

"Husbands, love your wives

and do not be embittered against them."

Colossians 3:19

There is an old saying that opposites attract. That isn't always true, but it was for me. The highest two areas of my profile are "D" and "C," with "S" as my third highest. If the "I" component of my personality were my heartbeat or brain waves, I would be in a coma. I have almost none. The highest areas of my wife are "I" and "S." These differences make life interesting, really fun, and at times frustrating, especially for her. We are perfect complements for each other.

We don't argue much. There are two reasons for that. First, her "I" personality likes to relate and have the approval of other people. Her "S" personality likes to get along and will quickly acquiesce to what others think or want. The second and primary reason is because I spend a fair amount of time arguing with myself. Yes, in my head, I argue with myself. My "D" personality says hurry up, make a decision, and go for it. The "C" part of my personality, which is almost as strong as my "D" is cautious and analytical. It says to slow down. Think about this more. Gather some more information. The "D" and "C" portions of my personality have some pretty heated and interesting debates in my head.

Then, there is the "S" portion of my personality which is not quite as strong. It's a peacemaker. It says, "Can't we all just get along?" It's talking to my "D" and "C" personality in the background saying calm down, work this out, and agree. The "D" part of me often tells the "S" part of me to shut up because I'm trying to have a debate with my "C."

So imagine the discussions going on in my mind. I argue with myself a lot. If I choose to argue with other people, I can often convincingly argue opposite sides of the same issues within the course of the conversation. I drive myself crazy at times. In fact, I used to think I was a bit crazy. Understanding my personality profile has helped relieve that tension.

Parenting

"Fathers, do not provoke your children to anger,

but bring them up in the discipline and instruction of the Lord."

Ephesians 6:3-5

Scripture tells us not to anger our children. As a practical matter, how do we keep from doing that? I was teaching a class on personality profiles once and a very agitated middle-aged man got my attention and asked if they made personality profiles for kids. I told him the profile did work for them too. As the discussion unfolded, he was actually talking about his 17-year-old son. This man was obviously a very high "D" personality. After asking a couple of questions, I discerned that his son was primarily an "S" personality. It was quite obvious to me that without some understanding and training for this man, he and his son would have trouble getting along. He would have great difficulty relating to his son in a way that would be constructive in helping him.

I heard a story about something Hallmark cards did in the prison system. They offered all the inmates free Mother's Day cards. Most of the inmates took a card and sent one to their moms. This was so well-received that they decided to do the same thing on Father's Day. To their surprise, very few of the inmates wanted a card for their father. Studies have shown a strong correlation between an absent father figure or father figure that doesn't relate well to their children and sons ending up in prison. It's very easy for fathers to anger their children. The more we understand about their hardwiring, the more we can relate to them in a way that is appropriate for them.

There's a difference between being fair to your kids and giving them what they need versus treating them the same. It's highly unlikely that they are the same regarding their personalities. So, how they need you to parent them will be different.

My son is very high "I" and "D." My two daughters have "S," "I" and "C" about the midline with their "D" below the midline. Trust me—they're very different in what they need. My son with the "I" and "D" personality needs a lot of freedom with some very clear boundaries to protect him. He's very capable. He's been quite successful as a business leader. But when he went to college, I knew his natural tendency would be to focus on social aspects a lot and the scholastic aspects less. I gave him a minimum GPA hurdle he had to reach each semester to stay in school. It was below his capabilities, but high enough not to cause him a problem getting a job when he graduated. I did not want to set it so high that it frustrated him and caused him to give up. But, I was not willing to set it so low it would cause a problem down the road. His GPA when he graduated was within 1/10 of a percent of the target we set. I have to say, and he would agree, that he had a really great time, too.

No such target was ever established for my daughters. Why? Their natural temperaments were to try hard and be very conscientious in their studies. A target for either one of them would have simply put unnecessary stress in their lives that neither one of them needed in order to do the best they could. I was constantly telling them to do their best and not to worry, their grades would be fine. And they were. They always did better than they thought they were going to do. But, the pressure of a target from me would have been hard for them even though they would have given their all to beat the target.

Work

> " ... and in the hearts of all who are skillful I have put skill,
>
> that they may make all that I have commanded you. "
>
> Exodus 31:6

God gifted people with all kinds of talents to express in doing His work. Maybe you've heard the age-old question, "Are leaders made or born?" Do you know who asked that question? Academicians! The same people don't ask if artists were made or born or if musicians were made or born. It's rather obvious they have a special talent or gift and that through much practice they develop and refine it. The same is true with leaders. They are born with a special gift or talent that they work hard to develop and refine. Can someone be trained to draw who is not a natural artist? Yes, but they will only be proficient to a certain degree. Can someone sing or play a musical instrument without being gifted musically? Yes, but there will be a limit to what they can do. The same goes for leaders. People can be trained with certain skill sets and operate at some level, but they can never be as effective as somebody gifted as a leader.

In the work environment, people can be trained to do a great variety of things. The key is to find what they're naturally gifted at and let them refine and perfect their natural talents versus trying to do something that takes a great deal of effort and they will never be great at. One of the things you're looking for in hiring people or giving them assignments is what they are naturally good at. What do they feel like they were just created to do? The hardwiring, or personality profile, of an individual will give us some help in knowing what a person is naturally good at.

The "D" personality likes to initiate ideas and come up with new projects or initiatives. They like to take charge or control the project.

The "I" personality likes to sell or promote the idea. They're concerned about the people aspect of the project. They like to handle the social part of the project.

The "S" personality likes doing things. They enjoy doing the work. They want to do whatever it takes to make the team successful.

The "C" personality likes to improve upon the idea. They are very technical and analytical. They are able to make most things work better.

The following chart illustrates the work that each personality enjoys most.

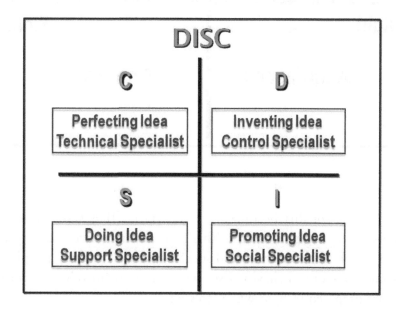

One reason why organizations tend to create problems in planning projects is because of how people interact on the team. The "D" personality, who came up with the idea, wants to control it and does a lot of talking. They tend to tell other people what to do. The "I" personality wants to be supportive. They start promoting the idea and they do a lot of talking. The "S" personality, who's going to do a lot of the work, wants to be accommodating and goes along with the idea. The "C" personality tends to see flaws in the plan, but unless they feel strongly about it will not speak up unless called upon to point out the potential problems. They fear being ridiculed or criticized for not going along with the team. Therefore, plans are made quickly and promoted without the solid input of people who know how to execute the plan or how to improve upon it. When plans get off-track, stress is introduced into the equation and the dynamics change further and get worse.

STRESS IS INTRODUCED INTO THE PROJECT

The dynamics change when stress is introduced into the equation. The chart below shows how people respond under stress.

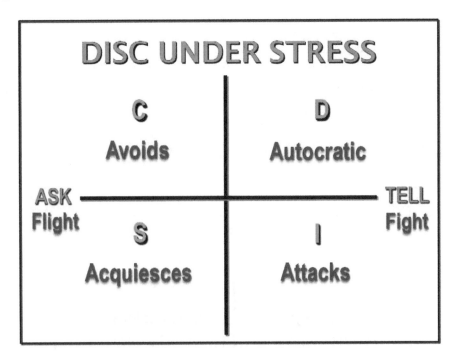

Under stress, the "D" personality becomes very autocratic. They start telling everyone what to do. The "I" personality begins to attack. This is counterintuitive and surprising. The person who has been the cheerleader and social specialist starts attacking people. This is one of the most surprising changes in behavior I see when stress is introduced. Both the "D" and "I" personalities are prepared to fight when stressed.

The "S" personality wants to make peace. They will give up their position to make others happy. Their stance is, "I'll do whatever you want me to do. Can't we just all get along?" The "C" personality tends to be quiet and reflective. Unless they feel strongly about it, they may not speak up unless called upon. Also, they will get very upset if they feel any criticism for the failure is being directed toward them.

Stress changes the dynamics of how different personalities interact.

These dynamics illustrate how things can get in such a mess in organizational life. Stress is usually introduced when something has gone wrong. The personalities doing the talking, the "D" and "I," don't know how to do the work or improve on the work but are giving the directions. The personalities with the most insight in how to get the project back on track, the "S" and "C," are acquiescing or avoiding the discussion altogether.

In this situation, a good leader needs to recognize the personality profile of each team member and the strengths each brings to the table. The leader needs to draw the "S" and "C" personalities into the discussion to get their expert perspective. Then, the "D" personality needs to chart a course, and the "I" personality needs to sell the new approach.

HCA went through a major merger in the 1990s. For my department, the teams of three former companies were being merged. I volunteered to handle the planning process to integrate the three former departments into one. All four major personality types were represented by the leadership teams of the three different departments. As you would expect, the person in the room with the highest "D" personality, besides myself, wanted to talk first and often. Next to speak were the ones that had the highest "I" components. As the facilitator, I let them talk. After an appropriate time, I asked that we listen to other team members. I called on the "S" personalities first. They knew most about how to get the work done. Next, I called on the "C" personalities. They tend to be most shy and generally will not talk unless asked their opinion in group settings. Yet, they will identify potential problems that no one else sees in the plan, ask deeper questions, and tend to improve upon a good idea.

After hearing from the "S" and "C" personalities, I asked the "D" personalities for their perspective on executing and controlling the project. I asked the "I" for input on how this would impact people and be received by them.

When we combined all these perspectives, we had a much better plan which engaged the entire team with their unique perspectives. It worked with fewer problems and adjustments later than if we had used a different approach.

COMMUNICATING

"Therefore its name was called Babel,
because there the Lord confused the language of all the earth;
and from there the Lord scattered them abroad over
the face of all the earth."
Genesis 11:9

One thing that can impact literally every other area of our life is our effectiveness in communicating. It impacts our marriage, parenting, work, friendships, and just about everything we do in life. Anyone not effective at communication is going to have great difficulties in life.

Our personality profile impacts how we like to receive communication. The "D" personality wants to know "the bottom line." They are focused on the action they will take as a result of the communication.

We like to communicate with others the way we like to receive information.

The "I" personality wants communication to be fun and interesting. They want to know about the impact on people.

The "S" personality wants the communication to be structured and non-confrontational. They do not want to feel like they need to make dramatic changes. This reminds me of George Bush Sr. who would often say, "Let's stay the course."

We should communicate with people the way they like to receive communication.

The "C" personality wants communication to be factual. They remind me of the old TV show, Dragnet, and Officer Joe Friday, whose favorite line was, "Just the facts, ma'am."

Here's an important thing to remember about personality profiles and communication. Our profile determines how we like to receive communication and thus how we tend to communicate with other people. For example, with my "D" and "C" personality, I like to hear the bottom line first. Then, depending on my level of interest, I may drill into very significant detail.

"What we have here is a failure to communicate."[4]

The question we have to ask ourselves in organizational life is "How do the people we're dealing with like to receive communication?" Unless we're dealing with people with our same profile, the answer will be that they like to receive communication in a different way than we like to give it. As a practical matter, this means we need to understand other people's profiles and structure our communication approach according to their needs, not ours.

"Do not look out merely for your own interests.

Look out for the interests of others."

Philippians 2:4

I get frustrated when people try to give me a lot of detail before I understand the big picture and the bottom line. This is why, in corporate presentations, you have an Executive Summary followed by detail. In most important business meetings, you have "D" personality profiles at the table that are going to make a decision pretty quickly, and you have to get your point across before you lose their attention. You also have "S" and "C" personalities in the room that want more information. The "D" personality is often going to ask their perspective before implementing a final decision. So you have to have the structure detail for them. If you don't have it, they will bring up all kinds of questions that have to be answered before the final decision is made.

Health

Medical health professionals have understood for a long time that stress in people's lives impact many things about their overall well-being, including their physical health. The various personality profiles handle stress differently. For example, the "I" personality profile is free-spirited, takes life a day at a time and deals with stress well. The "S" personality is calm and easy-going and tends to manage stress well.

"Better is a dry morsel and quietness with it

than a house full of feasting with strife."

Proverbs 17:1

I've seen that the combination of personality traits that appear to be in opposition tend to have high stress levels. For example, my "D" and "C" are close to the same levels, with "S" also being high. The "D" part of my personality wants to make quick decisions and take quick action. It's aggressive and risk-taking. It is also very impatient. The "C" side of my personality says slow down, gather more information, make the decision later, and be patient. The "S" side of my personality doesn't like sudden change, but the "D" side likes aggressive change. The "D" side of my personality is in constant conflict with the "C" and "S" components of my personality.

Let's go as fast as we can! Let's be careful!

Imagine driving a car with one foot on the gas and the other foot on the brake. What kind of damage would be done to that engine and brake system over time? One or both would wear out sooner than they should. If I'm not careful, that's what my life is like. I have one foot on the gas and the other foot on the brake, saying slow down. This causes internal tension which causes stress. About ten years ago, I had some health-related issues that I believe were caused by this constant stress. On one of my profiling systems, I rated poorly on the health tension index at that time. As I understood myself better and understood what was going on inside me, I made changes in how I thought and how I dealt with this conflict. Also, I sought spiritual solutions by turning to God and seeking peace in making the decisions. The good news is a few years later when I was carrying the heaviest load at HCA, I tested at much lower risk on the health tension index.

Certain personalities are prone to stress related health risks. Awareness can reduce the impact.

Being aware that you have a potential risk is pretty important. I was helping a church pastor from another state recently. His profile showed real risk in the health tension area. His three major components were "D," "I," and "S." His internal conflict was caused by the "D" component of his personality wanting to go fast and focus on the task while the "I" portion of his personality was saying to take time and be sensitive to the needs of people, and the "S" component of his personality was saying don't make rapid changes and keep the peace.

WHAT YOU WILL BE RESPECTED FOR

When dealing with people, it's important to know what they will respect you for during the interaction. The "D" personality respects you for speed. They want you to get to the bottom line so they can make a decision and move on. They don't like to chitchat.

RESPECTS YOU FOR:

"D" - Dominance
  → Speed of Accomplishment

"I" - Influencing
  → Verbal Care & Concern

"S" - Steadiness
  → Harmony / Friendships
  → Competency

"C" - Competence
  → Precise Standards

By contrast, the "I" personality very much enjoys chitchat. You need to slow down, take time, and use great verbal care and concern to maintain the relationship with them.

You don't want to be in a hurry with an "S" type personality either. They like harmony and a sense of friendship. They also know how things work, so you would need to show your competence with them. You can't gloss over things and maintain their respect. The "C" personality takes that a step further where you need to have precise standards for what you expect. These folks respect authoritative standards, not your personal opinion unless they consider you an expert.

FEARS

You will be more effective in dealing with people if you keep their fears in mind. The "D" personality is very competitive. Therefore, they fear losing. If at all possible, never set up a situation where they personally perceive you are in competition with them. Either defer to them or create a win-win situation. In win-lose situations, it will be a bitter fight to the end. Also, the "D" personality does not like scrutiny. They like big challenges and freedom to do things their way. If you make them feel like you're looking over their shoulder, you will meet a great deal of resistance.

The "I" hates loss of approval. These folks can accept constructive criticism. The key is to make sure they understand you still like them and still care about them. If they sense they lost your approval of them, they tend to go on the attack. Also, they don't like a fixed environment. They are free spirits and like the freedom not to be tied down. They don't like budgets either. I know; I'm married to an 'I' personality. The review of the household budget is like spousal abuse to them. If there had been a "1-800 budget abuse hotline," it would have gotten calls from my house over the years. "I" personality types just don't like limits. Also, they don't like their time audited either. If you have a significant other in your life with an "I" personality and they agree to do three things in a day and when they tell you they got two done, brag on them. They expect to be acknowledged for the two things they did. If you start questioning the one thing that didn't get done and try to show them where they could've been more efficient with their time, this is only going to hurt their feelings and eventually make them mad.

The "S" personality is easy-going, and they don't like big or sudden changes. These represent a loss of security for them, which is very important. They like tradition and sameness. They have a sense of how things should work and a strong dislike for unethical procedure, and they will resist it.

The "C" personality hates criticism. It's extremely difficult to find a way to offer constructive criticism to the "C" personality so that they don't take offense. They are perfectionist oriented. Therefore, they hate making mistakes. They're very hard on themselves and others. In the spiritual world, we would say they tend to be legalists. Also, they hate incompetent supervisors. The challenging thing is who they would consider incompetent. The answer is most other personality profiles. The "C" personalities consider themselves to be the experts unless they are dealing with another "C" personality of recognized "guru status." I know! I led the audit department of HCA for many years with a primary "D," secondary "C," and tertiary "S" personality profiles. This profile equipped me to lead the department. But, I'm sure there were many folks over the years who thought I wasn't as smart as they were when it came to the technical details. And the truth is they were right.

RESPONSE TO POLICY MANUALS

As organizations grow, so does the need for documentation, policies and procedures.

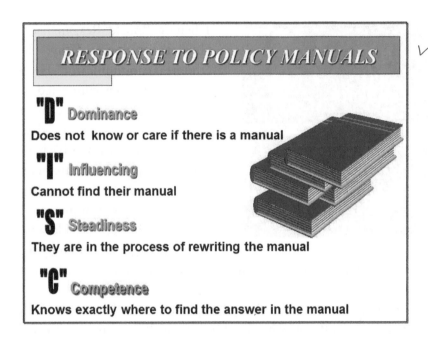

The "D" personality is not interested in the policy manual. They're okay with one existing as long as you don't try to apply it to them. They don't like to be controlled by policies and procedures, but they're fine with using the manual to control others.

The "I" type can't find their manual and has a strong distaste for policies and procedures.

The "S" personality always follows the manual. They understand the process and respect it. They wrote the initial policy manual and will likely do the revisions.

The "C" personality has great respect for the policy manual, particularly if it has clear standards and that make sense to them. They don't often have to look things up in the manual because they know exactly what the manual says. As a "D" personality, I seldom looked things up in the policy manual. However, a "C" personality was in the office next to me. I would simply shout next-door and ask him what the manual said. He could always quote it for me.

Your style impacts the team you need

I'm sure many people have the mistaken impression that you have to have a "D" personality profile to lead. That's not true. We see leaders with different profiles. What is true is that your style determines how you're going to tend to approach leadership and, therefore, the profiles you need around you to complement what you're trying to accomplish. For example, let's look at some presidents during my lifetime.

Your style determines the team you need around you.

I believe Ronald Reagan had a "D" and "I" above the midpoint. Why? He was known as "the great communicator." He usually had three to five points but connected well with people and connected with the camera. He was bold. Against the advice of his advisers, he made a speech saying "Mr. Gorbachev, tear down this wall." That is not a statement that any style other than a "D" personality would make. He liked and used humor consistent with the "I" personality profile. He was not known for working long hours or going into a lot of detail himself. Rather, he had a lot of "S"/"C" temperaments around him who executed his plans.

Bill Clinton's "I" is above the midpoint, likely complemented by "S" and "C." He is very charismatic and great with people. People who met him personally told me that he could walk into a room and change the dynamics. Unlike Reagan, who kept his list of speech points short, Clinton's list was longer which was consistent with his personality profile. He talked much about people and his State of the Union addresses were typically long because he liked to talk. His wife Hillary, with a "D"/"C" temperament, was a very good complement to his profile. When they collaborated, they typically covered all the bases.

George Bush Senior had an "S" profile above the midpoint. He was not a visionary like Reagan. He often referred to "the vision thing." Dana Carvey on *Saturday Night Live* used to do skits on Bush Senior. He used phrases like "stay the course" or "we're not going to do that, it wouldn't be prudent." These are typical of the "S" personality. He was not a great public speaker but did have substantial accomplishments when he was one-on-one with people. For example, one world leader at a time he put together the Gulf War coalition. All of these things are consistent with how the "S" personality leads.

Finally, there is Jimmy Carter who had a "C" personality about the midpoint. He managed the tennis schedule for the White House. He was involved firsthand in making decisions with the generals in the Iran hostage crisis. Once, he spoke of a discussion with a six-year-old daughter,

Amy. He said the primary concern she expressed was nuclear proliferation. Who talks like this? Well, a "C" personality does.

What I have said is not meant to be a political statement or affirmation of one president over another. This discussion is to show you that people with different profiles have been president of the United States. But, even in this high position people's natural hardwiring drives their approach to leadership and, therefore, the team they need around them to accomplish their agenda.

Reagan needed mixtures of the "S" and "C" temperament to execute his plans. Bill Clinton needed "D"/"C" temperament to balance him. George Bush Senior needed more "D"/"I" temperament around him to cast his vision and take credit for what he accomplished. Jimmy Carter needed more "D" temperament around him to help him let go of details and see the big picture.

SUMMARY CHART

The chart below helps put the four dimensions of behavior into perspective

	D = Dominant	I = Influencing	S = Steady	C = Compliant
Seeks	Control	Recognition	Acceptance	Accuracy
Strengths	Administration Leadership Determination	Persuading Enthusiasm Entertaining	Listening Teamwork Follow-Through	Planning Systems Orchestration
Challenges	Impatient Insensitive Poor Listener	Lack of Detail Short Attention Span Low Follow-Through	Oversensitive Slow to Begin Dislikes Change	Perfectionist Critical Unresponsive
Dislikes	Inefficiency Indecision	Routines Complexity	Insensitivity Impatience	Disorganization Impropriety
Decisions	Decisive	Spontaneous	Conferring	Methodical

PeopleKeys.com

The one-page chart above is a good summary to keep at your desk in order to remember and understand a great deal about what drives the behavior of each type personality.

DELEGATION

Our personality drives how we approach delegation. The employee's personality should drive how we approach it.

Personality profiles affect to whom we should delegate certain projects but also how we delegate. The "D" personality wants general direction and a lot of freedom. They like to do new things. They get bored with the status quo very easily. My son, Scott, is like this. He is an "I" and "D" personality. He likes a lot of freedom and broad boundaries. He lived on St. John Island as leader of an ecotourism resort. The freedom he was given in this job fit his style very well.

The "I" personality likes projects dealing with people. They don't want a lot of detail work. They prefer frequent conversation with their manager. They also like freedom and don't care for details. My wife, Debbie, is like this. She likes a great deal of freedom and doesn't like to get bogged down with detail. But she does like to get actively engaged.

The "S" personality likes clear guidelines and the ability to work with the team. They want an environment that is not competitive and free from conflict. My eldest daughter, Allyson, is like this. In college, she was majoring in fashion merchandising which fit the skills and passions she had. However, as she got into the program, she realized that the culture of the work environment was highly competitive versus team oriented and the best jobs were in major cities where she did not think she wanted to spend her life. She assessed other career paths that would use her natural talents that could be used in a more team oriented culture. Therefore, she has a job that she's doing great in that matches her personality.

One word of caution is due. "S" personalities are doers. They get things done and their managers like to keep them happy. Sometimes, because they do things so well, they get promoted to positions that don't match their "S" personality. The reason the Peter Principle exists, the tendency to promote people to their level of incompetence, is because "S" personalities often get promoted to stressful leadership roles they ultimately don't like.

The "C" personality likes analytical projects. They need a clear standard to meet and like detailed explanations about the project. My youngest daughter, Kelsey, has a lot of "C" personality along with good components of "S" and "I" like her older sister. She likes clear standards of what is expected. She will even ask for permission to change channels on the TV or turn it off if she's not alone in the room.

MOTIVATION

The "D" personality is very competitive and is motivated by unique accomplishments. I'm like that. I like to do things that people say can't be done or have never been done.

The "I" personality likes to be seen. They are motivated by recognition. My son is like this. He took great pride in driving a thirty year old orange International Scout in high school. There wasn't another one like it around, and it drew attention to him.

The "S" personality is motivated to get the job done and done well with others. They are motivated to maintain harmony. Often, they are the peacemakers on the team. My daughter, Allyson, is like this in the workplace. My daughter, Kelsey, is often like this at home or school.

The "C" personality is motivated to improve things. They hate criticism and are motivated to do things with perfection. Where the "D" and "I" personalities both love public attention and praise, the "C" personality is shy and appreciates individual, private praise.

People would be easier to understand if they simply fit only one of these four categories. But it doesn't work that way. People are a blend of all four styles. This can get complicated very quickly. Using a good profiling system like DISC gives you a good written and graphic perspective of an individual's personality.

APPLICATIONS

One time, I was touring the facility that ran a billing operation. The leader was talking about one employee who was high-energy, very likable, and talented, but they were away from their desk too much, visiting with people. I asked about the role. It was a data entry type function. I asked more questions and determined the individual had a primary "I" profile. I said to the leader, "This is not only non-productive for your operation but is really kind of mean to have a person with an 'I' personality in that kind of role."

I remember an employee was promoted to another part of the organization. He had a primary "S" profile. He was steady and dependable. He did what he was told to do very well. But the leader got frustrated with him because he wanted him to take more initiative. The leader constantly made comments about his good, hard work and talked about how good he could be if he would just be proactive. What the leader did not understand is that that trait didn't go with this guy's profile.

It is not uncommon for leaders to have really good employees but want and expect them to function in a way not consistent with their profile. And, frankly, it is very easy to do this. I have done it myself a number of times. You get under pressure and need things done. You go to people who operate well in tight timeframes and don't complain about doing the extra work. But, sometimes the work itself doesn't really fit their temperament. Then, we get frustrated at the employees for not performing well at a task they're not suited for to begin with.

Sometimes, small business owners or leaders and small non-profit organizations have limited staffs and ask good people to do things they do not have the personality profile for. These individuals are quite good at certain things, but the leaders get upset at them when they don't do the work they're not suited for well.

Once, I observed a situation like this at a church where I was consulting. The church grew, and the responsibilities grew. More and more responsibilities were added to this person beyond his original role. This individual finally got to the point where he couldn't do it all. He could not have done some of the work well even if he had more time.

The leadership got very frustrated with this individual and now, instead of being considered one of the best in the country, they were considered incompetent. This ended badly with hurt feelings that were unnecessary. The problem was not this individual. He was a good worker at the beginning and the end of this relationship. He never really changed. The expectations changed, and the environment changed. This person was expected to do the job that no longer fit his personality profile. And now he was labeled a bad employee.

NON-PROFIT APPLICATION

Volunteers

There is some tendency in non-profit organizations to hire or accept as volunteers those willing and showing an eagerness to do a job. Sometimes, non-profit leaders hire people who need a job versus those who really fit the job and can do it well. Non-profit organizations should be held to the same or even higher standard as any business for hiring capable employees who fit the job or accepting capable volunteers who can do the job well. There is often a mindset that non-profit organizations have to accept any willing volunteer because good volunteers are hard to find. The reality is that many potential good volunteers are like one of my friends. There is a non-profit organization that he really has a heart for, but he quit spending time with them because they wasted his time in how they conducted their meetings.

APPLICATION TO YOUR TEAM

Do you know the profiles of your leadership team or key employees? Based on what you learned in this chapter, graph the profile of each key team member.

Profiles of Your Key Team Members

D I S C

D I S C

D I S C

D I S C

— 86 —

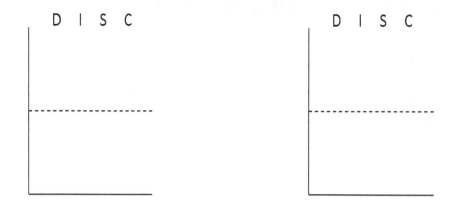

You might also try this for other significant working relationships like your boss, peers, contractors, etc. Try it for your spouse or "significant other" or your children.

Application

If you can't do this, you don't understand your team. If you don't understand your team, how can you lead them? If you were a mechanic and couldn't discern the difference between a screwdriver, a wrench, or a hammer, how good a mechanic would you be? If you don't understand the personalities of your key team members, how effective can you be in leading and managing?

Personal application

Do you understand yourself? Graph your disc profile below.

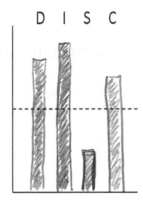

Now, explain the DISC system to some of your team members and ask them their perception of your profile. If you do not know and understand the strengths and weaknesses of your profile, how many mistakes are you making in leading your team? How do you know the people you need around you for the team to be successful without knowing your own profile?

Other profile systems

I have used some form of DISC profile for understanding my team for many years. There are a number of other good profiling systems on the market. I discovered one by Axiometrics International (A*i*) which I use in concert with the DISC. As an analogy, if the DISC is an x-ray of your personality, A*i* is an MRI of your personality. It goes much deeper, and it is difficult to manipulate as compared to simpler profiles.

For all leadership/management positions, I use the A*i* "Professional Profile" and "Professional Competencies (120) Profile." These show people's top ten leadership strengths and their top five areas for development. They also give views into leadership competencies as per the charts below.

Professional Profile – For leaders/managers

- Ten top competencies
- Five key development areas
- Leadership/management competencies
- Will you fit into the organization?
- How well can you manage yourself?
- How well can you think, solve problems, and make decisions?
- Can you lead?

Professional Competencies (120) assessment

Assessment of strengths/weaknesses in ten key areas of leadership:

- Interpersonal relationships
- Problem solving
- Decision making
- Time management
- Leadership
- Training and development
- Coaching and counseling
- Administrative
- Account development and management
- Management and supervision

To access the A*i* profiles, go to https://www.axiometrics.org. Once you are in the website, the login code is LEADERSHIP. You are invited to complete the profile and receive the "Career Pathfinder" report for free. The Axiometrics reports referenced above and their prices are listed on the website. You may purchase these at a 10% discount. (Note: these items will not work on mobile devices.)

To access a DISC profile, go to 48days.com and find personality profiles. When you're at the shopping cart, type the word "Leon" in the coupon box and you will get a 10% discount on this profile.

Chapter 9

CHOOSING THE TEAM

> **Thought:**
> How much more fun would leadership be if you
> had confidence in choosing your team well?

"So now send me a man skilled to work
in gold, silver, bronze and iron."
2 Chronicles 2:7

One of the most important decisions Jesus ever made was in the choosing of his disciples. After all, he knew that his ministry on earth would be relatively short, only three years. He knew that he was to train and empower twelve disciples to carry on his work and that he would impact all of human history through them. In fact, just before his death he told them that they would do more than he.

> *"Never doubt that a small group of thoughtful, committed people can change the world. Indeed, it is the only thing that ever has."* [5]

One man told his son, "Hire people who are mission driven—people who share your vision. If you don't, your business will struggle, or may never get off the ground. One of the reasons Steve Jobs is the entrepreneur of the era is because he has missionaries inside his company as well as outside." [6]

It should be no surprise that one of the most important jobs of the leader is picking the right people who fit the role and can be successful within the culture and the environment in which they operate. People who are not good at choosing the team can't be successful in the long run. They will be miserable, and the people on their team will be miserable. Further, these leaders will have ongoing difficulties with delegation. If they cannot choose well who to bring on the team, they cannot choose well in delegating work to others.

THE RIGHT PUZZLE PIECE

Jim Collins in *Good to Great* uses the analogy of putting the right person in the right seat on the bus. That's a good analogy. But, I like the analogy of the right puzzle piece given the growing complexity of organizations with multiple business units, departments, and functions, coupled with often times heavily-matrixed organization structures. It is one thing to find people that can do the job. It's quite another to find people that can do the job within a given culture and with the team they need to work with. To me, that's what makes selection more like completing a puzzle than the simple view of right person, right seat.

It's a real problem when people don't fit the puzzle. That's one reason why this whole leadership thing is so much more complicated when you actually have to do it than it sounds and appears to people who have never done it.

Now, let's remember King David and his charge to be a blessing to the people. Here's a perfect example of how we perform a key leadership function and bless people at the same time. We bless people by making sure that those whom we select fit our puzzle. We do them and the organization immeasurable harm when they don't fit. They're not happy or the most productive. We are not happy. Usually the rest of the team is not happy. And the organization suffers.

CHOOSING TEAMS ON THE PLAYGROUND

We played ball at recess when I was a kid in grade school. Two people always identified themselves as leaders and chose teams. One would choose a player, and then the other would choose. This continued until everyone was chosen. The best players were chosen first and the weakest players last. You always knew how good people thought you were based on how soon you were chosen. The process actually worked quite well in choosing talent. The leaders had observed you playing and knew what you were capable of. They assigned positions on the field based on their observation of your aptitude for that position.

Though this entire process was informal, the kids who were leaders did a good job of identifying talent and putting people in the right position so that the teams were fairly evenly matched.

CHOOSING THE TEAM IN AN ORGANIZATION

We finish school, go to college, get a job, and then get frustrated with this process of choosing people. It seemed so simple when we were in grade school. Why is that? We had multiple chances to observe the talent of the individuals over time before we chose them to be on our team.

Choosing the right people for your team is one of the most important things you can do as a leader.

We should not overlook the value of prayer as we choose our teams. Jesus had great insights into people, but he still relied on prayer as he chose the twelve disciples. Also, Jesus chose a number of different personality profiles as his disciples because he knew that was what was required to get the job done.

When we hire people outside the organization, they come to an interview with a resume´ and a game face. We have not had the opportunity to observe them nor do we know which position they play best. At the end of the interview, what we really know is how they come across in an interview. Plus, individuals and companies are making a living teaching people how to prepare for and handle an interview to get the job they want. Candidates are coming to the interview with great preparation. They are better at controlling the interview process than many executives who conduct the interviews.[7]

Next, let's look at what a good recruiting process looks like. We will also evaluate the common mistakes made in the recruiting and interview process.

COMMON MISTAKES IN RECRUITING

There are many mistakes you can make in the recruiting process. I know! I've made all of them. But if you do a poor job on any one of these, the process breaks down, yielding a poor result.

Mistake #1 – Not looking at the whole person

Looking at the whole person includes the individual's life before the things you see on the resume´ and those that go beyond the resume´.

Preparation
- Education
- Experience
- Accomplishments

Pre-Resume
- Calling
- Passion
- Personality
- Experiences

Post-Resume
- Expectations
- Potential
- Attitude

After giving it much thought, the visual above is what I would use to evaluate the whole person in an interview. Some of this I learned from my first boss. Some of it I learned by experience over many years. And, frankly, some of it I realize I should have done after studying Scripture and reflecting on the matter.

One of the deficiencies I see in most interview processes, and realize about much of my own after reflection, is that much of the process is based on looking at people's preparation, i.e. their experience and accomplishments.

My first boss spent the first part of the interview asking about the candidate's childhood, siblings, and parents. I used to think this quite odd. I thought an interview started with the resume´—not before it. Then, I realized he was finding out a great deal about some very major influences on that person's life that would tend to shape who that person was. He understood that what parents did and the associated work ethic would have great influence on the candidate. He also understood siblings have a great deal to do with how a person interacts as a member of the team. He understood that difficulties, challenges, and successes from early childhood would greatly impact the candidate's performance as an adult.

A pastor I know says that one of the most significant influences preparing him for his role in the church was the work he did for his dad who owned a TV store. He says that his interaction with the public did more to prepare him for his role as pastor than some of the things he learned in seminary.

I wish now that I had focused even more time on the candidate's personal life before the work experience began. I wish I had asked more questions that would have helped me understand the candidate's calling in life and passion. Often, people are driven by something that's happened to them in life having nothing to do with what is on their resume´. For example, a quality officer at a major hospital I know has a passion for quality even beyond the norm for that role. The reason is because she lost a teenage son to a clinical error in a hospital. I assure you she approaches her role with much more passion and zeal than the typical person in this role.

People's personalities are developed long before they enter the workforce. Understanding their unique personality as I discussed previously is key to knowing if they will fit the role. One thing I insisted on was having insights into the personality before they even came in for the interview.

People's work experiences and accomplishments can be gleaned from the resume´. But, I learned by experience it's wise to go beyond their accomplishments and experience to thinking about the future. I learned that it was important to ask about the expectations for the future and try to assess their potential for growth with the organization in the future.

I also learned that it is best to ask open ended questions versus leading questions in the interview process. I learned and developed this approach from my internal audit experience. It made a huge difference in the quality of my interviews. With open ended questions, people have no idea what answer will sound the best to you. Their best option is simply to answer completely and honestly. I tried to ask "most" and "least" questions. In other words, what did you like most about this situation or these people and what did you like least? This way the candidate cannot anticipate what you want the answer to be. They simply must answer candidly.

Mistake # 2 – Not spending the time and money on personality profiles

Without a clear understanding of the DISC personality profile needed, anybody with related experience is a potential candidate. You could potentially do in-depth interviews of a lot of people you shouldn't spend time with. You may hire the one you like best versus the one best suited for the job.

In business, church, and ministry organizations, I have dealt with this issue many times. A person comes highly recommended for the job. The leaders/managers feel like they just have to have this individual. Before I would interview the individual, I would ask about their view of the ideal profile and the acceptable range of personality profiles for this particular job. I would make some other inquiries into why a certain profile was needed to do a particular job.

Next, I would require that a profile be done before beginning the interview process. There were many times when the profile of the person the leaders thought they had to have was well outside the range they defined as ideal or acceptable. Sometimes, they hired the individual anyway because they liked the person and thought they could make it work. I never saw it work long-term, and usually it was a disaster.

I'll admit I did something similar myself. I knew the best profile for a particular position in our billing office was a "D" and "C." We had a person in an accounting role with a "D" and "I" profile. We reasoned that because he had the accounting degree and experience that he could adapt to the job. I liked him a lot, and he was a really hard worker. I was wrong! It didn't work out.

Some leaders and managers are not willing to spend the money on personality profiles for key candidates. There is an expression that fits this. It's called "being penny wise and pound foolish." I personally saved many hours and thousands of dollars on travel by not interviewing people who had enticing resume's but personality profiles that didn't fit the job. I also saved the company many more thousands of dollars by not putting the wrong person in a position and having poor performance or the enormous cost of making a change later. On top of that is the cost of having the wrong person in place for a period of time.

I'm familiar with a national ministry that recently made a change with one city director. The person clearly did not fit the role. The ministry could have spent $300 for a personality profile, known this on the front end, and avoided making this hiring decision. Instead, they spent $300,000 over two years for very little result and had to start over trying to find the right person for the role.

Using personality profiles does take some time and money. The problems they avoid and the "opportunity costs" they avoid usually have a payoff of ten and higher, easily.

Mistake # 3 – Not understanding the person's calling in life

People can learn to do many things. But, all people have a special calling in life—a purpose that God created them for (Psalms 139:16). Taking the time to find that out is key. If they can accomplish their calling while contributing directly in the role you are interviewing them for, you are making a potential long-term hire. To determine their calling, find out what they're passionate about. Ask them what they've always been good at. Find out what gives them joy and raises their energy versus what frustrates them and tires them out.

Ask people what they have always done well—things people seem to always want them to do and brag on them when they do it.[8] Ask people, "Is there something you enjoy doing so much and do so well that you feel like you were just made to do this?" Ask them, "Is there something you enjoy doing so much and that makes you feel so good that you would still do it if you didn't get paid for it?"

Mistake # 4 – Letting the candidates find you versus seeking out the ones most suited for the job

It's much easier to run an ad and let people looking for a job find you. For key positions, it is worth the time and effort to determine who is best in this field and to see if they match the values and vision of your organization. One of the best people I've ever hired was not looking for a job at the time I hired her. In fact, it took three different phone calls for me to get her to even agree to an interview. Often, the people best for the job aren't looking for a job. You have to go find them.

Mistake # 5 – Focusing only on your goals versus the candidate's goals

Some leaders, in fact most, leave out one very important dynamic in the interview process. They are pursuing what they want, trying to fill their needs and determining if the person they're interviewing can do the job and is willing to take the job. Something critically important is determining if this person truly wants the job. Not from the standpoint of "I must work and pay the bills," but from the standpoint of "Is this consistent with my personal goals and do I really want this job?" Does this job fit the vision, passion, calling and goals of the candidate? One of the best hires I was ever fortunate enough to make was a person who didn't think she even wanted to interview for the job. Let me tell you about Claudia.

Claudia may have had more educational credentials than anybody I ever recruited. She was personable, articulate, and as professional as anyone I've ever met. She knew what she was about more than anybody I ever met. She worked at a firm that worked for HCA, and she was quite happy there. I talked to her on the phone three different times about coming to an interview. She nicely declined each time. She did not want to send mixed signals to her firm, and she really wasn't interested in making a change.

This intrigued me. I asked her why she was so contented at the firm. She was able to clearly and passionately articulate her career goals and the impact she wanted to have. She clearly fitted the "cathedral builder" analogy. I listened intently to her goals. Then, there was this magic moment where I got very excited and passionate. I told her that I understood her commitment to her firm. I also told her that I thought she would be very happy there. However, I told her that I thought she could be even happier in the job I was recruiting her for. I went on for quite some time explaining the match between her passions, dreams, and life goals and how they could be carried out at HCA even better than her firm.

That began a process. I spoke to her three times in person and finally was able to recruit her into the company. In her specialty, she became like the "E.F. Hutton" in the company. After a few months, when Claudia spoke, everyone listened. She made enormous contributions to the company. Every time I spoke to her in subsequent years, she still loved her role.

Claudia was one of the best hires I ever made. But the face-to-face interview process would have never started with me focused on my goals or what was good for the company. I had to understand her goals and explain to her clearly how the company could help her meet them before I could hire her.

I continued to find that recruiting the very best people requires this approach. Often, the best people are not knocking on your door asking you to hire them. They are content working somewhere else where they are admired, respected, have great influence, are paid well, and treated well. To go get them, you have to show them how they can achieve more of their own goals in your job and your company than where they are. This requires that you listen intently to them about their goals and what they like about where they work. This is very counterintuitive to most leaders.

Mistake # 6 – Insisting on the right of first refusal

To my chagrin, as a young hiring manager, I actually did this once. The candidate was thrilled about the company, excited about the job, and asked when he could start. I sat there dumbfounded, realizing I hadn't even interviewed him yet and didn't know if I even wanted him!

Often, the hiring leaders/managers talk about the job and the company too early in the process. They want to convince the individual on why he should want to work for the company and why he should want this particular job. The problem with that is you don't know yet if you want the individual in the company or the job.

I'm convinced one of the reasons so many people get placed in the wrong jobs is because of poor interviewing techniques and human nature. Human nature is for candidates to come in and sell themselves as being a great fit for the job. Why? Our ego causes us to want to have the "right of refusal." If the candidates cannot sell themselves and get the offer, they have no "right of refusal" and they may feel rejected.

Conversely, the hiring leaders/managers often feel the same way. If they have a strong viable candidate on paper, they want to make sure the candidate is impressed enough that they can hire the candidate if they want to. Therefore, if you're not careful, you have two individuals telling the other what they think they want to hear without doing the hard work of determining if they really fit the job.

— 97 —

Mistake # 7 – Letting the candidate take charge

The next mistake is letting the candidate lead the interview. I've had many try this, especially those with "D" personality profiles. They talk about themselves and try to sell you on why they fit the job. Generally, if allowed, they will ask you a lot of questions about the job. If you answer them, it's human nature for them to position their comments and answers to your subsequent questions to fit what they think you're looking for. The value of the hiring professional taking the lead and asking structured, open-ended questions is that this scenario is completely avoided. They don't know what you're looking for and can only answer candidly. If they are not answering candidly, they will come across shallow or contradictory. I learned these questioning approaches through my audit experience.

RESUME´

Ask the individuals what they liked most and least about each of the jobs on their resume´. From this, I got a sense of the type tasks, activities, and environment they like most, as well as those that would de-motivate them. I've had times where, from a practical standpoint, the interview was over after these questions because I could see so many similarities between what they didn't like and what would be required in the job for which they were interviewing. I would continue to be kind but also honest with the candidate. Then, I would give them the chance to ask questions or talk about themselves so that they would not feel bad about the interview but also be respectful of their time and mine.

It is common for leaders to determine that individuals are only interested in the job they're interviewing for. I found it useful to probe deeply about what they liked and disliked about their last job. Were they outgrowing their job? Were they feeling restrained in their last job and looking for new opportunities? Were they looking for a slower, steadier pace with less change and therefore less opportunity? Probing deeply in these areas will give you a much better perspective on whether these individuals "fit your puzzle."

PERSONAL BACKGROUND

Try to understand individuals' personal background better. Ask what they like most and least about themselves. This will give you a good idea of their self-awareness, self-esteem, and ego. A person who likes a lot about themselves and can't think of anything they like least is usually going to be harder to lead. Generally, they have high ego needs, don't work well with teams, and don't take direction well. That doesn't mean don't hire them. Certain personality profiles are that way, and there are positions they fit. But, be aware of what you are getting.

By contrast, individuals too hard on themselves may have poor self-esteem. These people often are overly critical and negative. They can be generally critical of their teammates, their supervisors, and the organization.

You're really looking for a healthy balance—people who are aware of their strengths but also their weaknesses and can keep the two in perspective. It's good to ask about personal and professional goals they've achieved in the past that gave them the most satisfaction. Also, ask about their biggest disappointments or failures, both personal and professional. I personally like people who had some failures in life and were able to learn from them and put them in perspective.

Since I have their personality profiles, I already know a lot about their personal traits. Sometimes, I ask follow-up questions if needed.

Their personality is only part of the picture, though. I want to find out about their life experiences that have shaped how they think and feel. I want to know what they are passionate about. I want to see if they have a sense of "calling," i.e. this is what I was made to do—this is my unique purpose in life.

ATTITUDE – CONDITION OF THE HEART

"For as a man thinketh in his heart, so is he."

Psalm 23:7

Our thoughts and attitudes are very important to God. Scripture is very clear that God looks at people's hearts before selecting them for significant roles in His kingdom. For example, God looked at the heart and selected David to be king over Israel versus his brothers who were bigger, stronger, and looked the part. Samuel was surprised by God's choice because he was, in effect, looking at the resume´s. All of David's brothers seemed more qualified than David. After all, he was only a young shepherd.

When we are held accountable by God, He will not look at just what we did, but He will also look at our motives and attitudes. Wise and godly leaders will also discern the attitudes of people they hire and give significant job assignments to.

Ask candidates what they like most and least about peers, subordinates, and past leaders. Take your time. These discussions will give you great insights about candidates' attitude toward other people. If your leadership style is more like one of their favorite leaders from the past, you have a better chance of a good relationship. If your style is more similar to the leaders they liked least from the past, the relationship may not work. The same is true for their peer group.

If the individuals you're hiring will supervise others, you want to understand their attitude toward subordinates. If their view is not consistent with the culture you are trying to create for your organization, you should not put them in the position. Also, ask them what their leaders, peers, and subordinates like most and least about them. This will also give you a sense of their self-awareness.

I remember Frank, who was hired by someone else, but eventually reported to me. Over time, I noticed that he was very critical of every person he'd ever worked for. In his mind, they were all "idiots" or "jerks." It didn't take me long to figure out that no matter what I did, that would be his final assessment of me. Sure enough, after he left my department and went to another part of the company, he began "badmouthing" me. If I had been the original hiring professional using this interviewing approach, that characteristic would've been identified during the interview, and he would not have been brought into the company.

If individuals have never liked any organization they worked for in the past, there is very little chance they will like your organization. I never experienced an exception to that rule, but Frank and many others like him that I experienced convinced me how reliable it is. Ask what they like most and least about the organization or company they just left or are considering leaving. Listen for aspects of the culture they liked or didn't like. Listen for policies and procedures that annoyed them. Compare these to your own organization to see if they would be any happier. Listen for a critical attitude toward the organization. If you happen to know it's a good organization and they are very critical, it could be a red flag for you. If you happen to know it's not a good organization, listen and see if they can tactfully explain what they didn't like without a critical spirit. Remember the attitudes they have toward the organization will come with them to your organization.

FUTURE EXPECTATIONS AND POTENTIAL

Ask questions about their compensation history. Ask what they liked most and least about their overall compensation package. This will give you an idea as to what they value in the package. Some people like their salary packages with limited equity or bonus potential. Some people prefer less base play with more significant bonus or equity opportunities. Knowing this will help you structure a package that fits them best if you want to hire them.

The compensation discussion will give you an understanding of what they have become accustomed to in the past and their expectations about the future. If they have become accustomed to healthy annual increases and you're hiring them in at the top end of your pay range, you already know that kind of increases will not be possible in your organization going forward. Having a clear understanding of that will keep you from making mistakes.

Ask questions about their future aspirations and goals. Ask about their mobility. These may give you some insights into their potential and desire to grow with your organization.

Talk more about what they think versus what they believe you want to hear. I found that an interview following this simple approach, along with the personality profile done in advance, is superior to most approaches that I've seen used.

THE BOTTOM LINE OF THE HIRING PROCESS

To get the right person that fits your unique puzzle, what are you looking for? There are six key things:

- Personality profile — their hardwiring. You can test for this or you can be "penny wise and pound foolish."

- Talent — you can vet this through experience, follow-up on their resume´ and, to some degree, by an in-depth interview.

- Experience — you can do this through setting their resume´.

- Passion — you can discern this in the interview.

- Calling — you can discern this in the interview.

- Potential — you can discern this in the interview.

The key is it takes time, energy, and lots of listening to do these well. Leaders are typically in a hurry and do not spend the necessary time on this very important responsibility of theirs. As a result, they spend much more time dealing with the problems of not hiring the right person, plus the added costs of going through the process again trying to get the right person. It simply doesn't make any sense for a leader not to make this one of their highest priorities and to do it better than they do anything else. It will save time, energy, and money in the long run for them.

There is a great difference between what you *were* made to do (created for) and what you *are* made to do (forced to do). If you find people who were made to do, created for, the work you need done, you will have a productive and potential long-term relationship.

Application

I. On a scale of 1-10, how good are you at choosing people that work out well long term?

II. Do you have an interview process that considers the whole person? Yes_____ No_____

III. What changes will you make in your recruiting approach based on this chapter?

A. _____

B. _____

C. _____

D. _____

Chapter 10

MY PEOPLE DON'T FIT THEIR JOBS

Thought!
How effective could my organization be if everybody on the
team played their role well and were highly motivated?
How much potential and productivity is my organization
losing because I have people who do not fit?

*"You shall speak to all the skillful persons
whom I have endowed with the spirit of wisdom,
that they make Aaron's garments..."*
Exodus 28:3

God gave people natural gifts and talents that are to be exercised for the good of mankind while we're on this Earth. He also gave the spiritual gifts to be used for the building up of the church. These are outlined in Ephesians 4:11-12. The world works much better when people are working within the talent and gift set that God gave them. When they get out of place, you have a problem. Pride and greed often drive people to want more power or more material things. Many people are lured from their strengths to get more power or money and begin to operate outside their gifting. It's quite common in the non-profit and ministry world for founding leaders to want to be something they are not to maintain power and control. They may get so far outside of their gift set that they lose effectiveness or eventually fail altogether.

Sometimes, leaders come to the realization of "Oh, my gosh! I have people in place who don't fit the job. I have a 'square peg in a round hole.' Put another way, my people don't fit the puzzle piece I need anymore. They are either too small, too large, or just the wrong shape for what I need."

Organizations often blame failure on people for things they didn't cause or control.

It's not uncommon for leaders to be frustrated because a number of their people just don't seem to be meeting their expectations. The natural assumption of some leaders is, "I have bad people. I need to 'fire' them and get some different people." This is a simplistic and often counterproductive way to look at and deal with the situation. Start by understanding the reasons for underperformance.[9]

Did they used to fit but the circumstances changed or the work environment changed?

- Has there been a change in the people they work with and around?

- Has something changed in another area of their life that is impacting their performance? Is this change temporary or permanent?

- Were they ever suited for this position or was it just a bad hire?

- Has their performance changed or is it my attitude toward them that has changed? Am I under a lot of stress causing me to be more critical of the team?

The answers to these questions give some idea as to the current path you should take. Let's explore further. Let's ask the question, "Can the results needed be achieved with this person in the job?" If the answer is no, the only logical thing to do is make a change. But, many leaders seem very reluctant to do this. Some don't do it at all. And many do it much later than they should. In fact, many wait until they are in a crisis mode and mad or upset before they take any action. This only makes the situation worse or causes them to handle it poorly. Therefore, they are more reluctant to make a timely change the next time they need to.

TAKE A BIBLICAL VIEW

God created everyone with the ability to do something well and enjoy it. Why is it that leaders are so reluctant to make a change? If people go to a neurologist because a tumor is putting pressure on the brain and giving them severe headaches, does the neurologist feel bad about suggesting brain surgery? Does the neurologist apologize for suggesting brain surgery? Does the neurologist dread doing the surgery? Obviously, you want a brain surgeon who is empathetic with the person. But do you really want a brain surgeon who dreads doing surgery? I don't.

Neurosurgeons don't hesitate to take action to relieve the pressure from a tumor. Why do leaders hesitate to take action to relieve the pressure when people don't fit their job?

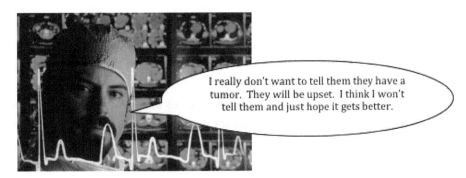

I really don't want to tell them they have a tumor. They will be upset. I think I won't tell them and just hope it gets better.

So what about people in a job that doesn't fit? Don't you think they feel some pressure? Don't you think they feel uncomfortable and perhaps even miserable? So if you suggest and move down the path of relieving the pressure, are you hurting these people or helping them? Our hesitancy is based upon a wrong view of this entire situation.

"But speaking the truth in love, we are to grow up in all aspects into Him..."

Ephesians 4:15

A major reason we aren't willing to make personnel changes is because we view it through a paradigm we learned in organizations versus a biblical view.

The person in the job is not always the reason for good results nor is he always the reason for poor results.

Let's take a practical example. I observed a lot of hospital CEOs over many years. Some didn't appear great to me. But they had the good fortune of being in growth markets, with stellar facilities, excellent medical staffs, great leadership teams, and good labor markets. They did not build or select the teams. They were just fortunate enough to be placed there. They were given the invisible "hero" label.

Conversely, I saw some CEOs that were exceptionally smart, worked really hard, and had stellar values. They had the challenge of being in difficult markets, having facilities needing access to additional capital, challenging medical staffs, weaker leadership teams, and an overall tough labor market. These CEOs seldom got the "hero" label no matter how hard they worked to improve their situation.

These experiences convinced me I should throw away my invisible "hero" and "goat" labels. When I did, my whole view changed of removing people who didn't fit the puzzle.

Does that mean these are bad people or poor employees? Maybe it's not their fault. If they never really fit the role, it's the leader's fault for putting them in it. If a team member is undermining them, it's the team member's fault. If the culture is a barrier for them, that's the problem.

No matter how good we become at selecting people, most of us are going to make a mistake. The question is what are we going to do about it? Unless it's really bad or until it gets really bad, most leaders do nothing. After all, it's a messy job. In the traditional view, we tell ourselves we have to "fire" the person. We hate that. And, I hope we do hate it anytime it's framed that way. We feel bad for the person and about ourselves for the "perceived negative" action we're getting ready to take.

Using a more biblical view, we are not always saying they are a bad person or a bad employee. I generally don't like to use the term "fire" or "terminate."

IS IT COMPASSIONATE TO KEEP PEOPLE IN ROLES THEY DON'T FIT?

So here's the question—are we being kind to people when we leave them where they don't fit? Are we helping them when we leave them in a situation where they can't do the job well? The simple answer is—no. In fact, I would make the argument that it is just plain insensitive and maybe mean.[10]

The most compassionate thing we can do for these people is to help them find a puzzle they fit. Please notice, I said <u>help</u>. They have to work with us and own the responsibility for accomplishing the transition. They are more likely to cooperate wholeheartedly if we kindly, clearly, and compassionately explain to them that it's better for them, better for the team, and better for the organization.

You are not helping people when you leave them boxed into a situation where they can't be successful.

I have a good friend, Jim Patton. Jim got a degree from a technical school with the goal of becoming an HVAC repairman making $20 an hour. He thought this would provide a good living and all he wanted out of life at the time. He tells the story in his excellent book, *Life in the Turn Lane*, about how his boss put his arm around him one day and said, "You're just not very good at this." He let Jim go. Jim was devastated and I'm sure his boss felt bad. But, it was the best thing that could have happened for Jim. His boss did him a favor. Jim was made to be a "dealmaker." And what a dealmaker he is! Jim has bought and sold over $2 billion worth of businesses in the past several years.

What if his boss hadn't let him go? What if he had told him he needed to buckle down and work harder and he could be an okay HVAC repairman? What if Jim had done that? He would have been trapped in a job that didn't use the potential that God gave him. He would have become increasingly miserable in it. By the way, his personality profile pegged him as a developer, i.e. a dealmaker. Just think of the pain and misery that could've been avoided had he known this before he went to school and if his boss had known it before he hired him. Jim was trapped in a job that he didn't fit.

If Jim's boss had not released him, he might never have become an enormously successful deal maker.

HOW TO DEAL WITH THIS PROBLEM IN A FAIR BUT COMPASSIONATE MANNER

First of all, look at all the possibilities. Sometimes, there has been enough growth and change that a job can be defined that fits this person and contributes to the objectives of the organization. Usually, this isn't the case.

Sometimes, there is something in the work environment that can be changed. I have a friend who is really claustrophobic. He needs to sit near a window. Sometimes, there is someone people are working with that is causing a problem; perhaps that person is the one that needs to be dealt with. I have had people on my team before that were catalysts for conflict versus team players.

Sometimes, the culture has changed and the employees no longer fit it or agree with it. If none of these can be changed so that success in the job can be obtained, the common sense thing to do is to relieve the pressure from these people and free them from a situation where they can't be successful or happy. The approaches for dealing with this depend on the answers to some of the questions we asked at the beginning of the chapter. The key is why don't they fit the role? Here are some possibilities and the approaches.

I MADE A MISTAKE

"Before destruction, the heart of man is haughty,

but humility goes before honor."

Proverbs 18:12

I've had occasions when I made a mistake in hiring someone. A couple of times, I hired people because they had experience that I thought would work even though the personality profile did not fit the role. It did not work, and I've never seen an occasion where it did work for anyone else.

What do you do in this circumstance? When I came to my senses, I simply admitted my mistake. I sat with the individuals, looked them in the eye, and apologized. I told them that I had done them a great disservice by putting them in a role that did not fit them and that I needed to correct my mistake. I've always been amazed at how well people worked with me when I owned my mistakes.

MY PREDECESSOR MADE A MISTAKE – I'M SORRY

Sometimes, you make a mistake in hiring and should accept responsibility for it. However, sometimes you are in a difficult situation. Either predecessors made a mistake in the initial hiring decision, or things changed and they did not act on the changes as they should. Nevertheless, you are left to deal with the problem. I've had many times when I had to deal with a predecessor's problem. I'm sure I also left some for my successors to deal with, too. In this case, don't throw your predecessor under the bus but acknowledge the mistake. Explain to the individuals it works to everybody's benefit to work together and resolve the issue. They need to understand this is better for them, the organization, and the team to deal with the situation versus leaving it unattended. I think it's fine to tell them that you personally like them, if that's the case. It's fine to affirm them in any number of ways that you believe are true. Tell them you're sorry they are in this situation and that you hate to be the one dealing with it. But it's your responsibility to do what's best for them and for the organization.

THINGS CHANGED — IT'S NOT YOUR FAULT

Many people, good at one time, no longer fit their roles. Given the rapid changes in organizational life, this happens all the time. Organizations are not stagnant entities. The marketplace changes, and the organization changes to meet the needs of the market or its constituents. As this occurs, well-defined roles that individuals used to fit will change.

It can happen in any position. So what do you do? I sit and talk to the individuals. I'm straightforward but kind and empathetic. I tell them things changed. You didn't change them. But, we both have to respond to the changes. I will point out what has changed that affects their role.

"Let no unwholesome word proceed from your mouth,
but only such a word as is good for edification
according to the need of the moment,
so that it will give grace to those who hear."
Ephesians 4:29

I affirm them for their talent and contribution to the organization. Then, I point out that since the position no longer fits their talents and passions, they will be increasingly frustrated and it's not really fair to them, the people who work around them, or the organization. Then, I begin talking constructively about roles that fit them inside my area, elsewhere in the organization, or outside the organization.

RESULTS OF THESE DISCUSSIONS

The results of these approaches have varied, but I've always had a better outcome than using the traditional approaches. I've remained very good friends with a number of people that I have had to release. I've been able to maintain a cordial relationship with others. Some have had hard feelings toward me but not nearly as hard as other approaches would have yielded.

Some people really press the point of trying to find out what they did wrong. They are so ingrained in the paradigm that if the job is not done, it's their fault, and they have trouble with a different view. They press the issue regarding what they did wrong or could have done differently so hard it becomes very tempting to offer up something just to appease them. I don't let myself get forced into going there in these discussions if there are other factors influencing the outcome of the job beyond their control.

Sometimes, there are things that people can improve on and learn from in this experience. I will discuss that with them at the appropriate time, but I do not mix it with the discussion about releasing them because this can be a difficult and emotional time. I pick a different time that seems suitable for individuals and make it clear that what I'm getting ready to discuss has nothing to do with them being released but rather some constructive suggestions they may find helpful in the future.

MISTAKES LEADERS OFTEN MAKE

Mistake # 1 – Keep underperformers too long

According to Harvey McKay, you should release a person the first time you think about it. I don't necessarily agree with that, but I do think many leaders wait too long to make a change. While that is benevolent, it is not a good long-term solution. Leaders will wind up giving the rest of the team the short straw, shorting their family or some other important areas of their life. I've seen businessmen in small companies put the wrong people in place and leave them there. It took a heavy toll on their own family, the rest of the business, and their health. I've seen much of the same thing in ministry leaders.

It hurts morale of the team much more than leaders are usually aware of. It makes the other employees less effective in their own job and perhaps what they are best at. It ultimately causes resentment and turnover of the best people. I've seen this done many times and caught myself doing it, too.

Mistake # 2 – Allow the person to be set up for failure [11]

I'm reminded of a ministry example. A regional ministry growing to a more national scope was expanding to a new city. I saw a personality profile on a city director. I had never seen this type profile work in the city director role and asked about it. The response I got was "We are trying to force him to grow or get out of the way."

Would you kick someone on crutches until they ran faster or fell over?

I was appalled! I talked to the national director. I asked, "Would you kick someone on crutches until they either ran or fell over?" He laughed and said, "No." I said, "Isn't that what is happening in this case?" He quickly agreed. We had a good discussion centered on the fact that this was not logical. You don't kick a person on crutches and expect him to run faster. It was not necessary because the discussion could be handled in an entirely different way. The person was boxed into a job that didn't fit. We discussed the fact that it was not fair. Nor was it a good spiritual approach to dealing with this matter. He agreed and discussed compassionately and honestly that the person was in a role that didn't fit him anymore.

Mistake # 3 – Not being clear about requirements

If you look closely at Scripture, you would have a hard time accusing God of not being clear about His requirements of us. In the very beginning, He gave Adam and Eve great freedom, but He was clear about the one thing that they were not to do. God was equally clear when He gave the Ten Commandments. Four of the ten deal with our relationship with Him and the remaining six deal with our relationship with each other . . . pretty specific and clear, wouldn't you say? It's very difficult for us to argue we didn't know what to do, or we didn't know what to avoid. Being clear about the requirements is the key to holding people accountable and saying they are "missing the mark."

Even though we've worked hard to hire the right people and give clear instructions, sometimes course correction is needed. So how are we to handle this? The first thing is to be sure that the expectations are clear.

I have had much experience in leading businesses and other organizations where there were a lot of dysfunction, lack of harmony, "firefighting" and, very importantly, mistrust among team members. I remember once leading an organization where one of the support staff was referring to another member of the support staff in derogatory terms. I asked, "Why do you think they do a bad job?" I got some general response. Then, I asked, "What specific expectation are they not reaching?" I got nothing but silence. This happened many times during that assignment. People repeatedly talked bad about others but couldn't articulate what the expectations were that had been agreed to. I see this in many types of organizations, but lack of clear expectations seems to be even more prevalent in some non-profit organizations.

Often people don't do what you want because the expectations aren't clear.

As an auditor in a big company, I had a lot of experience with evaluating operations against standards. HCA had operating indicator reports. For everything that was considered of major importance to measure, there was a standard, actual, and the difference. Everything we reported on as auditors had its basis in some company, industry, or generally accepted accounting standard or principle.

I coached the team to realize that where there is no clear expectation, there is no basis for an expectation gap. Their frustration was self-imposed. I went further by explaining that the person missing the mark the most was the one who had an expectation that had not been communicated clearly and agreed upon with the other person.

JOHNNY THE CRITIC

Johnny was a great guy in many regards but really bad about being critical of other people where the expectations were not clear or agreed upon. After a computer conversion, he called me in a rant about the printers in one of his physician practices being slow. To diagnose the problem, we sent someone to the practice to time the printer speed on the new system. There was no measurable difference between the times on the new system vs. the old one. It was merely a perception issue that was not based on any agreed-upon standard.

I remember having a long discussion with Johnny. I really liked him, but I was incredibly frustrated. I went over the idea that where there is no clear expectation, there is no basis for saying there's a problem. I said that if you don't have a clear agreed-upon expectation of the other individual or one of the support functions, you have no basis for your dissatisfaction. Your criticism is just seen as a non-productive whining.

I have observed that in big companies with decentralized operations and regionalized or centralized support functions, it is very common for the operations people to be highly critical of the support functions. Why? They have expectations that are not concrete, not measured, and not reported upon. Often they are not even realistic. Therefore, there's a perceived gap between what they expected and what they got. I've seen many times where processes were regionalized or centralized, and the measurable results improved substantially from when they were embedded in the operations. But the operations people were still critical of the support staffs.

A great deal of conflict is avoided when the core activities and contributions of people, i.e. what we expect of them, is clear, documented, and agreed upon among the team. In other words, no clear or agreed-upon expectation means no basis for an expectation gap. In those cases, if you want to be mad at someone, you should be mad at yourself.

Mistake # 4 – Not letting people know they are in trouble and helping them improve

"Treat others the same way you want them to treat you."

Luke 6:31

As I relate the Scripture above to dealing with expectation gaps, I think about what I would want if I was not meeting the expectations. Out of thousands of days I showed up for work, there was never a single one when I thought it was okay not to do a good job. And if I were not, I would want these things:

- Someone to tell me very clearly that there is a problem in a way I can understand it.

- An opportunity to resolve the problem and to know what happens if I can't.

- An opportunity to use my talents somewhere else in the organization if I didn't think I could resolve the problem. If not available, some time and support to find a role in another organization.

My human resources friends at HCA would agree, and the direction I always received from them was consistent with this.

Let me be very honest here. I worked in a very complex business and large organization with a lot of exceptionally talented people. There were times when I had doubts and fears about whether I measured up. When I would have those feelings well up inside me, I would have a conversation with the person I reported to and asked pointedly if I was meeting his expectations. He would tell me yes. Then, I would ask him for one favor: "If that ever changes, would you please let me know and give me a chance to deal with it?"

Let's think about how God deals with us. He gave us clear instructions through Scripture. He gave us Jesus as an example to follow. Throughout Scripture, He warned His people when they were off track and in the Old Testament sent prophets to explain the consequences of remaining off-track. He was patient in giving His people time to change their ways. He was consistent in delivering the consequences communicated by the prophets. Dealing with people the way God deals with us is generally going to include the following approaches.

BE CLEAR ABOUT WHAT YOU EXPECT

God was always very clear in His instructions to people. The problem was not His instructions but rather their listening and desire. The same cannot be said for many leaders. Many are very scattered, inconsistent, and unclear about what they expect. But they like to blame it on their employees.

ACKNOWLEDGE THAT YOUR EXPECTATIONS MAY BE THE PROBLEM – CONSTANTLY CRITICAL

"Therefore encourage one another

and build up one another..."

1 Thessalonians 5:11

I tend to be a management by exception person and don't live out this Scripture well. Do you know people who are constantly critical of their staff? I do. There are some leaders that just seem to never be satisfied with the team they have. Some constantly change the team. Some keep their team and constantly complain about them. For these leaders, I have a rather harsh message… "If you want a clear view of the problem, go look in a clean mirror."

If nobody is good enough for you, then you aren't a good leader.

I consulted with one organization where so much had been delegated to one team member with no clear set of priorities that he had no idea what to focus on next. Also, things had been delegated to him that did not line up with the strengths of his personality profile. Further, it would have taken two people to do the amount of work delegated to him. Guess what happened? This person who'd been labeled a "Hero" two or three years earlier was now labeled a "bad employee" and released.

The release was okay because he did not fit that job or any other the organization had at the time. But, the way it was handled was not okay. The problem was not that employee, but the person he reported to. The great irony was that the supervisor was mad at this really good employee. Mistakes the supervisor had made were the real problem.

I consulted for one organization where the leader said, "I'm a great leader. I'm up to the task of coaching a world-class team. The problem is my team is just not up to par. If the team could do their jobs as well as I can do mine, we would have a world-class organization." Folks, I'm just not creative enough to make up some of the stuff I put in this book. This guy really said that. I stood there dazed with the words of my daughter going through my head, "Really! Really! Are you kidding me?"

You cannot be a world-class leader and say that you don't have a world-class organization because your team is holding you back. You picked the team or can change it. You train the team and delegate work to them. If there's a problem with the team, you're the problem, not them. And while I'm on a roll, you would be surprised at how many leaders are surprised at that statement.

Great Summary of Leadership

BE TRUTHFUL [12]

Communicate to the employee kindly, but very plainly, that there is a problem. I've seen people terminated for poor performance where it is a complete surprise. When this happens, the greatest failure is on the part of leadership, not the employee.

Let people
Keep their
Integrity

Unless they know or clearly should have known better, employees should not be terminated until after it has been clearly communicated to them that there is a problem.[13] After an honest discussion, they should be given an opportunity to resign with dignity and find another job or try to resolve the problem. This is true as long as you think they have a chance to successfully resolve the expectation gap. Otherwise, give them the opportunity for a graceful exit.

"But speaking the truth in love..."

Ephesians 4:15

Help the employee understand the problem, to own the solution, and to be as clear as possible about the repercussions of the problem not being resolved. Having employed so many people over a long career, I've done my fair share of counseling people regarding their performance. People simply don't come to work to do a bad job and most don't leave work at the end of the day thinking they have done a bad job. In my experience, it has been fairly common for employees who needed counseling to be unaware of the expectation gap. Many times they were ignoring the obvious, but sometimes the expectations weren't as clear as they needed to be for that employee. I tried to help them understand the problem and the need to correct it as clearly as possible.

GIVE THEM A CHANCE TO FIX IT [14]

Human resources at HCA suggested that we have the employee create performance improvement plans to solve the problem with specific actions, timeframes, and, most importantly, results. Performance improvement plans should be more for redemptive purposes versus just legal protection. The key is the employee has to understand the problem must be solved and the employee is responsible for the resolution. It's fine and good for the leader to be willing to help the employee with the action plan. The trap I have seen many step into, however, is owning the action plan and result versus the employee owning it. Sometimes, new leaders get engaged in the action plan. The employee does the task on the action plan, but the problem still exists. Then, the employee is in a position to rightly say that he completed the tasks and did his best. The leader knows the problem is not solved but has difficulty doing anything. Why? Because the leader did not make it clear that the goal was resolution of the problem and the employee owned the action plan and problem.

If you own the action plan, you own the problem.

CLARIFY WHAT HAPPENS NEXT IF THE PROBLEM ISN'T FIXED

Be clear about the ramifications of the problem not being solved at the very beginning of the process. Not all problems are termination offenses if not solved. There are other repercussions to the employee that need to be understood. However, if release will be the consequence, it's especially critical the employee knows that from the beginning.

You may ask, since a leader's job is to bless employees, how is this a blessing to anyone? Well, let's think about it. Most people I ever worked with really wanted to do a good job and, while difficult to hear, wanted and needed to know if they were not. Good employees appreciate knowing when they're not meeting expectations versus being talked about behind their back, being disappointed at their annual review, or being disappointed over their raise. They especially want a heads up before they risk release or discipline of any kind. Telling people there is a problem is consistent with Paul's instruction to "tell the truth in love."

Now, the employees are in a position to determine if they can and will close the expectation gap. If they believe they can't because they don't have the skills or they don't have the motivation, they can look for a job while they still have a job or resign with dignity and find something they can be successful at.

Giving them the chance to develop and execute an action plan to solve the problem is as fair as you can be. Being sure they understand the consequences is also being as fair as you can be. Actually, what approach is fairer to the employee and the organization?

I think one reason leaders do not make changes in the organization at all or as timely as they should is because they are scared from a legal standpoint. I've seen the process just discussed used many times in very difficult circumstances and have seen it be very successful. In about half the cases, the employees were able to solve the problem and continued to grow in their career and do a good job where they were.

Sometimes, employees realized on the front end they either couldn't or wouldn't make the needed changes and resigned. Sometimes, as they worked through the action plan and realized they weren't achieving the results, they began looking for other jobs, found one, and resigned.

In my own experience, only about 10%-20% of the people who went through this process ever got to the stage where termination was necessary. Think about it. Taking people through a process that is fair and helps them avoid a termination is a blessing to them compared what happens often times in organizations.

INHERITED CHALLENGES

I had just assumed responsibility for a new corporate department and the vice president in charge told me he had a member on the team that was a problem but nothing could be done about it. He indicated there were three different sections of labor law that gave this individual protection. My view was this individual did not need protection if he was suited for the job and doing the job. But, it would be unfair to the individual to leave him in the job if it wasn't a good fit. We went through the process just described. The individual saw he was not meeting the expectations of the role and that he would not be able to. He found another job outside the company that fit him better and we did not have a lawsuit or any other repercussions from it. If we had not followed this process, I believe we would have had a very different outcome that would not have been constructive for the individual or good for the company.

SOLVING PEOPLE PROBLEMS

Mary was a young, intelligent professional. She had more than enough capability and a solid work ethic. Her attitude at times caused problems in her interpersonal relationships and thus impacted the team. We went through the process of identifying that there was a problem for her to solve, had her create an action plan, and we were clear that if the problem was not solved, that she would need to find a different environment to work in. Mary was diligent in solving the problem and worked with us productively for a long time. She simply needed to know there was a problem, what was causing it, and that she had the ability and responsibility to solve it.

BEING ON TIME

I once had an assignment in an organization where the norm was for people to show up fifteen to twenty minutes late for meetings. Since there were about fifteen staff members, starting every meeting twenty minutes late wasted a lot of time. The staff actually joked about it. Meetings scheduled to start at 8:00 A.M. would routinely start at 8:20 and the staff would say, "We are on Nashville time," meaning "We just tend to run late around here." Yet, some people showed up at 8:00, others at 8:05, others at 8:10, others at 8:15, and the last couple of stragglers at 8:20. The norm was to wait for the stragglers and to keep everyone else waiting. In this culture, it was considered rude not to wait on the stragglers but perfectly fine to make the majority of the staff wait.

I viewed it as unproductive to waste that much of the staff's time. I also viewed it is as rude to the majority to waste their time waiting on the stragglers. So I started meetings on time. When people walked in late, I would pause and ask them if they had some trouble that we needed to be aware of and help with. If so, I would acknowledge it and try to encourage them. If not, I would give a look of disapproval, pause for a few uncomfortable seconds, and continue on.

I also made it clear they were responsible for catching up with what had been talked about up to that point. Further, I made it clear that we would talk about some of the most important things at the beginning of the meeting and if they were not there, their input would be missed. People started showing up earlier.

After two or three times of the same people showing up late, I talked to them after the meeting and told them I expected them to show up on time because it was disruptive to the meeting for them to walk in late and rude to the rest of the team. They tended to get better.

There was one or two who still did not show up consistently on time. I dealt with it in their quarterly review. Yes, I did a written quarterly review and, if being on time consistently was an issue, I put that in the review with the expectation that it not be an issue the next quarter. Within six months, everyone showed up on time. If people had a problem or conflict where they would be late, they called or e-mailed in advance to let me know. When they came in the room late, they apologized to the team and engaged. Nobody was late without an acceptable cause after six months.

In any organizational culture, business, non-profit, ministry, or church where low expectations are accepted, it impacts the performance of the group. I'm a stickler for time. I don't just show up on time; I show up early. But, as strongly as I feel about it, if I'm in situations I don't control and I know that meetings aren't going to start on time, I don't show up on time either because the set time is not the real expected start time.

Mistake # 5 – Giving up too soon—God gives us many second chances

My early years in internal audit taught me the importance of not giving up on people before considering other options. The department was considered a training ground for the company. Sometimes, new auditors did a poor job. Often, people simply needed another chance. Some required more training and explanations than others. Often, if people weren't doing well, we simply needed to spend a little bit more time training them, which was advantageous versus finding someone else for the role and destroying someone's self-confidence. If you choose to train people, there are a few questions you have to answer before doing this. Do people have the right motivation to learn the needed skill? Is this skill consistent with their natural personality profile and the goals they want to achieve? If you spend the time and money to train these individuals, are you being a good steward for the organization? After answering these questions, you will know if training is an option.

Often, some of the average or even weakest auditors did the best job in other positions in the company. Being aware of a person's unique strengths and looking for matches within the company benefited a lot of individuals and was a far more successful approach for the company. We had some, but very few, that we did give up on. In most cases, the company was large enough that we had an opportunity to place them in a role they could be very successful in.

If you lead an organization of the size and scale that does not allow for this, you could go to your network of contacts and use a similar approach outside your company. This would be a blessing to the individuals you deal with and best for your company.

Mistake # 6 – Holding on too long

Sometimes, leaders don't deal with people situations as they should simply because the organization is meeting its objectives, and they are not forced to deal with it.

Leaders have enough problems to contend with every day, so there's a tendency to deal with the ones we have to now. But let's look at this from a stewardship standpoint. Often we are pleased when our teams are making a positive net contribution. For example, let's say the company's desired net profit is 10%. The team celebrates and everyone gets the bonus for delivering 10%. What if the potential of the team was really 20%, 30%, 40%, or even 50%? Should the team be celebrating? Should the leader receive a bonus? Too often, leaders look at how well they are achieving their target and do not exercise their stewardship responsibilities to optimize what is really possible with the resources available to them. This is a disservice to the organization and to the other members of the team.

Many tend to think of Jesus as a passive leader who didn't demand a person's best in following him. Yet at one point in his ministry, Jesus turned to his many followers and urged them to "count the cost" of following him. The reason he did this was because he expected a total commitment to his calling. We see this point made in other places in Scripture where Gideon was commanded to let everyone who was afraid go home. His army was eventually cut down to three hundred fully committed soldiers. In the New Testament, Ananias and Sapphira were struck dead in the church for misrepresenting their commitment. That seems severe to us. But Bible scholars explained that to have allowed this in the early church would have had a substantially negative effect. This is true in any organization. Half-hearted commitment of people impacts others.

I will take a very practical example. I go to a number of nonprofit and church gatherings. Some people leading meetings habitually wait for the last few stragglers to come in and, therefore, always start late. As I said earlier, I am personally a stickler for showing up on time. But when I am engaged with these organizations, I find myself showing up late because I know the meeting won't start on time anyway. There's high cost to keeping partially committed people in your organization. There's also a high cost of keeping people in positions where, for whatever reason, they are not doing a good job. Others on the team see it and either consciously or subconsciously it impacts their commitment and effort. I've experienced this many times.

As stewards of the organizations' resources, we have a responsibility to ensure the job is done by individuals in the role so that they do not negatively impact the attitude and effort of others.

Understanding this concept and dealing with it constructively changed my life as a leader. Often leaders struggle with the need to make a personal change way too long. We let ourselves get miserable and say things we shouldn't. But even worse, we leave people in positions they don't fit. They get more and more miserable and finally end up feeling like a failure. But, the reality is they're still good, talented people that have been impacted by change that they and their leader need to respond to.

APPLICATION TO NON-PROFIT ORGANIZATIONS

Because of the benevolent mission of many non-profit organizations, there is a real hesitancy not to deal with this issue. Given that many non-profit organizations are funded solely by gifts, I would contend that they have an even higher obligation to deal with this issue than a for-profit organization.

Mistake # 7 – Dealing with entrepreneurial leaders poorly

I've seen entrepreneurial leaders start new initiatives in large established organizations. They get the initiative going with great success. But, it finally grows beyond their leadership, experience, skills, and even passions. The creative startup phases of a new initiative are very different than running something after it gets large.

But since they started and grew the organization to a certain level, it's become "their baby." They have a hard time letting go. I have had occasions in business and ministries with these leaders and needed to make changes.

They looked at me and said, "So you are telling me that I can't run the organization that I created?" Answering that question, as framed, is a lot like answering the question for your spouse, "Does this outfit make me look fat?" I don't answer either of those questions.

I turn the discussion around. I compliment them on their strengths and thank them for the contribution they have made to the organization. And, I do so sincerely. I tell them they are gifted entrepreneurs. I compliment their creativity, high-energy, and hard work. I tell them they are wonderful at starting things and that I and the organization are grateful for what they have done.

Then, I explain the next phase of organizational growth and development does not play to their strength, their experience, or even their passions. I explain that they will get increasingly frustrated by the next leg of the journey. Then, I begin to talk about roles within the organization and, if necessary, outside the organization that fit their strengths and passions.

Sometimes, they almost try to force you into making a negative comment about them. I don't buy into that. I do not criticize them. I constantly go back to affirming their strengths and contributions and my appreciation for both. But I stay consistent with the message that their experience and skill do not match best with the next leg of the journey for this particular organization.

Did they like it? No, but it's more objective, more fair, and far less painful for them over the long run than criticizing them for what they are not. Or even worse, letting them stay in a position that ultimately lets them fail and then blaming them for it.

Starting something from nothing is hard work and entrepreneurial leaders contribute a lot to society and organizations. They should be treated with respect but not allowed to fail if their organization grows beyond their talents.

Mistake # 8 – Not staying on top of change

One of the most common ways a leader can bless people's lives is to make sure that their role fits their talents and passions. This is not a one-time job. It should be re-evaluated at least annually. As counterintuitive as it seems, sometimes the kindest thing we can do is to begin the process of removing people from the roles they do not fit.

Sometimes, leaders try to force the fit. Imagine trying to force a piece that doesn't fit the entire puzzle. Does that look very pretty? Of course not. Sometimes, leaders try to carve and reshape the puzzle piece so that it fits. Does it ever work? No! Does this mean that they can't learn or grow? No, that is not what we are talking about. We're talking about changing the passions and natural giftedness of the individual.

"For to the grace given to Me, I say to everyone among you not to think more highly of himself than he ought to think; but to think so as to have sound judgment..."
Romans 12:3

One of the things I disciplined myself to do every year was to ask myself if I still fit the role I was in. I would do as honest an evaluation of the issue as I could, while realizing I couldn't be totally objective. So, I asked my team and asked my boss how well they felt I fit my role. I challenged each of my direct reports to do the same thing and had a specific discussion each year on their fit for their role and how any changes were impacting their fit. If I thought I could foresee a time in the future when the role would change and no longer fit them, I had that discussion proactively.

Application

I. List the key people in your organization that don't fit their jobs anymore. What are the options to remedy?

   1.

   2.

   3.

   4.

   5.

II. What about you personally? Have you done an objective and honest assessment of how well you fit your job? Do you still fit? Rate your fit on a scale of 1-5. _____

   A. Do you need some new training? If so, what training will you get in the next year?

   _____

   _____

   _____

   B. Should you consider a transfer within your organization? Yes_____ No_____

   If yes, what role might fit you better?

   _____

   _____

   _____

C. Should you look outside your organization for a better fit? Yes_____ No_____

If yes, what do you see in the marketplace that fits you better?

_____

_____

_____

III. Priorities

God gives us priorities to live by . . .
Be transformed from trying to have and do it all
to realizing what is important.

"The way is narrow that leads to life"

Matthew 7:14

"Seek first His Kingdom and His righteousness

and all these things will be added to you."

Matthew 6:33

Questions to Ponder

- How would you like to cut your schedule of activities by 20-50% and feel like you're accomplishing more?

- Are you overwhelmed with all the activities in your life?

- Do you seem to want more out of many areas of your life, yet seem to be getting less?

- Do you know your top three priorities in life, for this week, or for today?

- Do you know your top three priorities for your job? If you don't, do you think your team can be clear about their priorities?

- Do you feel like you have enough balance in your life?

- Are your spiritual priorities clear?

Issues Covered in this Section

- How to accomplish more by doing less.

- The most common mistakes leaders make regarding priorities.

- The leader's role in helping people with priorities.

Chapter 11

LESS IS MORE!

Thought!
How much time are you wasting and how much extra stress are you enduring because you're not focused on priorities?

"The way is narrow that leads to life."

Matthew 7:14

"Seek first His Kingdom and His righteousness and all these things will be added to you."

Matthew 6:33

I had heard all my life that "the way is narrow that leads to life." The problem was I didn't really get that. I did not understand that less in God's kingdom means more. I really believed that more meant more. In my foolishness, I tended to want it all and think if I worked hard enough, I could have it all. So, I was busy all the time and worked really hard. In the process, I ignored my wife, kids, family, friends and relationship with God. I gave up so much of what would have given real joy in life to chase things that, in the end, didn't matter. You don't have to do that. And you don't want to do that. The life the narrow way leads to is what Jesus referred to as the abundant life. It was wholeness in life. It was everything that the person needed to be whole and experience joy and satisfaction in life.

Scripture says that it's impossible for a person to have two masters. We will love one and hate the other. That seems harsh. Can't we love both—some? I look at my own life and realize for big portions my priorities were getting the tasks done versus loving the people, accomplishment versus relationship, and acquiring things for people that I cared about versus simply being with them in relationship. The Scripture is true. If the task is your priority, the people aren't. If accomplishment is the priority, the relationships aren't. I gave up much in my life being task and accomplishment oriented versus more relationship oriented. There is much more joy in having the right relationship with people.

Everywhere I go, it seems executives keep getting busier. There aren't enough hours in the day. The work backlogs get bigger, and the stress seems to increase. I understand. My life has felt this way many times. Let's understand the concept of "less is more" better through a couple of illustrations.

BAKED POTATO

This a true story about a couple I know. The thrifty wife wanted to have hot baked potatoes for Sunday lunch. She put the potatoes in the oven before she left for church and set the temperature to 150°. Three hours later, the family sat down for lunch. The husband put his fork in the potatoes, and it made a crunching sound. He stuck the potato again with the same results. He said, "Honey, this potato isn't done." She said, "Of course it's done. It should be nice and hot and soft in the center." He stabbed it with a fork again so she could hear the crunch and said, "Well, it's not." She contended, "Well, it should be." He proceeded to cut the potato open and have her examine the cold, hard center.

She said, "I don't understand. Normally, I bake a potato for 1-1½ hours at 350° and it's done. This potato baked for three hours at 150°, which is the same as 1 hour at 450°. It should be well done, instead of cold and hard. This doesn't make sense." The husband said, "Well, your math is right and I'm not a physics major, so I don't know why it doesn't work. I just know it doesn't." She said, "It should." He said, "Well, let's think about it this way. If it's 75° in here and we laid the potato on the counter for six hours, mathematically that's the same as one hour at 450°. Do you think that will work?" She said, "Oh, I get it now."

Now you may ask what the story about the baked potato has to do with priorities. The point is, just because something makes sense doesn't mean it's true or right. Because the math works, that doesn't mean you would get the results you expect. In a world where every ounce of our logic and fiber says that the only way to have more is to do more and that more is always better, we need to accept the fact that because it *seems* true doesn't *make* it true. The key to time management is priority management. If we can truly manage our priorities well, we can actually accomplish more in our lives and our organizations, even though that seems very counterintuitive.

Not Work More, Work on what Matters

THE EXAMPLE OF THE RIVER

Picture in your mind's eye a river. The river is two miles wide and has barges and boats and dinghies on it. They are spaced a safe distance apart with each carrying a cargo. A certain amount of goods can be moved in a day's time on this river, even without any other power source, because it is flowing at five miles per hour. If you wanted to move the most goods down the river in the least amount of time, what would you do?

Let's assume you had the ability to narrow the banks of the river. Now instead of being two miles wide, it's a mile wide and flowing at ten miles per hour. For this to be safe, you have to take the sailboats and dinghies off the river and all you'll have left are the barges. In this scenario, would you be able to move more goods in less time? Of course you would.

Now, let's think about any area of your life and see if this isn't also true. Let us take work for example. Let's compare the width of the river to the breadth of the project lists and activities you have. As leaders, we have many choices to narrow the number of activities we engage in and the number projects we pursue. Now let's compare the barges to those projects and activities that really "move the needle," as the leadership used to say at HCA. We had some very savvy operators who were very focused, not on small items but those things that "moved the needle." When you see boats on the river, especially sailboats, they normally have a name on them. They appeal to our pride, and they are flashy and fast compared to a barge. Let's compare the boats in organizational life to those projects or initiatives that have particular individuals' thumbprints on them. It is a matter of pride to them. These are smaller projects that can move quickly, but over time they don't do much to "move the needle." The only sailboat type projects that should be left in place are those that have the potential for barge type impact later.

Now let's compare the dinghies in organizational life to those pet projects of the leader. These are small blips on the radar screen, and the leader can control these, but these things do nothing to "move the needle." These things in organizational life still take administrative time and effort to follow up on, and they take some resources. I have seen many times in a big company that when the focus is narrowed to the big projects that really move the needle, more progress is made in a shorter period of time. We see this in the Bible in the book of Nehemiah. The Great Wall of Jerusalem was rebuilt in fifty-four days, a task thought unachievable. How did this happen? It was the single focus of all the people, and they did more than they thought possible during that timeframe.

I read multiple books on time management. Most of them have a number of tricks and techniques that are useful in helping you be more efficient with your time. But I know through experience that narrowing my focus and concentrating on the high potential projects always yields better results.

WHAT MOVES THE NEEDLE FOR LEADERS?

So what are the things that move the needle for a leader? This will depend on the nature of your organization and its size and scale. I will share the "needle movers" in my last organizational role. Leading the team in planning to come up with clear priorities and breaking those into strategies and goals by department and individual took about 5-10% of my time each year. This was one of the most critical activities I did each year because it directed everyone's focus.

Putting the right people in the right place took another 5%-10% of the time. From years of experience, I can tell you that having the right people in place is the difference between a good life for the leader versus misery for them and the team. As important as it is to get the right people in place, I observed frequently that often otherwise good leaders would get really busy and not put the necessary time and focus into interviewing and filling positions timely with the right people. There were times in turnaround situations when I literally had to make leaders give a priority to people selection. They kept "putting out fires," not realizing there was no end to it until they got the right people in place and delegated to them appropriately.

Accountability took about 10%-15% of my time. Setting up good control systems with exception reporting and variance monitoring can take more time early on. However, once established, determining whether you are within the boundaries and what needs to be done if you are not only takes a small portion of your time.

This is the approach I used at HCA to expand the service offerings of Physician Services and when I was leading Physician Services, the company's temporary nurse staffing organization, and playing the role of executive pastor at my church. For each area, we made sure we had good plans that everyone understood and were rightly connected to. We put the right organization chart in place and put the right people in the proper positions. Then, we implemented measurement and control systems to monitor if we were proceeding according to plan. I delegated much to capable leaders. Following this approach allowed me to do many different things without running out of time. We made progress in all of those areas.

I also used this approach in writing this book. After thirty-five years in the business world, there are numerous principles and experiences I could have chosen to discuss in this book. From the beginning, I narrowed the focus to a much smaller percentage of the possible options. What I could have written about would have been too much. I believed the narrower focus with the highest impact experiences would be easier to use and result in more good for the reader rather than more material.

I also tried to follow clear priorities in how I organized the book. You may wonder why I didn't start with the progress section. After all, that's what you're interested in—making progress. I started with purpose because without a clear purpose you're not going to make meaningful progress no matter what you do. You might make progress in a direction that doesn't make any difference. People were next because without the right people, it's nearly impossible to make meaningful progress. I covered priorities in the third section of the book because without clear priorities, it's very hard to keep people or yourself on track toward the vision of the organization. Power was next because without understanding how to truly empower others, the organization would never grow beyond your personal ability and effort.

<u>Summary</u>

① ② ③
Once you have a clear purpose, the right people in place, with clear
④
priorities who are properly empowered, then you have the chance to
⑤
make real progress, but not before.

Great Progression Plan

KEY PRIORITIES FOR MANAGERS AND SUPERVISORS

Leaders have a number of managers and supervisors in their organization. What are the key priorities that leaders help them focus on? Let's look at what I consider the top three:

Key # 1 – Avoid a "firefighting" culture

"Where there is no guidance the people fall,

but in an abundance of counselors there is victory."

Proverbs 11:14

In organizational life, everyone is trying so hard for the big breakthrough, "the grand slam," that the basics are often overlooked and problems occur resulting in big setbacks. These setbacks require an enormous amount of time, energy, and resources just to get back to even. Take British Petroleum (BP) for example and the explosion of their oil rig in the Gulf region. According to TV reports, a few more dollars spent on backup batteries and a little bit of time on the follow-up of backup routines by managers and supervisors could have saved British Petroleum $20 billion and untold stress. The list of corporate examples could go on and on.

Avoiding a fire fighting culture results in a much better organization. Why? Because organizations that don't are always solving a problem that didn't need to occur. And in their hurry to solve that problem, they tend to create their next series of problems, unintended consequences, by not thinking them through. "Firefighting" organizations never make substantial long term progress.

I mentioned early in the book a trip to London during which time I decided to walk across Hyde Park back to my hotel room versus taking a taxi. I didn't know the way, so I asked someone and they said it was to the right side of the park. I headed that direction. After walking a while, I asked someone else if I was going in the right direction. They pointed me to the other side of the park. This happened about three more times. I finally got to my hotel, but realized that I had zigzagged across a five hundred acre park and had extended more than twice the walking, energy, and time than if I had been going in a straight line. This reminds me of organizations where priorities are changed frequently. They go one direction, then another, then another. The employees are much more aware of the fact that everything to the left and right of a straight line is wasted time and energy. And, they are very aware that they waste a lot of time and energy when their leaders are changing directions. Think about it. When you're not going in a straight line, everything to the left and right, even if you're going in right direction, is completely wasted.

Key For Me

Key # 2 – Right people

Jesus prayed all night before he began choosing his disciples. Why? Because it was that important. This handful of men that Jesus would choose would change the course of human history after he was gone. One of the first places to avoid future pain and time is making sure you have the right people in place. When I first began to lead Physician Services for HCA, there was one division out of twelve where 60-80% of the complaints came from. There was weak leadership in that division. This was complicated by the fact that this was a matrix management system and the division president thought these people were very good. I couldn't unilaterally make changes. It took about six months, but I finally found someone that I thought would be great in the role. Rather than criticize the people in place that the division president supported, I simply acquainted him with a much stronger player. It's kind of like driving your old car. You're satisfied with it until you go to a dealership and smell the leather in a new car.

Changing one key person in your leadership team can make a huge difference in your life as a Leader.

Then, you're not happy anymore. I showed the division president a better set of options. He agreed. We went through an appropriate process to put a stronger leader in place. Within eighteen months, this division had the fewest complaints that required my attention and 80% of the unsolicited compliments for Physician Services came from the same division.

That one personnel change made an amazing difference in my life as a leader. Remember, I said earlier that putting the right people in place in your organization only took 5%-10% of my time, but it is one of the keys that make a significant difference. This change was a strong example for me of just how valuable that principle is. Here's the point that should not be overlooked. The change not only made my life better but also made life better for the hospital CEOs, the Physician Services employees, and for the physicians who were employed in that division.

Putting the right people in place in an organization brings blessing and wholeness to many people. And by the way, some of the people who needed to be displaced were put in other positions in the division where they could be effective. Remember we talked earlier about transferring people to other positions within the organization where they are a better fit. We did that, and it worked.

Key # 3 – Training and delegation

"The things which you have heard from me in the presence

of many witnesses, entrust these to faithful men

who will be able to teach others also."

2 Timothy 2:2

In ministry, they call this discipleship. Elsewhere, it's called training and delegation. But regardless of what you call it, it's important. Jesus knew its importance. He knew the rest of human history would be impacted by the few people he shared his work with. The Apostle Paul knew its importance, and he was teaching Timothy the importance of training people and sharing the mission and work with them. Jethro, father-in-law of Moses, knew how important it was. He gave Moses some good advice regarding training and sharing the work with others.

Most leaders I know feel like they need more time, but they spend very little time training people because they don't have time. It seems to be a vicious circle.

It's amazing how often leaders do work out of habit instead of thinking of who they have on the team that can do the work. The more common issue is leaders being reluctant to train others to do the job. Their response is "I don't have time to train anyone." That very well may be true. But, if you don't take time to train someone, how will you ever gain more time for yourself?

In my experience, taking time to train others for some of the tasks you do is the key to leaders having more time and freedom. This freedom gives you time and energy to make sure you plan properly, select the right people, delegate well, and follow up promptly on exceptions in performance from your control system flags. These, in turn, produce greater progress and save more time in the future.

I know many entrepreneurial leaders who never seem to have enough time. Yet they never slow down and take the time to train people within their organization to give themselves more flexibility and time. They seem to just keep running in circles.

The Four Most Common Mistakes Leaders Make Regarding Priorities

Mistake # 1 – Unclear priorities

"Let all things be done decently and in order."

1 Corinthians 14:40

I remember assuming responsibility for a new corporate department. I tried to assess the priorities. It quickly became clear there was no true sense of priorities among the department. They were simply trying to make the operators they were dealing with at the time happy. There was much wasted activity. Substantial money was being spent on plans and projects that had no hope of being approved. There was much other wasted activity with no sense of direction. Some of the activity even worked against the company in the long run.

I led the team to assess strengths, weaknesses, opportunities, and future threats. From that, we put together a set of goals and priorities and had them endorsed by senior management. The team saved millions of dollars and did a better job for the company with much less stress and anxiety because they had clear priorities.

How did we save so much money? We did it by having a process in which we sought approval of senior management before spending substantial money on projects that would eventually be rejected. How did we do a better job for the company? We did it by having everyone's focus on high-priority projects that would make a difference and would be approved. How did we reduce the stress and anxiety for the team? Prior to this process, everyone in the department had

Teams waste enormous time and energy when priorities are not clear.

the stress of keeping each individual operator happy. The corporate team had the stress of realizing that sometimes what operations wanted and what was best for the company were at odds. But, they felt they would ultimately get evaluated based on keeping each individual operator happy. When the new process was implemented, it was senior management making the decisions on project priorities before a great deal of money and time was spent on weak projects. The people in the corporate department were not "pitted" against the operators in the field. The operations satisfaction ratings of this department went up. The team had much greater satisfaction and less stress. They spent time on high-impact projects. They were not chasing projects and spending time that would ultimately be wasted while stretching them too thin. Eliminating unproductive work and enabling people to make progress on things that "move the needle" blesses the people.

It is not uncommon in large companies for people in support areas to work really hard to make whoever they're dealing with happy but with no real sense of priority for the greater good of the organization.

Non-profit organizations frequently experience mission creep. Therefore, it is common for the priorities to become blurred.

Mistake # 2 – Too many priorities

"On these two commandments depend

the whole law and the prophets."

Matthew 22:40

Having too many priorities is the same as having no priorities.

One of my group vice presidents came back from a division president's meeting and was quite excited about the priorities the division president presented. I looked at the sheet and quickly said, "Problem." He looked at me astonished and asked what was wrong with the priorities. He asked me which ones I didn't like. I said, "Each of them is fine. The problem is there are twelve of them. Can people focus clearly on twelve different things?" My experience has shown if you go beyond five to seven objectives/priorities for an annual cycle you start diluting the effort, and people lose focus.

**News Flash, Leaders!
If you have a bunch of them,
they aren't all real priorities.**

So, how does focusing on priorities in your organization bless people? It creates focus. It brings simplicity to complexity. It makes sure people are pulling together toward the key priorities resulting in greater accomplishment and satisfaction for them and the whole team. It assures the leader and employees are more on the same page, resulting in fewer expectation gaps, conflicts, and confusion.

Priorities in organizations act like river banks. Initiatives flow faster the more narrow they get.

Let's think about how a river works. The more the river banks narrow, the deeper the channel gets, and the faster and stronger the water flows. Priorities in organizations act like river banks. Initiatives flow faster and stronger. Priorities create "tipping points" in organizations like the great waterfall on a river. Things move with great speed and a powerful, almost unstoppable, force is created. It has great power and a certain beauty about it.

YOU OFTEN SEE TOO MANY PRIORITIES IN CHURCHES AND MINISTRIES

One time I was consulting with a large church that was getting ready to double in membership. In working with the staff, I tried to assess the priorities. In a team meeting, I asked people to share their priorities. The chief administrative leader had a page of activities front and back. I said, "I think that's too much for you to get done. What are your top three priorities?" He lifted his hands with a bewildered look and said, "I have no idea." If the lead administrative person has more than they can do and no sense of priority, what do you think that was like for the team? There was chaos, confusion, and anxiety among the team. In fact, if things proceeded on the present course, I perceived it was only a matter of time until high turnover would occur. Even though this was a church, I hardly saw it as an environment where employees were being blessed. And, here's the point. This leader and the whole team were really good people. The church was a good church. Everybody had good intentions. People worked hard and did their best. But with lack of clear priorities, anxiety, chaos, and confusion were rampant in the lives of these people.

If the leader is confused, it's safe to assume the team is too.

Mistake # 3 – Over controlling

"From any tree of the garden you may eat freely;

but from the tree of knowledge of good and evil you shall not eat..."

Genesis 2:16-17

You can make your organization non-competitive by over controlling.

God doesn't over-control us. In fact, He gives us great freedom coupled with great accountability. We see this in our analogy of the river. The river banks do not micromanage each drop of water. Rather they guide the flow of the water via the path of least resistance toward the ultimate destiny of the river. When the river banks get too narrow, the water overflows its banks. I've seen this in an organization where such restrictive controls were put in place. The operations people began to work around them, resulting in a complete lack of control.

I started my career at HCA as an internal auditor. The typical mindset of an auditor is that you should control at the perfection level. The problem with this is operators are held accountable for results. The parable of the talents in Matthew 25:15 teaches us that there is some risk of loss when you make an investment of time, energy, or money. God was not pleased with the steward who was not willing to take any risk. The key is taking measured, prudent risk.

I am reminded of my experience on the farm with the hogs and the electric fence. The hogs were shocked so many times touching the fence that we had a very difficult time getting them to leave the hog lot even though the gate was open and there was no fence across it. When people are exposed to excessive control environments where there are severe penalties for making mistakes, they no longer show any initiative or take any risk outside of what they see as the boundaries. This can have a devastating effect on organization in the long run where restrictive controls are put in place, and overly punitive measures are used as punishments.

Teaching this principle to a group of auditors was challenging, to say the least. As we began to implement this in our thinking for planning and executing audits, we were able to accomplish far more and get better results for the company than continuing with our perfectionism.

As I write this portion of the book, we have a national debate going on regarding government regulation of business. We are in an environment of high regulation with businesses screaming that it is causing them to be less competitive. Clearly, some regulation is needed. However, once the controlling goes too far, the costs get too high, and business competitiveness and creativity are inhibited. This tends to happen the larger and more bureaucratic an organization becomes.

Also, the wrong personality profiles in key leadership positions will almost always result in over-controlling.

So what does this discussion have to do with bringing blessing into people's lives? People want to be prudent, but they also want to be productive. They see the need for good planning and a reasonable level of controls. They also get worn out when the planning cycle never ends and when they are not allowed to plan to a certain degree and then get started. They get really frustrated when they feel they're over-controlled and that the controls stifle productivity. Over-controlling is like narrowing the banks of a river until water flow is blocked. Good controls give direction, protection, and create steady organizational flow. Over-control stops the flow and is counterproductive. This happens quite frequently in government and other non-profit organizations. Be careful not to misapply this concept. In legal matters, safety, and health issues, the goal is 100%.

Mistake # 4 – Favoring efficiency over effectiveness

The leader's job in today's world seems a lot like farming. The work never seems to get done. There never seems to be enough time. Leaders are often driven individuals who lean toward being competitive workaholics. Therefore, their solution is to work longer hours and require others to work longer hours. This goes on until higher and higher turnover results. Then, the leader eventually may experience "burn out."

Sometimes, enterprising leaders say, "We need to be more efficient." They may read time management books for the latest ideas on efficiency. They may call on the team to come up with efficiency ideas. This is what my internal audit team did when I challenged them to cut the length of the work day to reduce turnover. Many times organizations can be more efficient. But this begs the question, "Is it more important to be efficient or more important to be effective?"

When I led the internal audit department, it was not uncommon for the teams to work until eight or nine o'clock at night, have dinner, and then work more in their hotel room. Needless to say, we had high turnover. People left on average after six months to one year. It seemed we were always hiring, always training new people, and always trying to do complicated work with inexperienced people.

I noticed that these late nights were the norm with some supervisors while other supervisors completed their audits with more normal hours. After much discussion with the leadership team about employing efficiency techniques, we actually went the route of looking at effectiveness issues/priorities. Auditors like to dot every "i" and cross every "t." But not all work in any audit is of equal value. We started talking about working smarter, not harder. This meant that we would have to determine what truly high priority was. We prioritized the steps that were mission-critical. We never compromised on those. We held open the option of changing the scope of the audit depending on the time available. With that change, we were able to make the schedules reasonable and retain people for much longer, resulting in higher qualified people doing better audit work.

I proved this again for myself many years later when I was responsible for the Physician Services department. This was a function with substantial responsibilities and a good deal of complexity. I really thought I was managing my time well and was highly focused on only the most important priorities. Then, I had a major surgery. I had to transition back into work first two hours a day, then four, then six, and then finally a regular schedule. I discovered that I could do all my high-priority work in two to four hours a day. The rest of the time was really spent on lesser priorities, meetings, miscellaneous administrative tasks, and bureaucratic activities that I got a "pass" on during this time.

Application

I. For your organization, what objectives, goals, or activities drive most of your results?

1. _____

2. _____

3. _____

4. _____

5. _____

Are you zealous about protecting the time to do these activities, appropriately staffing them and funding them at a priority level? Yes_____ No_____

What changes will you make?

_____
_____
_____
_____
_____
_____

II. As the leader, are you clear about your activities that are like barges and will move the needle?

What are these?

_____

_____

_____

Do you give appropriate time and attention to those activities that will be responsible for most of your results? Yes_____ No_____

What will you do?

_____

_____

_____

_____

_____

_____

III. For your direct reports, do they know the primary goals or activities that will produce most of their results? Yes_____ No_____

If no, what will you do?

_____

_____

_____

_____

_____

_____

Chapter 12

A PRIORITY DRIVEN LIFE REQUIRES PRUNING, BALANCE, AND FOCUS

Thought:
Have you ever considered that your true joy, greatest impact and progress toward your real purpose in life is being blocked by lesser goals and activities in life?

Yes and it's terrifying

"I came that you might have life and have it to the full."

John 10:10

"Jesus grew in wisdom, stature and favor with God and man."

Luke 2:52

Different authors have similar but different ways of categorizing areas where we set goals. Dan Miller has one version; Chuck Swindoll has another version. And, finally, Zig Ziglar has his version as illustrated below.

According to Dan Miller's *"No More Dreaded Mondays,"* **we set goals in seven key areas:**[1]

- Career
- Financial
- Family
- Spiritual
- Social
- Physical
- Personal Development

Chuck Swindoll offers this breakdown of priorities:

- Family
- Career, vocation or calling
- Job (not necessarily the same as career, vocation, or calling)
- Health
- Finances
- Possessions
- Friends
- Spiritual Development

Zig Ziglar illustrates it this way.[2]

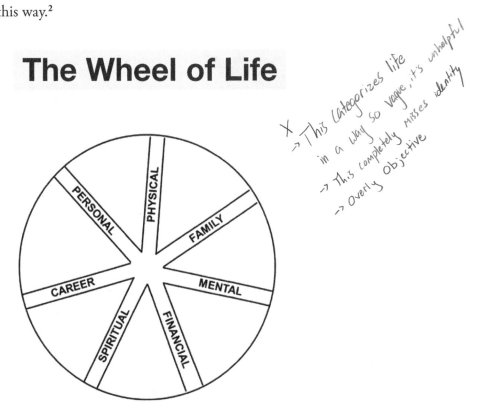

[handwritten note:] X → This categorizes life in a way so vague, it's unhelpful → This completely misses identity → Overly objective

Everywhere I go, I notice that people seem busy and stressed. It seems just to be getting worse. When I ask questions, it seems that people are chasing what they consider the good life. They look at the various components of their life, and their answer seems to be that they want more in each of these areas of life. They truly believe that *more* is the key to happiness. Jesus said, "I've come that you have might have life and have it more abundantly." Some translations say, "I've come that you might have life and have it to the full." There's a difference in the busy and heavily scheduled life that most Americans are living versus the full life that Jesus intended.

[handwritten note:] [?] What is Life?

THE PRIORITY DRIVEN LIFE REQUIRES SOME PRUNING

I would make the argument that less is more in all areas of life. I don't think you can make your life better just by being busier in any area. I grew up on a farm, so I tend to think that we have a lot we can learn from nature. One counter-intuitive thing in nature teaches us that in order to have the healthiest and most robust plants, they require pruning. Yes, you have to cut things back, prune them, for them to reach their optimal health, growth, and beauty. Dr. Henry MacCloud, in his book *Necessary Endings*, teaches us this through his illustration of pruning rose bushes.

The most healthy, beautiful rose bushes were pruned properly.

There are three kinds of branches that need pruning on a rosebush:

- **Dead branches that are taking up space needed for healthy ones**. Evaluate all areas of your life. What are those activities that are dead—those that bring you no joy, give you no feeling of purpose, and are not necessarily helping anyone else. You do these out of habit or obligation. Cut these out.

- **Sick branches that aren't going to get well**. These are activities in any area of your life that have some life. They aren't totally useless, but they don't bring real joy or meaning, and that's not going to change. Cut these out.

- **Healthy branches that aren't the best.** My pastor, Mike Glenn, always says that "Good is the enemy of best." There are activities in your life that are good. They bring you joy, help other people and you see purpose in them. Yet, they take time that could be spent on even more purposeful activities with more impact for you and others. Cut them out to allow time for the best.

Less is more in all areas of life.

PRUNING YOUR BUSY LIFE

Let's look at all key areas of life and think about pruning that needs to be done in each area.

Career

Most people I know have jobs with too many projects.

Too many projects and too little sand in the hour glass!

Isn't that what we face in our jobs? We have more projects than time. Our choices are to decide which projects we are not going to do so that we can spend our time and do the projects that "move the needle" well, or we can spread limited time among all projects and risk doing all of them poorly, resulting in failure.

We actually accomplish more over time by choosing a few high-priority projects and doing them well versus spreading limited time among too many projects. In doing this, we prove that "less is more" because we accomplish more in the long run. Also, we experience less stress and frustration because we are not stretched too thin. We aren't stressed over giving inadequate time to important projects.

You accomplish more doing a few high priority projects well vs. doing a lot of projects poorly or with mediocrity.

There was a time I had flu-like symptoms and could not work a normal schedule for about two weeks. I thought I was being a very good time manager. But, when I looked at my schedule and eliminated everything that was not mission-critical, I was able to cut my schedule in half. **Less is More on the Job!**

i.e. More Quantity will often hurt Quality. And Quality is what Matters.

Family

Everywhere I go, I see families busy and worn out, especially the mom and dad. Many parents I know feel like taxicab drivers. They're always taking kids from one event to the next. They eat fast food and seldom have time for a meal around the table. Many are talking at, not with, their kids. Most people I know with children work really hard at having a good family life, but almost none are really content with the family life they have. Why? They're trying to do too much. They think that more is more versus realizing that less is more. If they scheduled fewer activities and put more time into meaningful activities together with a purpose, their family life would be greater, not less.

My kids almost never talk about all the ballgames and other activities we spent so much time and energy on. They talk about the family times where we spent a block of time as a family doing something special together or helping someone. Being busy all the time didn't make family life better. **Less is More in Family Life!**

Your full focus and attention means more to your family than a lot of activities you wear yourself out doing for them.

My kids taught me good lessons in this area. One time, my son called wanting me to do something. I thought I was being responsive and efficient by taking care of what he needed and sending a message back through my executive assistant. She came to me and said, "Scott is demanding to talk to you." I picked up the phone and he "lit into me." He said, "I am your son. I get to talk to you!" He reminded me of a very important principle. Sons and daughters do have special privileges. As sons and daughters of God, we have special privileges. We are always welcomed to go to the throne of grace because we often need it. Having genuine communication is really important in family life.

I had a similar incident with my daughter, Allyson. She asked me for some help. I did everything she asked and more. But, I sent the message back through my assistant. She got very upset, thinking I had ignored her.

My rule became that if my kids ever called, it didn't matter what I was doing. I wanted to be reached, and I wanted to talk to them. Kids want and need the undivided time and attention of their parents more than they need all the busy activities that we often spend so much time on.

Spiritual life

Most churches I know are brimming with programs. There are activities seven days a week. They are all well-intentioned. Many are good, and some are excellent. Yet, the activities of many churches need to be pruned. Some of the activities and programs are truly dead. They have no impact. They are continued because the program has a strong advocate or simply because it is hard to eliminate any program in a church. Other programs are anemic, and they are never going to be robust and should be cut. Some programs or activities are good but still not the highest and best use of the time and resources. They should be cut to allow all the time and energy on achieving the true purpose for the church. I'm convinced less would have more impact for the church.

It's particularly easy for people in the ministry to consider their job such an overarching priority that they sacrifice health and family for the job. It is a common occurrence for people in ministry to burnout after a few years. One of the reasons is they put so much focus on their job that they have no balance in the other areas of their life. They try for a while to do it all but can't, and they burnout. Often, they sacrifice their own families while trying to minister to other people's families.

In our own spiritual lives, we are so busy with spiritual activity that we often don't experience the spiritual depth that God has for us. The Bible says, "Be still and know that I am God." We are an active people. I've seen in the lives of others and experienced in my own life that less activity often creates more spiritual growth. Less really is more.

In my own ministry activities, I've noticed that less is more. I'm a very active person and left to my own devices would tend to fill up my calendar. God has shown me that a less busy schedule can have a greater impact. For example, Bill invited me to lunch to talk about raising children. Bill worked sixty to eighty hours a week as a consultant and routinely charged twenty hours/week less than he worked. He also charged a rate less than half of his true value. He explained he did this because he wanted to go the "extra mile." I commended him for wanting to go the "extra mile," but questioned how much of it was the desire to go the extra mile versus fear. He acknowledged a great deal of it was fear. Then, we talked about stewardship. I asked how much good could be done if he charged at or near market rate and charged for most of his time versus twenty hours per week less. He had not thought of it that way.

Less activity can create more spiritual growth and impact.

He was considering going to a smaller church where his kids could get involved in hands-on activity. I asked what difference it would make if he charged for most of his hours at a fair rate, worked fewer hours, and took his children to a Third World country on a mission project to see how the rest the world lives and minister to children in poverty. The lights came on for him.

I spent an hour lunch with Bill and a few hours since. He is positioning himself to work fewer hours at a much higher rate resulting in a better income for his family, more giving to ministry, and more time for his kids. He is discovering that less is more. But, God is also showing me that less is more. In a handful of hours, God gave me the opportunity to impact two generations of people. That's much more impact than I would have in a typical day of being very busy. In ministry, being available to strike at the right time is more important than being busy all the time. ← *Well said!* Jesus took time out to go and rest. He often encouraged his disciples to step aside from their busy activities and rest with him. Less is More in Spiritual Life and Ministry!

Social

People I know who seem most content and fulfilled in community work are those that pick an organization or an initiative to support. They have a much greater impact on the community. Those who try to be involved in everything seem more stressed and less fulfilled. **Less is More in Community Life!**

Some people wear themselves out on their recreational activities. The people I know who get the most of their recreation are the ones who focus on one to two hobbies or activities. They become really good at one activity or hobby, and it seems to make their life far better, but not just busier. **Less is More in Recreation!**

Physical

I know people who go through aggressive training to run marathons. A lot of people make it a point to jog or exercise at least an hour a day. There is nothing wrong with this if a person enjoys it. Some do it as a simple act of discipline, thinking it's required for optimal health. The latest research on exercise physiology supports the idea of "surge" training. This is short bursts of intense activity with rest in between. A full workout takes about eighteen minutes three to four times a week. Studies have shown that a person's overall health is as good or better doing this as jogging an hour a day seven days a week. **Less is More in Exercise!**

How many of you were taught to clean your plate as a kid? It didn't matter that you weren't hungry. You were supposed to eat it all. In fact, when I grew up, kids got complimented for eating hearty. We Americans like our food. Studies in recent years, however, have shown that cultures with less calorie intake actually have longer, healthier lives. **Less is More in Health!**

Personal development

I had a friend one time that seemed to listen to every new seminar series and read every new book that came out related to business. I told him that he needed to quit listening to seminars and reading more books. He seemed surprised and asked me why. I told him he had already studied enough topics that it would take him three lifetimes to implement. I suggested he narrow the focus and begin making changes in areas that would be most beneficial to his life. People seem to do a lot of self-development in many areas without ever mastering anything. You would be more productive to master a topic in the area of your strengths, passions, calling, and purpose in life. Think about the impact your life could have. **Less is More in Personal Development!**

A new agricultural agent was placed in a job in a big farming community. He wanted to teach some courses on agriculture. He went to the most progressive farmer in the community, hoping to enroll him. The farmer declined. The agricultural extension agent was surprised and asked him why. The farmer said, "I don't need to learn anything else. I don't do as well as I know to do now." Isn't that the case with most of us in many areas of life?

Non-profit application

Ha! ...And sadly so true.

Who should be the most balanced people in our society but often aren't? Who should encourage balance in people's lives but often don't? Who should reduce guilt in our lives but often add to it? Often, it is the leadership in non-profit organizations. Why does this happen? Because there is a philanthropic mission, these leaders often do not do a good job of balancing their own lives. They intuitively believe that you can't give too much to their mission. But you can. And your life can get out of balance. Luke 2:52 says that Jesus grew in wisdom, stature, and favor with God and man. Do you ever see Jesus being in a hurry? Do you ever see people who do a lot of volunteer work with non-profit organizations being in a hurry? I do! Balance is needed in this part of our lives just like any other portion.

Sure, but how?

Application

I. What do you need to cut out of your life? Look at each of the seven areas and list things that you need to prune.[3]

	High Priority – Keep	Low Priority – Prune
Career		
Financial		
Family		
Spiritual		
Social		
Physical		
Personal Development		

II. Are you clear about the purpose that you're pruning your life toward? Write it out below.

_____

_____

_____

_____

III. What are you doing that causes you to be anxious? How can you cut it out of your life?

_____

_____

_____

_____

Notes

Chapter 13

LEADERS SHOULD HELP PEOPLE BALANCE THEIR PRIORITIES

Thought!
Have you ever considered how much stronger your
organization could be in the long term if you
helped your team be more balanced?

"Do not merely look out for your own personal interests,

but also for the interests of others."

Philippians 2:4

PEOPLE NEED BALANCE

You accomplish more in life with balance. Plus the ride feels smoother.

Life is like the wheel on a car.[4] If it gets out of balance, it feels lonely and uncomfortable. Most people I know feel their life doesn't have the balance they want.

Sometimes, leaders think the organization can't be successful if employees are encouraged or allowed to give significant priority to other goals in life. I'm reminded of the story of the hare and the tortoise. The tortoise won the race instead of the expected finisher, the hare. It's been my experience that people who are very conscience of the choices they are making and feel good about the balance they have based on their "calling" in life actually contribute the most to the organization and accomplish the most in every area of their life.

I remember a movie about a dogsled race. The team that took periodic rests actually beat the teams that kept going all the time. This is the principle of observing the Sabbath day. People can actually get more done by resting every seventh day than by continuing to work all the time.

When I think about it, it is sometimes surprising to see what people will give up in life to achieve a particular goal or complete a project at their job. It's not a matter that what they're working on is not important. But, often people make significant trade-offs for projects they won't remember a year later. I remember many times almost insisting that employees take time off to be with sick parents or to be at some significant event for their children. These were cases where I'm really convinced they would not have done it without my encouragement. I was impressed by their dedication but marveled at their lack of insight regarding the true priorities in life. I say that remembering decisions I made myself, especially early in my career. There were many times I wish I had back, to make a more holistic and conscious decision about what matters most in life.

Jesus never seemed in a hurry. He was stressed at times, but it didn't come from a full schedule, too much to do, and worry over not getting everything done on his "to do" list. His earthly ministry was three years, and on the cross he said, "It is finished." He completed all the work that he was assigned to do. Yet, Jesus had balance. I'm told that the checkerboard square, which is a brand symbol of the Ralston Purina Corporation, was created by the founder to show the balance in Jesus' life.

Luke 2:52 says, "And Jesus increased in wisdom and stature, and in favor with God and man." In other words, Jesus grew mentally and emotionally, physically, spiritually, and socially. Jesus had goals and spent time in the four balanced areas of life. Yet, he did so without anxiety and stress over a busy schedule.

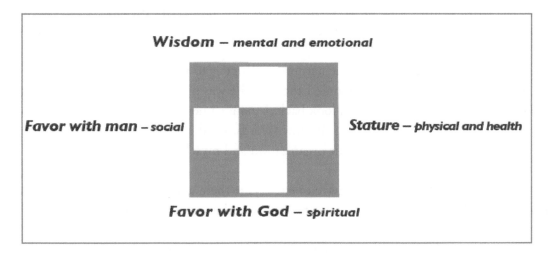

Wisdom – *mental and emotional*

Favor with man – *social*

Stature – *physical and health*

Favor with God – *spiritual*

I once interviewed what appeared to be a bright, aggressive young man. I remember asking him where he wanted to be in ten years. He said he wanted to be sitting in my chair. I said that was great because I had other goals, and I wanted to be sitting in another chair by then anyway.

Later, I offered him a job, which he promptly turned down. I asked him why. He responded that he had a dog and that he could not be out of town and leave his dog that much. I told him I respected his concern for his dog, and there's nothing wrong with being that attached to a pet. I did, however, go on to explain to him that he had an important decision to make. I explained that he had lofty goals he would never achieve if his goal of being at home with his dog took priority. I reminded him of saying his goal was to sit in my chair in ten years. I explained that sitting in my chair or one like it would require some changes in his priorities.

Striking a healthy balance is something that people seem to struggle with. Leaders are in a position to make the struggle harder or easier for people. We can help them or hurt them in the process. If we are going to bless people, that means we should help them.

BONNIE MADE A GOOD DECISION

Bonnie reported to me in a key leadership role. She was great at her job, loved her job, and her people loved her. I never thought Bonnie would do something different. I remember making a goal-setting speech. Within two weeks, Bonnie told me she was resigning from her job. She thanked me for my speech that helped her reach this important decision. I asked her what I had said that made her reach that decision. I said jokingly, "I may want to take it back or clarify what I said!" She told me how much she loved her job and the people that worked for and with her. But, she explained she had been feeling some internal tension which had been growing over the past several months. She explained that as I discussed this topic she realized it was the tension between her focus on the job and the travel versus wanting to be closer to her family, community, and church. She explained the goals she had in those areas

Help people think about career goals balanced against their dreams, passions, and purpose in all of life.

and the fact that she just could not do it all. She was passionate about the fact that she needed to give up this job to get one that required less travel so that she could pursue her other goals.

Nobody likes to lose a great leader. The natural tendency is to want to talk them into staying. I resisted that urge and instead told Bonnie I thought she was making a good decision. I encouraged her to feel good about it and not look back. I thanked her for all that she had done for the organization and how valuable she was. In other words, I did everything I could to support her decision even though I felt a loss for the organization and myself.

If we as are going to bless people, we have to encourage them and affirm them for making decisions that are right for them even when we feel a loss to the organization and ourselves.

HELPING YOUNG PROFESSIONALS FIND BALANCE

When I led the internal audit department of HCA, I dealt primarily with a large number of young professionals. They were ambitious, hard-working, and eager to please. Most importantly, they were very impressionable. I used to teach goal setting sessions based on material from Brian Tracy and lead them through the goal setting process. I never required them to discuss goals in any other area of life other than the job. However, I strongly encouraged them to set goals in all areas of life and led them through the process. I also offered to look at their entire set of life's goals at the same time I was looking at their career goals. Why? I explained to them that I did not want to lead them in the process to set career goals and ignore the fact that they were whole individuals with goals in many areas of life. In the more than fifteen years that I did this with literally hundreds of people, I never had the first person who did not very willingly share their entire set of goals with me.

Consequently, I was able to help them think about their career goals in light of their overall life goals so that they achieved the balance that was consistent with their dreams, passions, and purpose in life. Where their purpose was not clear to them, I tried to help them achieve clarity. It wasn't about my doing what was best for me as the leader of the department. It was about what was best for the individual. It may seem like you're getting ahead when you lead people to blinded loyalties to you or your organization. However, first of all, this is wrong morally and ethically. Secondly, it never pays off over the long term. When people are not moving toward their true calling and purpose, they eventually become unhappy and leave the organization anyway. In fact, often when they are unhappy, it's most manifested or felt in their job, and they blame the job or their leader for the unhappiness whether the job is the problem or not.

When people achieve their goals and you do what's best for them, it helps the organization over time. Why? Because you have people there who are balanced and content with being there. But, most importantly, when you develop a reputation for doing what's good for people, you have a lot of other people ready to join your organization as the replacements. If you have a reputation for taking advantage of people, it's much harder to fill open positions with the caliber people you really want.

I really helped people look at their entire set of goals because I knew morally and spiritually that was the right thing to do. I didn't need another reason to do it. Many times when I was making those decisions, I thought I was hurting myself in doing the right thing. It was only years later after doing the right thing consistently that I saw how it all came back around and actually benefited the organization.

A PRIORITY-DRIVEN LIFE NARROWS THE FOCUS

People, especially leaders, are the busiest I have ever seen them. Leaders want more time, more freedom, and less stress. How is that even possible in organizational life today? The key is how you approach life. Are you going through life like a rifle bullet or like a shotgun blast? Let me explain. A rifle bullet is much smaller than the shotgun shell. It has less powder and less lead. It takes less powder because there's only one piece of small lead at the end as it leaves the barrel moving straight toward its target. It takes less powder to propel the smaller piece of lead a great distance. By contrast, a shotgun shell has much more powder and more lead. The lead is a bunch of pellets, called buckshot. They look like small BBs. They come out of the barrel of a shotgun and scatter. They hit a bigger target area since they scatter. The shooter can be less accurate with a shotgun and still hit the target. Since the buckshot scatters and is small, it doesn't go nearly as far as a rifle bullet.

This analogy is like some people's lives. Some people are highly focused on the singular objective or a limited number of objectives, and they can go far. Other people's lives have so many activities that they are more like a shotgun blast. They cover a lot of territory but don't make as much progress as the person who is more focused.

You get further when you narrow the focus.

Jesus modeled a life that had three critical components. First, he already had balance. Second, he had a clear purpose that he lived his life toward. And, third, he was extremely focused on a narrower set of goals than most people believed he should pursue. Jesus was extremely focused in his life.

Right. And if you have many goals, consolidate them into a small set or even single objective or project

Application

I. Do the people on your team have a balanced life? Yes_____ No_____

    A. If no, are you doing anything to help them find balance? Are you encouraging a lack of balance by your example or expectations of them?

    B. What changes do you need to make to encourage balance for your team?

_____

_____

_____

_____

II. Do you affirm people when they make hard personal choices to achieve balance in their lives, even if you feel it is a loss for you? Yes_____ No_____

_____

_____

_____

_____

Chapter 14

SPIRITUAL PRIORITIES

Thought!
Have you ever considered the opportunities
and joy you miss or the pain you endure
by not following spiritual priorities?

"But his delight is in the law of the Lord,

and in his law he meditates day and night."

Psalm 1:2

The New Testament speaks to the tendency of people to worry about having the basics of life. Jesus said to them:

"Seek ye first the kingdom of God and His righteousness

and these things will be added to you."

Matthew 6:33

Jesus understood the importance of right priorities and clear priorities in life. There are Ten Commandments in the Old Testament. A lawyer once asked Jesus which was the most important commandment. He summarized all the Old Testament by saying:

"Love God with all your heart, soul, and mind

and your neighbor as yourself."

Matthew 22:37-40

KING DAVID

Have you ever considered what it costs a person not to follow the simple commands of God? Let's look at the life of King David again. God called him "a man after his own heart." David truly lived an outstanding life by anybody's standards, especially for the time in history where he reigned as king. But, he strayed from these commands at times.

BATHSHEBA

His affair with Bathsheba is an example. He wasn't putting God's kingdom first, nor did he love his neighbor as himself. He was self-focused. He took what he wanted. And he had a good man killed in battle to cover up his crime. The prophet Nathan told him that he would be forgiven, but he would pay for this seven times over. We see through studying his life that this did cost him seven times over in personal and family difficulties.

NUMBERING HIS ARMIES

David once became prideful and wanted his armies counted to show how powerful he was. He did this even over the objection of the commander of his armies. He wasn't thinking about God's kingdom when he did this; he was thinking about his own. A plague struck the nation of Israel and 63,000 people died because of David's pride.

> *"Pride goes before destruction,*
>
> *and a haughty spirit before stumbling."*
>
> *Proverbs 16:18*

[handwritten margin note: Convicting. What do I count to gain that sense of security?]

The good thing about David was that when he strayed from the path of God's priorities, he genuinely repented and returned to God. That's why he had a long, successful, and famous impact as a king. His leadership over time came more from his shepherd's heart and less from his position as king.

PERSONAL EXPERIENCES

It's hard for me to assess objectively what I've lost by not following God's priorities. I am aware of the anxiety and pressure I feel because I didn't start on this book immediately when God told me to write it. But, I can look back at some significant experiences and see what I gained from putting God first.

When I was about thirty years old and in the number two position of HCA's internal audit department, I was frustrated. My boss did not have a good relationship with some of the company leadership. It would be years before he retired, and I felt stuck. I was Assistant Vice President of Internal Audit, and it looked like that's all I would be for many years. I was recruited by another healthcare organization that was smaller. They offered me a 30% increase in pay, an expensive company car, a company paid country club membership, and what seemed like a great stock option package. As I talked to friends and advisers, all of them but one person told me it was an offer "too good to refuse."

My pastor was the only person who encouraged me to turn it down. After much prayer, I did turn it down. The reason was that when I looked at my immediate family, extended family, church service, community service, and so on, there was a loss in all those areas. The only one benefiting from this move seemed to be me. I swallowed hard and turned it down. I had a strong sense that this was what God was leading me to do.

[handwritten margin note: I.e. Hedonism was the only gain]

Within nine months, the company that offered me the job was in bankruptcy, and all the senior officers were being sued. I would have been one of the senior officers if I had made the switch. Also, my boss at HCA retired, and I had the top spot in internal audit at HCA, which had been a serious goal of mine for a long time. Over the next few years, the compensation and stock options that I got at HCA were much more than I was offered at the other company. Making God my priority and loving others more than myself led to the right decision and made a deep impression on me.

A few years later, HCA was acquired through a merger, and the senior executives had an opportunity to leave with a nice financial package or stay. All of my natural intuition and business intuition said, "Take the money and run." But I sensed in my spirit God telling me to stay, so I stayed. My natural and business intuitions proved to be more right than I could've ever imagined. It was a difficult season of life for me and many others.

Yet, God was working in this, too. Jeremiah 29:11 came to my attention many times: "I know the plans I have for you, plans to prosper you, not to harm you." I was given many opportunities to lead departments outside of internal audit. I was eventually given the opportunity to lead Physician Services for HCA. These various leadership opportunities gave me the experience that I needed to write this book and do many things that I will be doing in the future.

The move to Physician Services created the opportunity for me to have an office off the main campus a mile down the road from my church. After a season of downsizing Physician Services, I had margin in my schedule. That allowed me, with the approval of HCA's leadership, to devote a block of my time in the "role" of the executive pastor at my church. After that, Physician Services experienced much growth in size and in many new functions that we started in group. I learned much from these experiences that are incredibly valuable today.

What I went through felt bad, looked bad, and was very confusing to me at the time. But I knew it was what God was telling me to do. Looking back, I can see how clearly God was training me and positioning me for what I would be doing fifteen years later. It prepared me to create Vision Leadership Foundation to mentor, train, coach, and consult with business, non-profit, and ministry leaders.

Sounds like 'Disciples' Table...

Application

I. Do you follow the Scriptures at the beginning of this chapter in making business decisions and personal decisions? Yes_____ No_____

II. Remember some times that you did and make notes below revealing the difference it made.

_____

_____

_____

_____

_____

III. Recall some times that you didn't and make notes on the difference it made.

_____

_____

_____

_____

_____

IV. What really is your main spiritual priority? What effect could it have if you followed it wholeheartedly?

_____

_____

_____

_____

_____

Notes

IV. POWER

God empowers us . . .

*Be transformed from trying to grab more power for yourself
to empowering others to achieve their calling in life.*

*"For even the Son of Man did not come to be served, but to serve,
and to give his life a ransom for many."*

Mark 10:45

"But the greatest among you shall be your servant."

Matthew 23:11

*"But it is not this way with you, but the one who is the greatest among
you must become like the youngest, and the leader like the servant."*

Luke 22:26

Questions to Ponder

- Do you wish you had more power?

- Do you wish you had more influence on other people?

- Do you understand the difference between positional power and real, lasting power?

- Do you know the key to becoming a leader and staying a leader?

- Do you have problems delegating to people?

- Are there things you want to delegate but don't have anybody you trust to delegate them to?

- Are you confused about motivation? Do some of your people seem very motivated while others aren't? Are you wondering what you're doing wrong?

Issues Covered in this Section

- What is real power?

- How do leaders get power and how do they keep it?

- A key to being able to grow from a small organization to a larger organization.

- The negative effects of micromanagement.

- The results of abusing power.

- The impact of culture on attracting people and keeping them.

- The leader's influence on the motivation of people.

- The three keys to effective delegation.

- The most common delegation mistakes leaders make.

Chapter 15

REAL POWER — CHOICE OR FORCE

> **Thought!**
> How much would you enjoy your work if people
> did what you asked willingly and eagerly,
> without grumbling or complaint?

"Just as the Son of Man did not come to be served,

but to serve, and to give his life a ransom for many."

Matthew 20:28

- Do you have the influence with people that you want?

- Do you know healthy ways to influence others?

- Do you use destructive approaches to influence others?

- Do you know the difference?

Power can be a great thing or terrible thing, depending on whether it is used constructively or destructively. Great power rests in the hands of leaders in organizational life.[1] I've seen it used for great good and, sadly, seen it used many times with great destructive effects. And I have to admit I personally have done good at times, but at other times I have been destructive in my own leadership style. I see this in business organizations, non-profit organizations, ministries, and churches I have engaged with.

A BIBLICAL PERSPECTIVE

Let's look at power from a biblical perspective. At the time Jesus entered human history, the people had one primary understanding of power based on the system of kings and emperors they were accustomed to. These rulers had totalitarian control over the lives of people to the point of life and death for them. These regimes most often were controlling, harsh, and corrupt. God's people were looking forward to a Messiah who would come as an earthly king and be a military and political leader. They expected Him to overthrow the Roman government and exercise power for the benefit of the nation of Israel. When He came as a servant leader and said, "I came not to be served, but to serve and give my life as a ransom for many," this mystified the people. This was not how a king thought and acted, at least not what they had seen.

Jesus had no intention of governing as a totalitarian leader. He would not force people to follow him. They would follow him out of choice based on the gratitude and love they had for him because of his sacrifice on their behalf. In Revelation 3:20, he says, "Behold, I stand at the door and knock, and if anyone will open the door, I will come in and eat with him and he with me." Notice that Jesus never forces his way into anyone's life. He initiates the relationship but waits for the invitation to come into a person's life. He asks for complete surrender, but it's based on the person's loving choice to follow him willingly, not by force.

Jesus was the perfect example of the servant leader. Think about the example he gave us. He created everything. Then, he left heaven, where he had no limits, to take on the limits of the human body. The creator of the universe became a carpenter to make a living for his family. He taught and served his disciples and people everywhere throughout his ministry. Then, he gave his life on the cross in excruciating pain and humiliation so that we could have a relationship with God.

PEOPLE WANTED A KING TO FIGHT THEIR BATTLES FOR THEM

As we search Scripture further, we see that the people in the time of Jesus were the same as the people thousands of years earlier. Right after the time of the judges in the Old Testament, the people asked God for a king. This was when Samuel was a prophet. Samuel felt like the people were rejecting him as leader. God told Samuel that it was God himself they were rejecting. They did not want God to rule over them (1st Samuel 8:10-18). God never intended for his chosen people to live under the reign of an earthly king. Yet, the children of Israel in the Old Testament wanted a king. Scripture says they wanted somebody that would fight the battles for them and protect them. God warned them about the future consequences, but they ignored those warnings. It was my personal experience in thirty-five years of leadership that people want the same thing. They want protection. They want someone to fight their battles for them. And they want you to provide for them. People will gladly follow leaders who will do those things for them.

LEADERSHIP CHOICES

This review of Scripture gives us two clear choices. Are we going to rule like kings, the autocratic, controlling and sometimes abusive, totalitarian leaders? Or, are we going to lead like Jesus? Will we lead as a servant? Will we train, mentor, and empower people the way Jesus did, or will we abuse them?

TEMPORARY POWER VS. LASTING POWER

The tyrants of long ago had great power because of their totalitarian governments. Their power was temporary however. When they no longer had the position, people no longer followed them. Yet, with Jesus, the disciples followed him wholeheartedly and followed him all of their lives—freely and by choice. Disciples today still follow Jesus. Yet, we follow obediently and willingly. Would you rather have a workforce that follows you because they want to or because they feel like they have to? Which one will serve your customers and constituents best over time? Which one will be the best to lead and work with? Which ones do you want to be associated with? How do you want to be viewed as a leader—tyrant or servant? Robert K. Greenleaf and others have written much about servant leadership in our generation. There is a growing number of books on the subject. Yet, we need to look no further than the examples we see in the Bible of Moses, Nehemiah, the Apostle Paul and, for the ultimate example, Jesus himself.

USING PEOPLE OR ENGAGING THEM

I believe through my experiences that understanding the use of power biblically is a key to being an effective leader. It was also a key to my spiritual growth in many ways.

In my early years, I approached power from the perspective of using people to achieve worthwhile projects. I was not focused on how I could bless people by engaging them in worthwhile projects that they had the passion, personality, and preparation to help accomplish. I'm reminded of King Solomon in the Old Testament who had a visiting queen from a foreign country who noticed how happy and blessed the people were under Solomon's leadership (though sadly Solomon later failed miserably). I'm reminded of Nehemiah and how the people joined together and said, "Let us rebuild the wall." They had a shared vision, and everyone had a part of it. This stands in stark contrast to "We've got a big job; let's get to it," or "That's what we get paid for," or "If you can't get it done, I will find someone who will."

What's the key difference in this way of thinking? Basically, it's rooted in Scripture—loving your neighbor as yourself, as Jesus said, or thinking of others and not just yourself, as Paul said.

When I got my spiritual attitude right, I began to think differently about how I engaged with people. I changed from how can I control them and get them to do what I want, to how I empowered them to do something they wanted to do that helped achieve the vision. There's a big difference in the attitude and output of people when they are complying with you versus cooperating with you. When they are doing what they want to do, it's an opportunity which is followed by energy and passion.

Some leaders fear that if they soften their approach with the team and do things through spiritual means, they will be seen as spiritual but not strong leaders. Most of us have the view that being a strong leader means being tough with people. That's not the case at all. To be an effective leader, we have to make tough decisions, but seldom do we need to flex our muscles with the team. Nehemiah is a perfect example. When he went to Jerusalem to be the governor, he didn't exert himself and his power. Rather, he rallied the people around a vision so they, with one voice, said "Let us rebuild the wall." (Later, he did have to challenge some of the people about how they were not living out some of God's word by how they treated the poor, and he did not shy away from the issue. Instead, he guided the people to make the right decision.) I learned by experience that I had the most real power when I thought about the team and what was best for them and the company, ignoring the impact on me personally.

YOU DON'T HAVE TO BE THE "TOUGH GUY" TO LEAD

There is a widely held perception today that a leader has to be a "tough guy" to be taken seriously. Otherwise, as the perception goes, you are seen as weak and unable to lead. This is the way many people see Jesus as a leader—weak and passive. This is not what I see at all when I take a close look at his leadership. He had many enemies, but he was not fearful or anxious. Many tried to trick him, but he always had an appropriate answer and never lost a debate. He was kind and gentle to the sick, the disadvantaged, and, in general, the underdog. Yet, he was very bold with the religious leaders of his day. He called them "whitewashed tombs" (Matthew 23:25). He rebuked them publicly. He overturned the tables of the moneychangers in the temple, single-handedly driving them out.

These examples are not when he was the strongest though. The Apostle Paul said, "When I am weak, then I am strong" (2 Corinthians 12:10). Jesus was actually strongest when he appeared the weakest. For example, when he was in the Garden of Gethsemane praying and sweating, he still mustered the courage and self-control to yield his will to God. When the centurions came for him, he did not run or resist arrest. Instead, he was strong enough to forgive his enemy Judas, kiss him, and call him "friend." The soldiers fell back when Jesus presented himself and freely turned himself over to them. When he faced Pilate, he did not feel the need to defend himself or try to talk himself out of a horrible situation. He did not defend himself in front of the people. But, where his strength was most revealed, in apparent weakness, was when he allowed himself to be beaten, stripped, thorns placed on his head, and crucified without opposition. Remember Christ said he could call down ten legions of angels to protect himself. Yet, he was strong enough to suffer wrongfully and horribly without exercising any of his rights as an innocent man, much less the rights he had as the Creator and only Son of God.

There are a lot of benefits to not trying to be the "tough" corporate leader. Your best people stay with you. People cooperate with you versus simply complying. People follow willingly versus being manipulated. Other people are drawn to your culture so that you have your choice of the best people at all times. By contrast, the really tough leaders burn people out. Their people operate in cultures of fear and don't take risks and are, therefore, less proactive. They leave when they get a chance. Other good people are not attracted to those cultures. I have seen those cultures sustain themselves for fairly long periods of time as long as there are enough financial incentives to keep the people. But, when those cords are cut, people will jump ship very quickly.

USE OF POWER

So what is power? A possibility to influence others.[2] It is clear that leaders have power and have the ability to use that power for great good. You may say, "I want

Power is a possibility to influence the actions of another person.[2]

— 171 —

to be a leader and have power so that I can make a difference." That's a worthy ambition. So, how do you become a leader? How do you stay a leader?

What is it that makes a leader different from other people? What do leaders have that others don't? You may say intelligence, good looks, or high-energy. Jim Collins refuted all that in his description of "level five" leaders.[3] I've seen examples of people with all these who weren't great leaders. I have also seen examples of people with none of these who are.

Why did people follow Jesus? Peter followed Jesus because he appealed to the "I" portion of Peter's personality when he told them he would make him a fisher of men. Judas obviously followed Jesus because he wanted access to military type power and wealth. He thought Jesus would be a political and military leader and would overthrow the Roman government. He wanted to be part of the reigning class. James and John followed Jesus because they thought he would be the source of their positions in heaven. They wanted to occupy the thrones to the left and right of him in heaven. Their mother wanted the same for them. The bottom line is that everybody who followed Jesus expected something from him.

Great insight to Leadership

In pursuing what they perceive is best for themselves, people pick leaders throughout their lives to follow. The people they follow are not always good people. They do not always lead to good results. They are not always good-looking, caring, or even intelligent. They are simply someone that they think will do something for them.

HOW DO YOU BECOME A LEADER?

Maybe you remember Dale Carnegie saying that "You can achieve any goal or dream you have if you're willing to help enough other people achieve their goals." Or maybe you remember the words of Jesus who said:

*"It is not this way among you,
but whoever wishes to become great among you shall be your servant,
and whoever wishes to be first among you shall be your slave;
just as the Son of Man did not come to be served, but to serve..."
Matthew 20:26-27*

*"But the greatest among you shall be your servant."
Matthew 23:11*

*"I came not to be served
but to offer my life as a ransom for many."
Mark 10:45*

I recently had a social lunch with the leader of a large privately owned physician practice. He had just fired one of the doctors in the practice. This doctor had chewed out one of the support staff for scheduling a patient that was not convenient for him. He told this person never to schedule people at an inconvenient time. Many doctors I know are compassionate and considerate of other people's needs. But, there are some who do not have a selfless/servant heart.

Jesus' own people rejected him because he was not the political, military leader who would exert power and control over people that they expected. When he led and died as a servant to rescue his people, they just didn't understand it. And many today still do not understand it. The purest form of power is when people follow you because they want to. People do what you say out of **force** or **choice**. They follow you with their heart out of **choice**. They comply out of fear with **force**.[4] Only one is lasting. When the fear is gone, people no longer follow out of force. They will always follow when it is their choice. In Revelation 3:20, Jesus makes it clear he does not force his way into people's lives or override their will. He wants people to follow him by choice, not by force.

STANDING ON FAITH

How about us? As leaders, are we able and willing to be misunderstood, rejected, ridiculed and humiliated without having to defend ourselves or our reputations? Are we willing to sacrifice for the good of others or even suffer for the good of others if it comes to it?

There is a strong perception among many who want to be leaders in the business and nonprofit sectors who think they have to fit in to get ahead. They are afraid to speak up for their faith, thinking they will be seen as weak and be bypassed for promotions. Scripture has some good examples where this wasn't true. Joseph was upfront about his faith and was ultimately promoted everywhere God placed him, including prison. Nehemiah was a captive in a pagan kingdom. He was the cupbearer for the king, which is one of the most important positions in the kingdom, and the person the king trusted the most in the entire kingdom. Daniel was also a Jewish captive serving a pagan king. He was promoted above all the other king's assistants and highly regarded by the king. In fact, his integrity and devotion to God was the only fault the jealous bureaucrats in the kingdom could find in him.

STRONG THROUGH SERVICE

Early in my career, I led more like the "tough guy." Then, I transitioned more to the other end of the spectrum, though I was never satisfied that I had arrived. Early on, I was working, striving, and competing to get ahead in my career. I did, but it was hard on me and hard on others. I actually discovered that I got ahead most when I quit trying to get ahead and simply tried to serve the company well and help my team progress. I realized that leading God's way makes you a stronger leader. It also helps you to grow spiritually. Here are some of the changes I made and how I grew spiritually when I quit worrying about me and started helping others get promoted:

From controlling to empowering — Because of my natural personality profile, my training as an accountant and further development as an auditor, I was strongly oriented toward controlling everything. I wanted to do too much myself. I had a hard time letting go and even found it difficult to take vacations because I did not feel in control. I saw many examples in HCA of effective leaders who empowered others but who had good accountability systems. I learned from them and began to empower people. I gave them substantial freedom coupled with accountability. My people liked it better, and it was an entirely different life for me. The spiritual growth occurred by moving from pride and thinking I knew best to counting on and engaging other people. I went more from autocratic announcements to truly engaging people. In fact, in the last chapter of my career, I can barely think of any initiative or project of significance my team pursued that was my original idea. All the best ideas came from the team in group brainstorming sessions.

From achieving my goals to serving the company well and helping other people achieve their goals — I remember reaching a significant marker in my career and thinking, "Now, what's next?" The problem was there wasn't anything next for me that I found exciting. Thankfully, what I did find exciting was deciding to help as many other people as I could achieve their career ambitions and places of service that would benefit the company most. I quit thinking solely about what made my job easiest or made me look best as the leader. Instead, I focused on what was best for the company and what was best for each individual that I was entrusted to lead and train. When I did this, I did a much better job for the company, was appreciated much more by my people, found greater satisfaction and joy in my work, and was given opportunities to do things in the company beyond what I ever thought would have been possible.

In hindsight, that seems so clear and right. But, I remember many times how hard it was. I gave up key people to other parts of the company, which was best for the company and best for those individuals. But, it left me scrambling and re-training to try to replace them. The people using the "tough guy" approach in the company restricted people from being promoted outside their function or division, or at least strongly discouraged it. Over time, their people began to resent it, and certainly it was not what was best for the company. It takes strength to let somebody leave who is a key member of your team. It only takes selfishness to prohibit them. The strongest leader is one who can let go, not the one who can hold on the tightest or longest. I learned after the fact that God has a pleasant reward for those who can let go. When you get a reputation of doing what is best for people and for the company, the best people are willing to work with you, and the company trusts you with greater levels of service. You see, I got what I had been striving for earlier but achieved at much greater levels when the focus was not on me but on others.

From taking the company line to advocating for employees while supporting the company — Rules, policies, and procedures exist for a reason. Certainly as an auditor, I knew that. But sometimes the rules just don't make sense in certain instances for individuals and, therefore, are not in the best long-term interests of the company. "Tough guys" tend to use the policies to give them power. It takes a stronger person to challenge the policies and advocate for an individual when you know that's the right thing to do. Often, the people you are opposing made the policies and could use them against you later if you made them mad. Enforcing policies doesn't make you strong. Going against them when you know it is the right thing to do is what requires real strength.

From just doing my job to getting out of my box — In doing my job, I often did what the Bible would call "going the extra mile." Yet, I mostly did that either out of fear, to get noticed, or to get a promotion. When I quit worrying about those things and quit being preoccupied with what was in it for me and just looked for ways to serve the company, I worked outside the box that my role called for. Sometimes that makes bureaucrats in the organization mad. Sometimes, it's risky because you become involved in things that you can be blamed for if it doesn't go well. I used to think being in complete control of an area was a sign of great strength. I later learned that venturing beyond your spot in the organization chart to serve required more strength.

From trying to get recognition and credit to giving it to others — I think this was perhaps my most difficult lesson and one of the harder areas of spiritual growth. We all seem to want the accolades of others. Proverbs 25:6 says, "Don't call attention to yourself in front of the King, but rather let others praise you." I can remember many times the team wanted me to do or say things to call attention to the department so that we would get credit. We found by experience that taking on small initiatives and leading successful pilot projects was a better alternative. We would identify initiatives that we thought had potential. Then, we would find a willing pilot in the operating group. After the initiative succeeded, we would give them the credit and offer to help the next willing participant. We did this with several initiatives over the years. I can remember how hard it was to give others the credit, knowing we had started the project and done much of the work. Another pleasant surprise from God was in learning that was a temporary situation. Eventually, our contributions were recognized. In the boardroom, when somebody is praising you, that makes a lot greater impact than if you grab the same headlines yourself. Patience is one of the fruits of God's spirit. It takes patience to wait for the credit you know is yours. It takes humility to wait and sometimes never receive the full credit that you know is yours. Both make you stronger and more durable in tough times.

From answering or defending against every criticism to taking it for what it was worth and trying to improve where I could — The typical "tough guy" always has a response for every criticism and tries to put the other people back on their heels. I was especially prone to do this. It just seems like the thing a "tough guy" does. You don't let your opponent have the last word. Do you realize how much harder it is be criticized, say nothing, and simply learn from it—to see if there's any value in what is being said? Some of my greatest opportunities for spiritual growth and best models of my faith came from these experiences. My team would say, "Leon, you know that's not right. Why didn't you prove them wrong in front of the group? Why didn't you take up for yourself?" If it served some purpose, I did set the record straight, and I did take up for the team. But, there are times when you serve no purpose in defending yourself. When the truth comes out, people will respect you more for holding your tongue and not embarrassing them in a meeting. It actually takes more strength to do that than to "cut them off at the ankles" when you have the chance though you may seem weak at the time.

POSITIONAL POWER VERSUS REAL POWER

Positional power, also called "legitimate power," is the power of an individual because of the relative position and duties of the holder of the position within the organization.[5]

In my positions at HCA, I had a great deal of what I will call "positional power"—sometimes called authority or formal power. It is derived from a person's position in the organization.[6] Because of my position, I could influence or require people to take certain actions. But, I discovered after many years that the power I wanted most was not positional power. What I wanted most was the power a leader has without regard to organizational position. This is where people follow you because they want to. Positional power stays with the position when you leave it. Real power goes with you wherever you are.[7]

I can give you numerous examples of where people did not do what I asked or directed, even though I had substantial positional power at the time. There are also numerous examples of people who did what I asked where I had no positional authority. I had helped them many times before. They knew I cared about them. They knew I would help them.

THE KEY TO PEOPLE FOLLOWING YOU

"Do not look out merely for your own interests.
Look out for the interests of others."
Philippians 2:4

The bottom line is if you want people to follow, you must help them achieve their goals. Notice that we keep coming back to the importance of the goals of the individual. Claudia was one of the most capable people I ever hired. She was willing to work with me because I was able to convince her that HCA would help her reach her goals.

Positional power stays with the position. Real power goes with you.

Selfless leaders

In a healthy organization, leaders are looking at their team trying to figure out how to guide and support.

> *"...that one wants to serve, to serve first.*
> *Then conscious choice brings one to aspire to lead."* [8]
>
> *"The work exists as much for the person*
> *as much as the person exists for the work."* [9]

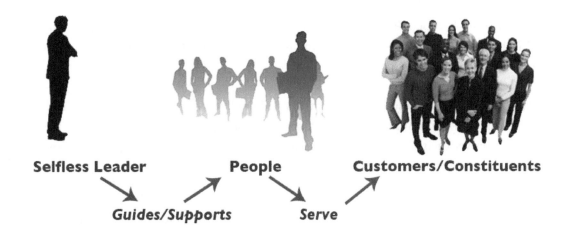

Selfless Leader   **People**   **Customers/Constituents**

Guides/Supports   **Serve**

In this organization, all the people and activities are focused on providing a good or service to others. They look to the leader for purpose, vision, and support, but their daily focus is on providing a quality product or service.

DR. FRIST SR.

Let me tell you a story about Dr. Frist, Sr.—one of the three founders of HCA. My aunt had been diagnosed with pancreatic cancer. She was in horrible pain and wanted a second opinion from a physician in Nashville. The family asked me who was best. At that time, I was a young executive and had no idea whom she should see. I asked for an appointment with Dr. Frist, Sr. My only goal was to ask him for the name or names of the best physicians for her to see.

He said, "Wait a minute" and quickly turned around and got a physician on the phone. He said, "I have someone I want you to see when are you available." It was Friday, and the physician apparently said Tuesday of the next week. I was traveling that week but learned that Dr. Frist, Sr. met my aunt and family in the physician's lobby. He talked to them before and after they saw the doctor.

That's the kind of company I grew up in. Our founders were servant leaders. They had a heart and compassion for people. Work was never a game for them, and they took every day seriously. They didn't play games with people's lives. They made people's lives better, not worse. The remarkable thing about the story of Dr. Frist, Sr. is that this is one of hundreds that could be told about the man. I shared this one because it was my own experience.

Dr. Frist, Sr. had a favorite saying, which was "Good people beget good people, and bad people beget bad people." His point about the law of attraction certainly holds true in organizational life. Good people know other good people and are able to attract them into the organization. Bad people know other bad people and tend to pull them into the organization. Again, this shows the vital importance of being diligent in hiring to make sure you have strong people with values aligned with those of the organization.

I learned through studying Jesus in the Scriptures and the lives of real role models that real lasting power isn't what you claim or possess through organizational positions of authority. It's the power people give you over their lives and actions because they believe you will help them. How do we use our power as leaders to most effectively serve people? We serve people by:

- Helping them set goals that give them a clear direction and feeling of importance while helping the organization achieve its mission.

- Empowering them with systems, policies and procedures, etc. that provide boundaries, but don't discourage them.

- Creating cultures conducive to doing the job with energy and creativity.

Leaders who are secure in their relationship with God are able to serve better. When we find our identity in our relationship with God and live in the awareness that we are His sons and daughters, we don't have to strive for power. We don't have to compete to be better than other people. We realize He made us uniquely for a special purpose. We are not competing with anybody else to live out that purpose. That allows us to give power away. It allows us to serve well. We don't have to worry about image, reputation, or being better than someone else. We only need to focus on living out who we are and the purpose God created us for.

We don't need to strive for power when we realize we are a child of God.

CAN YOU HELP TOO MUCH?

Jesus was known as "the suffering servant." However, his goal was not to make his disciples co-dependent on him. Let's take a look at this approach. First, he prayed in selecting the right group of men. Then, he called them to join him and his purpose. Then, he began training them. He taught them sermons in the synagogues and in the wilderness. He taught them as they walked from place to place. He taught them in the context of small groups when they were together over meals and in the evenings.

Next, he showed them. He demonstrated his powers of healing, casting out demons, and so on. Next, he watched them try to live out the life he was leading them toward and gave them coaching and direction along the way.

Then, he sent seventy-two of them out in pairs with specific instructions. They went and did the things Jesus had been doing. Then, they reported back to him how things went. Finally, Jesus commissioned and encouraged them. He told them he would be going soon, but they would do greater things than he had done. It's really amazing when you think about it. He spent three years training and equipping his disciples who would carry on his work and change the known world at the time. He did send the Holy Spirit to strengthen, guide, and comfort them after he was gone. But, they were not dependent on his physical presence.

Jesus was the model of the selfless, servant leader, always willing to help and guide. But, he created strong, independent disciples who could carry on without him.

Many leaders do the opposite. They create organizations where everyone is dependent on them for the answer to the next major decision. How do you think this makes people feel? What happens when the leader is not around? How strong is this organization without the leader?

You may think if being willing to help people is good it would be impossible to help them too much, right? Well, is it possible to help people too much? Yes, when employees become too dependent on the leader to do their job.

We bless people and organizations when we are willing to help them but not when we make them dependent on us for their next move. That makes employees anxious and angry when we are not available to help them. The leaders become their crutch.

If you help too much, you can become a crutch for your people.

My wife was always great about being willing to help the kids with their homework. They were like their mother, so they were smart kids. Yet, she helped so much and got in such a routine with our youngest that Kelsey, though very smart and capable of doing most of her homework on her own, got to the point that she felt like she couldn't start, or wouldn't start, unless her mother was sitting with her.

Owners of small businesses or new leaders tend to lead in a way that makes people too dependent upon them. When people have clearly established goals and are empowered to achieve them, they are most productive.

In the complex organizational structures of today's world, most people sometimes find themselves needing their leader's expertise and support at times. So, being willing to help when needed is good. But making employees or volunteers constantly dependent on your help or approval is unproductive and lowers morale. We need to empower them. This is one of the keys for being able to grow an organization larger.

Application

I. In what ways do your people need help?

_____

_____

_____

_____

II. Do you want to help them? Yes_____ No_____

   If no, what will you do?

_____

_____

_____

_____

III. Do they know you are willing to help them? Yes_____ No_____

   If no, what will you do?

_____

_____

_____

IV. Do you have people on your team that you have helped too much, and they have become dependent on you? Yes_____ No_____

If yes, what will you do?

_____

_____

_____

_____

Chapter 16

ABUSING POWER

Thought!
Have you considered how much you damage your
organization and hurt yourself when you abuse power?

"He spoke to them according to the advice of the young man saying,

'My father made your yoke heavy, but I will add to it;

my father disciplined you with whips,

but I would discipline you with scorpions.'"

2 Chronicles 10:14

"You know that the rulers of the Gentiles lord it over them,
and their great men exercise authority over them.
It is not that way among you, but whoever wishes
to become great among you shall be your servant..."
Matthew 20:25-26

My desire for the wrong kind of power came when I was just a boy. I've abused it and learned a valuable lesson. You've heard the saying that power corrupts, and absolute power corrupts absolutely. It started with me early in life. And I tend to think it starts very early in life with others, and we either grow beyond it or stay trapped in it.

I was raised on a small farm, which I'm grateful for. We had dairy cows but also raised hogs to sell. The hogs were a problem. They tended to get outside the fence and root the grass in our fields. So, Daddy bought and installed an electric fence. He would test to see if the electric fence was working by taking a shovel, sticking it in the ground, and leaning the metal part against the fence. When it was working, it would create a small spark.

Sometimes, when we fed the hogs, some grains of corn would fall close to or under the electric fence. The hogs would touch the fence, get shocked, squeal, and jump back. As a kid, I thought that was funny. Sometimes, I would drop kernels of corn leading up to the fence, knowing the hogs would focus on the corn and touch the fence. It worked 100% of the time. They always went after the corn and hit the fence. I wasn't doing it to be mean. I just thought it was funny.

Then, I decided to escalate the game. I tied a string to an ear of corn. The hogs would go for it, and I would pull the corn toward the fence. In going for the corn, two or three hogs would touch the fence, squeal, and jump back. I felt smart, in control, and it seemed funny to me.

I got creative and decided to escalate the game again. I climbed up the fence and climbed from the top of the fencepost to the top of a small shed which was about nine feet high. I tied an ear of corn to a string and lowered it to the ground. The hogs would go for it, and I would pull it just out of their reach. They would chase it, and I would continually pull it just out of their reach. That was entertaining for a while. Then, I decided I wanted to see if I could make them dance. So, when they were fully engaged in going for that piece of corn, I lifted it just above their heads. They would stand on their hind legs snapping at the ear of corn. I had made them dance!

Sometimes, they would get the ear of corn in their mouth, and I would jerk it out. A couple of times, they got a good hold on the corn and were able to jerk the string out of my hand. The string burned my hand. Plus, I had to climb off the roof to get the string again.

I decided enough of that. So, I wrapped the string around my hand so that they wouldn't be able to jerk it out so easily. What happened next was rather predictable. I was confident they couldn't jerk the string from my hand, so I took a little more risk. I let them get the corn in their mouth and jerk it out. There was one five hundred pound hog that was standing straight up on her hind legs. She got the ear of corn locked firmly in the back part of her jaw. She flicked her big strong neck, and I came sailing off the roof like a small missile.

It had been a while since the last rain. So the once muddy hog lot now had dry, hard, lumpy clumps of dirt. As the hog dragged me across those rock hard lumps, my chest and groin area were catching the brunt of the punishment. Thank God, after a few yards, the string broke. The hog had the corn, and I was free.

THE MORAL OF THE STORY

- You may not be as smart as you think you are. I wasn't!

- Don't lock yourself into an all or nothing position.

- It's not okay to have fun at another's expense, even if the other is a hog.

- When your goal is simply to entertain yourself, the game continues to escalate and the risk gets higher, and someone's going to get hurt.

- You will likely be the one that gets hurt the most.

At the point in this story where I said I wanted to make the pigs dance was your first thought, "I wonder how he's going to make a pig dance?" Or was your first thought, "Why would you want to make a pig dance?" You see, *why* I wanted to make a pig dance showed a lot about my motives. I wanted power and control. I wanted to be entertained at the pig's expense. That was wrong, and it was costly.

APPLICATION TO CORPORATE LIFE

I thought of this experience on more than one occasion in corporate meetings. I saw sophisticated, educated, polished, professional managers (notice I said managers, not leaders) at times do the same thing I did with hogs at nine years old. These people were supposed to be mature adults. And to be honest, there were times when I was tempted or did play the game again with people. So, what does this look like in corporate life?

First, executives forget about the primary purpose they are to be serving. They begin to see it as a game to be played versus a purpose to be served, a mission to be achieved, or a vision to be realized.

Next, they begin to entertain themselves at other people's expense. This causes anxiety, confusion, and sometimes very deep emotional pain. But that's okay with these leaders because they see the people they are impacting as lesser beings to be toyed with.

Then comes boredom with the game, and it escalates. This evolves until the managers must show their superiority, their higher intelligence, and finally their power over others. At some point, there is going to be a power-play. And these insensitive, immature, and ego driven executives are going to win a lot of the power games. Each time they win, they feel smarter, more secure, more powerful, and more invincible. Thus, they take greater and greater risks.

Finally, they lock themselves into a position believing they can't lose. But they have grossly underestimated the power of the opposing force. They are jerked hard from their pedestal. They're not like I was—a poor farm boy who could only afford a grass string from a bale of hay versus a rope that wouldn't break. I've often wondered how much damage would have been done to my body if I had a rope tied to that ear of corn. Anyway, these people are locked in with the metaphorical triple cord rope, and they are metaphorically dragged as far as their opposer wants to drag them. It's an ugly sight.

The last thing they saw was the gleam in their opposer's eye that said, "I got you now." Believe it or not, I saw the same gleam in that hog's eye just before she flicked her neck and jerked me from the roof. I've seen this many times in corporate life and in non-profit organizations and ministries. I've seen many professionals jerked from their pedestals like human missiles. The lessons are the same.

- Our work has a purpose that should be taken seriously.

- Others are not there for our entertainment or sport.

- When you start entertaining yourself, the game escalates, and someone's going to get hurt. You will hurt many others along the way.

- You may very well be the one most hurt in the end.

How God views power

We need to lead by God's way if we are going to bless people. This begins with viewing power the way God does. God's way is not that power is something to be hoarded or abused. God gives power away. We see this view of power in God the Father, God the Son, and God the Holy Spirit as follows:

- When Adam and Eve were created and placed in the garden, God gave them dominion over everything.

- Jesus gave up the heavenly throne to come to earth. Here, he lived as a man and a servant and gave his life for others. "Although he existed in the form of God, did not regard equality with God a thing to be grasped . . ." Philippians 2:6

- Jesus trained his disciples and empowered them. He empowered them supernaturally through the Holy Spirit. But he also empowered them naturally through training them and releasing them to do his work. He told them that they would do and accomplish more than he did.

- The Holy Spirit empowers people for the work that God has given them to do. The Holy Spirit never draws attention but rather points the people to Jesus.

- God the Father raised Jesus as King of Kings and Lord of Lords. After the resurrection, He granted him all power in heaven and on earth. You see clearly that with God there is no grasping for power or clinging to power. There is a sharing of power and empowering of others. If we are going to be godly leaders, we need to share power and empower others.

Application

I. Do you pit people against one another in your organization? Yes___ No___

II. Do you tend to try to manipulate and control your people? Yes___ No___

III. Do you at times see organizational life as a game? Yes____ No___

IV. What changes do you need to make so that you don't hurt yourself or others?

_____

_____

_____

_____

_____

V. Do you give power away, i.e. empower people, routinely or do you try to hang on to power?

Give it away_____ Keep it_____

If you tend to try to keep it, what changes will you make?

_____

_____

_____

_____

_____

Chapter 17

POWER — KEEP IT OR DISTRIBUTE IT

Thought:
Have you ever wondered why some businesses, churches, and other organizations seem to stay small while others tend to grow larger and larger?

"Then the Lord God took the man and put him in the Garden of Eden to cultivate it and keep it."

Genesis 2:15

"Then teach them the statutes and the laws, and make known to them the way in which they are to walk and the work they are to do. Furthermore, you should select out of all the people able men who fear God, men of truth, those who hate dishonest gain; and you shall place these over them as leaders of thousands, of hundreds, 50s and tens. Let them judge the people at all times; and let it be that every major dispute they bring to you, but every minor dispute they themselves will judge. So it will be easier for you, and they will bear the burden with you.

If you do this thing and God so commands you, then you will be able to endure, and all these people also will go to their place in peace.

So Moses listened to his father-in-law and did all that he had said."
Exodus 18:20-23

I have noticed a tendency for small businesses to hit barriers and stay small. Non-profit organizations spring up everywhere but only a few get large. There are several mega-churches in the United States, but most churches are small, under one hundred people. Why is that? Why do so many businesses/churches and other organizations tend to plateau and can't grow any further. The key is how they approach the use of power. Are they going to approach it like Moses did when he started out? He kept all the power, and people gathered around him waiting for him to judge their cases and give them direction. Or, are they going to approach it like Jethro suggested to Moses? That is, identify capable leaders, provide training, and empower them to act on most cases, keeping only the hardest cases for himself—management by exception.

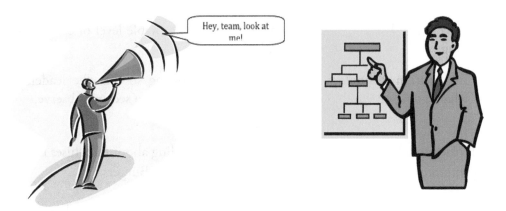

Today, we would tend to refer to these as the "mom and pop" or sole proprietor versus the franchise approaches to leadership and empowerment. I observed these as I grew up in a small town at the local grocery and hardware stores. They had few employees, and everything revolved around the owner. HCA gave me the opportunity to experience a different style of leadership as is common in large companies and franchises. In the first, the power is retained by the owner or by the founder if this is a non-profit organization or ministry. In the second, power is distributed to a number of other people. It works the same way in large, sophisticated organizations as it does in a franchise organization.

THE LIMITATIONS OF KEEPING THE POWER

Small businesses and organizations stay small because the focus is on the owners/founders. They always have ownership and control of the organization. We see this model throughout society. We deal with local businesses, and the owner is always there making the decisions. When they're out, the employees have to call or wait for them to return before making the decision outside the norm.

However, when the organizations are led only in these ways, they never outgrow what the individual leaders can touch. What's the difference between a person owning and running one restaurant and the same person owning and running ten, twenty, thirty or even one hundred restaurants? With some basic skills in the restaurant business, people can run a single restaurant. However, to run ten restaurants or one hundred, they have to approach it much differently, like a franchise. What makes franchises and large organizations like HCA different? A lot of things such as:

Think About This

— 191 —

For Training

- Operating manuals for each key aspect of the organization indicating how things are to be done.

- Measurement of certain key activities and standards for what is expected.

- Checks and balances so that activities have an acceptable level of control but not stifling.

- Information technology and management reporting so that the leaders can know what's going on without always being there physically to see and observe.

Note: I learned much and clarified much of my understanding about franchises through my discussions with Steve Lynn, former CEO of Sonic and Backyard Burgers.

Franchises require goals for individual business units and goals, coupled with good training, for each position in the organization. They have great policy and procedure guides, operating manuals, training systems, and control systems. Managers are carefully selected and trained to operate successfully within acceptable boundaries.

Sole Proprietor

Check with me and I'll tell you what to do

Note: When you keep power, everything revolves around you.

Franchise or large organization

Policies and Procedures, Operating Manuals, Training and Documentation

Vision & Goals

Enabling Control Systems

Note: When you give people power, goals give a strong sense of direction and freedom within the broad boundaries of policies and procedures. Goals are like the current of the river. Policies and procedures are like the banks of the river. They keep the flow consistent.

In franchise systems, the owners/leaders can't be in every restaurant every day. But when the operating parameters are properly established, levels of service quality and profitability can be consistently achieved. With good management reporting systems and controls, the owners can know where each restaurant stands in a timely manner.

that's it?

So what is it that large organizations do that small organizations don't? They are more sophisticated in using documentation, training, policies, procedures and so on to guide the organization. Small organizations tend to be pretty low on the scale of developed and refined operating manuals, written policies and procedures, control systems, and management reporting systems. They tend to accomplish things by the owners'/founders' individual engagement and oversight. Therefore, they can't grow beyond what the leaders can be engaged in.

EMPOWER PEOPLE LIKE FRANCHISES AND LARGE ORGANIZATIONS

In this model, like I experienced at HCA, goals are established with the people. They are empowered to operate within these goals. There are policies and procedures in place to empower decision-making but also to guide it. These models are not dependent on the leader's continual presence day-to-day for their functioning. People know what to do, how to do it, and are empowered within certain guidelines to take action. I experienced this the times I was out for extended periods of time.

Let's go to our river analogy. Rivers have movement. They have power. It is very easy to get caught in the current of the river and be swept way. Rivers have direction. Rivers have banks which are boundaries that give the river direction. The goals give individuals power and movement. Goals, policies, and procedures give them direction. Policies and culture give them boundaries, just like the banks of river.

FUNCTIONING WITHOUT THE LEADER PRESENT

I remember many years ago when the CEO of HCA had an accident which kept him out of work for several weeks. He came back and was pleasantly surprised at how well the company had done without him. But he also felt bad because he felt like the team really didn't need him in order to be successful. The truth is he was a great leader who had put in place the right team with the right policies, procedures, systems, and goals. And he had empowered them. His value was continuing to envision the future, casting the vision, and making sure the team grew and evolved to the vision versus being involved so much in day-to-day activities.

This man was an entrepreneurial leader who put a chief operating officer and others around him. He empowered them to run the day-to-day operations of the company. Of great significance, he was able to trust the people he put in place and let them do their jobs without interference. Letting go and trusting others with the organization are two of the greatest obstacles I've seen that most entrepreneurial leaders/founders encounter in taking the organizations that they started to the next level. HCA continued to prosper because its founder had:

- Clear plans—mission, vision, and objectives;

- People in place with clear goals who agreed with the mission, vision, and values of the organization and were competent for their roles; and

- Control systems to know that things were on track.

THE KEY TO BEING ABLE TO GROW TO THE NEXT LEVEL

In small organizations, the power, control, authority, and expertise is centered on the owners/founders. In larger organizations, others are empowered, policies and procedures guide, clearly established and agreed-upon goals direct and information systems support, monitor, and control.

This discussion of large organizations versus small organizations does not mean that large organizations are good and small organizations aren't. Often, people enjoy working in small organizations. They can also become very frustrated working in large bureaucratic organizations. Policies and procedures can be constructed in a way that frustrate and cause anxiety for people. This is true in both large and small organizations. However, using these tools properly gives leaders great freedom and improves morale and productivity of the employees in both small and large organizations.

A SMALL BUSINESS OWNER MAKES THE TRANSITION

I knew a man who was working seventy hours per week and incredibly frustrated much of the time. He had quite a profitable small business and was doing well financially but worn out from working so many hours. Then, he implemented a leadership style of using the franchise model of leadership over the next year. He was able to reduce his hours to thirty to forty hours per week with profitable results.

EARLY PERSONAL EXPERIENCE

Early in my career, I felt like I always had to be there to ensure everything was done. I worked five and six days a week and long hours. I never took the vacation time allotted each year. Once I learned how to lead like others in the company, that all changed. I took time off and didn't have to work as many hours.

Some years later, while I was in Physician Services, I had a major surgery and was out of the office for an extended period of time. I phased back in slowly working two hours a day, then four, then six, and so on. Physician Services accomplished its goals just as well while I was gone as it did when I was there. So, did I not matter? Well, if I had not gone back, there were many developments of service lines such as Anesthesia Services and Hospitalist Services that never would have been developed without my engagement to help create the vision and plans, to staff the organization with the right leadership, and to ensure that systems and controls were created to run those lines of business. But, I didn't have to spend all my time every day engaged only in the existing service lines.

I had a radical change in my view from early in my career when I felt I had to be there all the time to ensure that things ran well. I changed to the view that if I had to be there daily for things to run smoothly, I did not have it set up right. I viewed my role as that of envisioning and helping create the future with most of my time, and then being available to support the team and maintain culture with the rest of it. My goal was not to be needed on a day-to-day basis for the organization to achieve its goals.

The Dream

APPLICATION TO NON-PROFIT ORGANIZATIONS

Let us look at a biblical example: Moses. Even though he led a large number of people, he functioned more like the new entrepreneurial leader. He cast the vision of freedom from Egypt and going to the Promised Land. Because of the miracles that God performed through him, the people eventually admired and followed him. Yet when it came to the day-to-day leading of the people, we see Moses trying to do it all just like small business owners, small church pastors, and small non-profit directors. The first leadership consultant I see in the Bible was Jethro, Moses' father-in-law. He paid the family a visit out in the desert and observed. He noticed three things:

- Moses trying to do it all

- The stress and strain on Moses

- How long and tiresome it was for the people standing in line to get a decision from Moses

The first thing he did was say, in essence, "Moses, you need an organization, you need a system, and you need some guidelines and training programs for your leaders and people."

"The thing that you are doing is not good.

You will surely wear out, both yourself

and these people who are with you, for the

task is too heavy for you; you cannot do it alone."

Exodus 18:17-18

"Then teach them the statutes and the laws, and make known to them

the way in which they are to walk and the work they are to do.

Furthermore, you should select out of all the people able men

who fear God, men of truth, those who hate dishonest gain;

and you shall place these over them as leaders of thousands,

of hundreds, 50s and tens. Let them judge the people at all

times; and let it be that every major dispute they bring to you,

but every minor dispute they themselves will judge. So it will

be easier for you, and they will bear the burden with you.

If you do this thing and God so commands you, then you will be able

to endure, and all these people also will go to their place in peace.

So Moses listened to his father-in-law and did all that he had said."

Exodus 18:20-23

Proper Authorities

He said, "You need to choose some leaders, and here are their qualifications. Put some in charge of thousands, some in charge of hundreds, and some in charge of fifties." Then, as now, choosing the right leaders to empower is key to the success of the organization. It's also key to taking the stress and strain off the top leader and making it better for all the people.

Proper Training + Boundaries

Jethro said to Moses, "Assign the leaders and their teams, teach them the rules, and empower them to make decisions and then, Moses, you only take the hard cases." This freed Moses up to spend time praying, thinking, and planning so that he could keep the vision before the people and make wise decisions rather than being worn out and wearing the people out who were waiting on him.

BLESSING PEOPLE BY EMPOWERING THEM

How are people blessed in organizations that empower them? First of all, they have clear goals and are empowered to act without always being told what to do or someone always looking over their shoulder.

I remember one of my direct reports, who lived out of state, saying that he had received four e-mails from me in two years and all of those were responses to his e-mails. He said, "I don't think I could ever accuse you of micromanaging." This was a very capable leader who had a clear set of goals. All he needed from me was occasional support and occasional discussion to answer a question. God instilled a need for freedom in people. He actually runs the universe by giving people clear directions. He gave an operating manual, the Bible, to guide and instruct us. And, the Holy Spirit is available for day-to-day specific guidance. God gives His people a great deal of freedom but with guidance and accountability.

Proper Freedom

People like freedom, need freedom, and seek freedom. God gave man great freedom when He created him. Man could eat from any tree in the garden except one. When you hire people who can achieve their personal goals by doing what they're called to do and using their gifts and passions to do what they want to do and what your organization needs done, you can give them great freedom. It's like water flowing in the river. They just naturally fit and flow with the organization. I experienced and observed at HCA that when employees become dependent on their leaders to take action, it causes a great deal of frustration and anxiety. They don't feel the same sense of ownership and control of their lives as when they're given clear goals consistent with what they want to do and are empowered to act, knowing they have their leaders' support.

Efficiency Drain...

It's hard for people to be efficient if they spend too much time each day waiting for the leaders to give directions or make decisions for them. They feel drained when they spend too much time and energy waiting on decisions and instructions. *Or worrying or second-guessing*

Also, since dependency on the leaders is reduced, the team feels more empowered, more free, are more productive, and have higher morale because they feel like they have a level of control and

Authority as guiding People with goals to Freedom

trust. They feel more like kids than adults when someone is always looking over their shoulder. People feel energized when they've had a productive day.

People don't always like being told what to do by their leaders, particularly people with personality profiles like mine.

Let's look at a simple example. Companies have expense reporting forms and guidelines for how to report expenses of what is acceptable. This is uniform for all employees. They complete it and abide by policy with little complaint. If there were no policy and standard form and they were questioned individually by the managers, they take that as looking over their shoulder and offensive. People thrive much better with goals, guidelines, and procedures than with constant one-on-one oversight.

Organizations are sustained when people are empowered. If the operations are based on the owners/founders being there, what happens when they are gone? What happens when they get sick? What happens when they are ready to retire? What happens when they pass away? The answer is obvious. The organization can't continue to function unless somebody like them takes over and carries on. Often, in small businesses, this is passed on to the children who may not have the temperament or skill set to pull it off, and the business suffers. When the business suffers or fails, it can be really bad for the employees. Good employees can work diligently for a long time and find themselves out of a job in small organizations with no "go forward" plan.

SUMMARY

So what are the benefits of operating like a franchise or large organization versus a "mom and pop" operation? First, it is more efficient. It's hard for people to be efficient if they spend too much time each day waiting for the leaders to give directions or make decisions for them. Secondly, the team feels more empowered, more free, are more productive, and have higher morale because they feel like they have a level of control and trust. Last, but certainly not least, is the issue of leadership stability and succession planning. When everything revolves around the leaders, the organization shuts down and/or stops progress with the leaders' absence. Yet, when there's a clear mission, clear vision of the future, documented priorities, individual goals, clearly established accountability, and a wholesome set of values that the organization operates by and are ingrained in the culture, the leaders can be absent for extended periods of time, and the organization continues to make progress.

Empowering people changed my life as a leader. When I finally understood how to empower people like a franchise operation versus trying the other approaches to leadership, it changed my life as a leader for the better. I got more done in less time. Actually, by using this approach, I had a better handle on what was going on and knew in more detail how we were doing. I had more freedom day by day.

Application

I. On a scale of 1-10, how much do you lead through franchise type techniques? _____

II. What changes do you need to make to empower people more?

_____

_____

_____

_____

_____

_____

[?] Must a business operate either with strong direct personal Authority or strong clear standards?

How Can Standards, Authority and Individuals work better with one another?

Notes

Chapter 18

A MODEL SURE TO FAIL — MICRO-MANAGING

Thought:
Do you have any idea how much productivity and morale
are actually lost by your micro-management?

*"Then the Lord God took the man and put him
into the Garden of Eden to cultivate it and keep it.
The Lord commanded the man, saying,
'From any tree of the garden you may freely;
but from the tree of the knowledge of
good and evil you shall not eat.'"*
Genesis 2:15-16

People tend to see God as a micro-manager. But the Scripture above shows what great freedom He gives people. The antithesis of using goals to lead an organization is the perfectionist oriented leader. You may say, "Well, what's wrong with being a perfectionist? Don't you want things done right? Do you have perfectionist tendencies yourself?" I used to see them as a strength but have come to understand they can also be a great weakness in leading people. Also, you can't get or keep the best people with this approach. Certain personality profiles tend to be perfectionist oriented. For example, the "C" competent/compliant profile tends toward perfectionism. Real leadership and micro-management are at opposite ends of the spectrum. Micro-management is poor management by itself, but it especially has no rightful place in the life of a leader.

> **People hate being micro-managed and you do too even if you are a micro-manager yourself.**

THE EFFECTS OF MICRO-MANAGEMENT

What's the problem of being a perfectionist manager? Notice I said manager, not leader. Managers tend to want to control people and processes and are more likely to be perfectionists than leaders who cast vision, attract people to it, and help set priorities and strategies. Perfectionist managers pick at small things; employees get focused on lesser priorities.

Remember the 80/20 rule. Not all tasks are of equal value. Make sure the 20% of tasks that drive 80% of the results get the focus. When you start focusing on the 80%, that only drives 20% of the results and require perfection that disorients and actually detracts from employees staying focused on the real priorities.

God is a God of order, not of chaos. God is not a micro-manager. Many people do not believe that. I have sat with many people in church and in private who ask why God doesn't strike other people with lightning because of the evil they've done. You only have to wrestle with this issue for a while to see that God clearly is not a micro-manager. He does hold people accountable, but He does not micro-manage their daily lives. When managers nitpick, they create confusion for employees or volunteers. They disorient some. They frustrate them. They throw them off track. And, over time, they cause them to be less effective in their job. In most organizations, the work environments today are simply too complex and have too much going on for everything to be a priority. But, don't misapply this. Some things have to be perfect—like healthcare and air travel.

WHAT DO YOU DO IF YOU ARE A PERFECTIONIST LEADER?

Being aware of your perfectionist tendencies is a good first step. Controlling those tendencies and avoiding them in your leadership style is your next step. The way I have personally dealt with this is to explain my thinking to employees. I point something out as a learning opportunity, because they could do the same thing the next time in the same or less time. I let them know, though, this is not a high priority. "I don't want you to change this. Here are your real priorities."

I had an extremely capable executive administrative assistant. There was always a lot going on, and I delegated a lot of work to her. Being so conscientious, she wanted to do it all and wanted to do it well. Being perfectionist-oriented, I wanted it all done and done well. I had to constantly remind myself to communicate with her daily on the high priorities. I would say, "Here's why they are priorities. Do these first. Do these well. These other items do when you have time, and they don't have to be perfect." This kept the focus on the priorities. When I did this well, it took a lot of pressure off my assistant.

Having high expectations is fine. Adhering to high quality standards is good. In the airline industry and the healthcare industry, lives are at stake if quality standards are not maintained. I'm not talking about not maintaining quality standards. I'm talking about not "nitpicking" employees in administrative organizations on low priority activities. *i.e. Not everything matters the most*

WHAT IF I WORK FOR A PERFECTIONIST-ORIENTED LEADER?

I had one boss that was perfectionist-oriented. He wanted it all done and done at a high level of quality. When I would see it was not possible to do everything at quality standards, I would proactively go to him and ask about the priorities to make sure we stayed in sync. I never had a time when he wasn't glad to discuss priorities. Actually, 100% of the time he told me not to worry about the lesser priority items. That gave me freedom to focus on the high priority stuff and let the lower priority items go.

Application

I. Do you have perfectionist tendencies? Yes_____ No_____

What changes do you need to make so that you don't confuse your team?

_____

_____

_____

_____

_____

II. Do you work for a perfectionist? Yes_____ No_____

What changes will you make in your approach to dealing with them?

_____

_____

_____

_____

_____

_____

Chapter 19

EMPOWERMENT THROUGH INFLUENCING MOTIVATION

Thought!
How much more could your organization achieve
if everyone on the team was highly motivated?

"Whatever your hand finds to do, do it with all your might..."

Ecclesiastes 9:10

Are you confused about why some of your team seems motivated and some don't? One of the more misunderstood roles of leadership relates to motivation. Walk into any room of leaders/managers and ask them for a definition of motivation. I've always gotten pretty diverse answers. Ask them about their responsibility for motivation, and you get even more diverse opinions. So, is the leader responsible for motivating the team? Most people I've asked say yes. Most leaders say yes. Yet, most leaders acknowledge being frustrated in not having a highly motivated workforce.

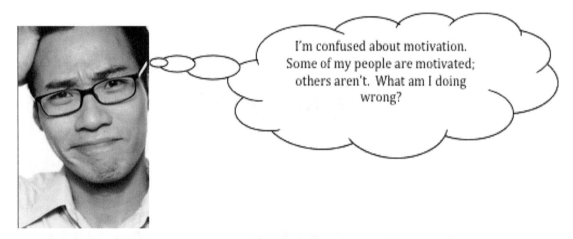

God intended for us to enjoy our work. In the beginning of creation, work was not a drudgery; it was a gift. It's been made difficult by the fall of man. But, it is still a gift. So how do we reconcile the command to do our work with all our might and the words of Jesus which said "My yoke is easy and my burden is light?"

We can easily work at something with all our might when our heart is in it. What does it take for our heart to really be in our work?

THE ROCK QUARRY

I formed an opinion on this topic before I graduated from college. I had the opportunity to work in a rock quarry during the summers. I made minimum wage and worked long hours in very hot and dusty conditions. I was genuinely grateful to have the job. I respected and was grateful to the manager, Vernon, who hired me. My attitude about the job was radically different from some people who were doing the same work for the same pay as I was. In fact, over the course of four summers and doing various other jobs around the quarry, I noticed more and more people doing the same work for the same pay and for the same leader, but their attitudes and motivation were really different. That's when I decided there's more to this motivation thing than just what the leader does.

So let's break this down and see how motivation really works. We will answer these questions:

- What is motivation?   [?] Not Answered

- Where does it come from?

- What causes it?

- How does the leader influence it?

Why was I motivated to work for minimum wage in a rock quarry? I was raised on a dairy farm. We milked cows twice a day every day. I got up at 4:30 in the morning. We finished the evening milking usually around 6:00 P.M. In the summers, we often worked more after that. I love the fact that I was raised on a farm, and there is much about it that I liked and still miss. But it was not how I wanted to make a living. It was not what I felt called to do. My goal was to work in a business environment. I decided at an early age to take that direction. There was something inside me that took me in this direction. It wasn't someone else's influence but what I wanted that drove me.

"Here is what I have seen to be good and fitting:
to eat, drink and enjoy oneself and all one's labor
in which he toiled under the sun during the few years of his life
which God has given him: for this is his reward."
Ecclesiastes 5: 17-19

As a kid, I thought this was my goal just because I wanted to be cool in the summer and warm in the winter, which the office job offered. It was years later that I discovered my goal was based on far more than that. I have a real passion for organizations and working with people. Nevertheless, my goals to get a college education and work in business drove me to work hard at the rock quarry and appreciate the opportunity. For me, that job was a means to an end. For some, it was a transitional job. For others, it felt like the end.

BIBLICAL SOURCES OF MOTIVATION

I realized from experience that it is possible, and even likely, for particular leaders to have some people working for them who are motivated, while others are not. But I've always been bothered by the number of leadership trainers and written sources that make reference to leaders and their responsibility for motivating people.

Also, I will acknowledge from my own experience, some people in leadership roles universally have highly motivated people while others have universally unmotivated people. I will sort through all of that later. But, for my baseline understanding, I went to the Bible to understand motivation. In Scripture, I see three sources of motivation:

- Love – given by others laying down their lives. *(A Show of identifying so strongly beyond pain or consciousness or position)*

A Sling-Shot in hopes of another For one's kingdom

- Desires of the heart

- Pain or fear of discipline

LOVE

"For God so loved the world that he gave his only begotten son..."

John 3:16

God gave his only son to die for the sins of mankind out of love. In fact, God's motive for everything He does is love. God was not lacking anything. He began creation out of love. The whole Bible is a story of God's love for His people.

Jesus taught his disciples about love. One of his last instructions to them was to love one another. John 13:34-35 says, "Greater love has no man than this that he lay down his life for another." This teaching was just before his crucifixion where he would do the very thing he was teaching them.

Love motivates people to do the most amazing things. Parents make amazing sacrifices for their children out of love. I am still astounded at the sacrifices I saw my mom and dad make as they raised six children on a small dairy farm. We did not earn the sacrifices they made nor did we deserve them. They sacrificed for us out of their love for us. Numerous volumes of books have been written on the amazing feats people perform and sacrifices they made out of love for someone in their life.

I deal with leaders in a number of nonprofit ministries. One of the things that distinguish the most outstanding among them is when their people are serving people from the depths of their hearts out of love. These people do amazing things. Yet, it's not only people in nonprofit organizations that have this capacity. There are numerous examples of CEOs, leaders, and others in profitable organizations that also pursue a mission or passion about providing a good or service out of love for the people they are serving. The examples I can think of from my years at HCA are too numerous to mention.

Remember the story about three people laying bricks as discussed in the first section of this book? I'm often asked by people in organizations how to get people to move from being bricklayers to builders to cathedral builders. I think the key to this one is love. Until people care deeply and passionately about something and someone beyond themselves, they will not likely have the vision of the cathedral builder.

I have listened over the years to some of the great coaches in college athletics. One thing I hear most from some of the greats are how they coach their teams on selflessness, i.e. how much players care about the team and each other versus their own success. I have come to discern by listening to the coaches and watching the teams that the ones who care most about each other have the endurance and put forth the effort to be champions.

So what does this have to do with influencing the motivation of a team? Very simply, it is by placing people in positions where they can do the things they love doing because they love and want to serve others.

Remember my previous example surrounding the flooding we had in Nashville in May 2010 and the flooding I had in the basement of my house? One of the hourly workers that came to help on the project was a lady named Janine. She showed up at my house one Saturday morning after working two weeks straight at sixteen hours a day without a break. This was her first day off since the flood. She said she woke up early Saturday morning and remembered something about my house that she wanted to check to see if there was moisture. She checked and indeed there was moisture and mold in a spot that anyone else would've missed. I had a long talk with Janine trying to understand her motivation for the hours she put it in and why she took part of her day off to help me. She said, "I just love helping people." As we talked further, it was obvious to me that she was a person of faith who loved God deeply and, therefore, was able to love others as well. This is the kind of person it takes to be a cathedral builder. Her motive was love.

Excellent

It was love that caused Jesus to leave heaven and hang on the cross for us. It was love that caused Moses to tell God to blot him out of His book of life but to spare the children of Israel. It was love that caused Paul to say that he would be willing to be eternally damned if only his people would come to know God. And, I'm convinced that if you do anything extraordinary, your motivation will be love.

Desires of the heart

Psalms 37:4 speaks of God granting his servants the "desires of your heart." There are many places in Scripture that talk about the desires of the heart. In fact, Proverbs 4:23 says that out of the heart come the issues of life. What is the heart? It is the seat of decision making, our will, and our emotions. What is a desire of the heart? In simple terms, it's something that we desire deeply. I can remember when I was a young boy living on the farm, and I wanted a pony. I wanted one so badly that I asked my dad about it every week until he finally gave me one. There was nothing noble or self-sacrificing about this desire I had. It is just something that I wanted deeply enough to keep asking my dad until he decided, out of love, to give it to me.

I remember well when my son was a teenager. I had a hard time finding an approach to get him interested in any kind of work. Then, one day he started talking about an orange International Scout that he wanted to buy. He already had a vehicle I had bought for him that was better than the Scout. I told him that if he wanted the Scout to go get a job and earn the money to pay for it. He went to work for a landscaping crew and worked really hard all summer to make the money to buy the Scout. At that time, it was a great desire of his heart, and he was willing to do what it took to get it.

With great desire goes great effort. Dan Miller, in *No More Dreaded Mondays*, talks about some things that remind me of this idea of desires of the heart. He said to figure out what makes you mad, glad, or sad. The thinking here is that if something invokes a great emotion in you such as some injustice that makes you mad or some need of other people that makes you sad or something you want that gives you a deep gladness, you will be highly motivated to pursue these things.

What do the people on your team care deeply and passionately about? If they are in positions that let them do what they love to do, you will have a good solid builder. If they do it for the sake of others, you will have a cathedral builder.

The potential for reward is part of this. Peter once told Jesus what he had sacrificed and asked what he would get in return. Jesus did not rebuke him but rather told Peter what he would receive on this earth and hereafter. Jesus often spoke of the rewards of heaven and the punishment of hell. Is it inherently wrong to desire reward for right behavior? Nehemiah asked that some of his sacrifices be remembered and rewarded by God.

Discipline/Pain

The final motivation Scripture refers to is discipline or pain. In Deuteronomy 30:15-20, God outlines His requirement for blessings and also for the curses if people did not follow his ways. Throughout the Old Testament, God's prophets were sent to his people when they strayed to warn them of the judgment if they did not change directions. Judgment or pain was used by God in dealing with His people to change their behavior but only as a last resort and after much patience.

Now think about this in organizational life. With what type people do you most frequently need to invoke some discipline or pain? Isn't it the bricklayers? Isn't it the ones there just for the money, just because they need a job? Isn't it all drudgery to them? Remember what would be a drudgery to one person might be a great joy to another like Janine who loved to help people.

My suggestion is that if you have people on the team who constantly need discipline, they would be happier in another organization in another role.

THE GREATER THE PAIN THE MORE LIKELY A CHANGE

Country comedian, Jerry Clower, expresses this idea very well. He tells the story of coon hunting with his cousin Marcell. They treed a coon, and Marcell climbed up in the tree to shake it out. He soon discovers they had treed a bobcat, not a coon. The bobcat squalls, and Marcell screams. This goes on for quite some time. Finally, Marcell yells out to Jerry, "Just shoot up in here amongst us. One of us has got to have some relief." Marcell was a man desperate for something to change. We would say he was highly motivated.

If pain, physical or emotional, causes us to want to change something, are we motivated every time we are in pain? Let's take a common issue for lots of people, myself included. Are you happy with your weight? Are you happy with your overall health and how much you work out? Most people I know would say no. Yet, most people are not distressed enough to take any action to change. Therefore, we would say they are not motivated. They are just unhappy at this point. Marcell fought with the bobcat a while before he began experiencing enough pain to tell Jerry to shoot up into the tree.

I'M MISERABLE!

Most people get motivated to go on a diet or start exercising the day they stand in front of a mirror, observe themselves, and either break into tears or a string of profanities and say something along the lines of "I can't stand this anymore." That level of emotion is usually required to take some action.

When I was a kid, my favorite cartoon was Popeye. In every episode the villain, Brutus, would push Popeye to his limits. Just before Popeye would eat his spinach so that he could be strong enough, here is what he said: "I have stands all I can stands, and I can't stands no more." That's when Popeye would take drastic action to make everything right. That's when we tend to be motivated, isn't it, when we can't stand how things are anymore?

ORGANIZATIONAL APPLICATIONS

Desires of the heart

What does this look like in our personal and organizational lives? Brian Tracy would say it is setting goals. He says goals are like heat seeking missiles. I've always been a goal setter by nature. It comes from my "D" dominant personality. But Brian Tracy had the earliest and most significant impact on me as a young professional in setting goals and using them in organizational life. I've learned through experience that if you can understand people's goals, you can begin to understand what they do—like my son when he wanted the International Scout. When I helped people set goals they agreed to and believed in, that impacted their performance.

A key to leaders influencing motivation is knowing what people want. Leaders can help illuminate wants and needs that people already have. This is an appropriate thing to do to influence motivation. You might raise this question: "Should we help people want more?" After all, the Bible says to be content with what you have. It says godliness with contentment is great gain.

How do we deal with that? The Bible tells us to be content with what we have. It did not tell us not to want to do more or have greater impact for God and other people. In fact, it says we are to outdo one another in doing good. I'm reminded of the prayer of Jabez. He asked God to expand his boundaries so he could have a greater impact on people. God answered his prayer. Helping people to understand their passions, dreams, goals, and potential in life for God and others is something good leaders should do.

When I led the internal audit department for HCA, I spent considerable time helping to illuminate the passions, dreams, and potential goals for the team. Sometimes, people's passions and dreams get buried. They've been hurt or failed at some point in life and are just trying to survive, so they put their dreams on hold. Sometimes, dreams and passions are ignored or forgotten. People get busy doing what's necessary and forget about doing what they dream about or are passionate about.

You can help illuminate dreams, passions, and goals that people have inside.

Sometimes, people just can't see their potential. I spent a lot of time working with people identifying their potential and "calling it out" in them. I told them they were setting their sights too low. They didn't have enough self-esteem or enough confidence. Sometimes, I pointed people in a different direction because they didn't have good self-awareness.

I don't believe there is such thing as average, above average, or below average people. People's talents vary, and their effectiveness in using them varies. Therefore, there's average, above average and below average performance. But people are unique. They have a specific calling and purpose that God created them for. When people understand and accept their calling, they will be motivated by the desire that springs up within them to live out their calling.

All people are unique and capable of unique accomplishments.

Science tells us that God did not create any two snowflakes that are identical. As complicated as the human being is, do we think God ran out of ideas on people? Do we really think people are not unique? Whatever purpose God created people for, they are unique for that purpose and better suited for it than anyone else. Seeing and "calling out" that unique potential in people is a way leaders bless and serve those on their team.

A 90-YEAR-OLD MAN MARRIES A 70-YEAR-OLD WOMAN

I remember a comical story along the same lines. Two 90-year-old men were talking. One told the other man that he was marrying a 70-year-old woman. His friend asked, "Is she pretty?" The first man replied, "No." The friend asked, "Does she kiss good?" The man replied, "No." The friend asked, "Well, is she rich?" The man replied, "No." The friend, exasperated, said, "Why in the world are you marrying her?" The man said, "Because she can still drive."

A WOMAN WANTS TO BUY CYANIDE

A lady went into a drugstore and asked the pharmacist for cyanide. The pharmacist looked surprised. He said, "Ma'am, I can't sell you cyanide. It's poison." She didn't respond verbally, but simply pulled a photograph and laid it on the counter. It was a picture of her husband and his wife together in an intimate situation. The pharmacist stared for a moment, shook his head, and apologized. He said, "Ma'am, I'm so sorry! I didn't realize you had a prescription for the cyanide." When you understand people's goals, you can understand what they do.

During my HCA career, I was given several opportunities to turn around a department or functions that were perceived to be off-track by the company's leadership. One of the first things I always did was to listen to the team to get a perspective of the organization's strengths, weaknesses, opportunities, and threats. From these, we set measurable objectives as a team. From these objectives, we set goals for everyone on the leadership team. These goals, to which they would be accountable, significantly re-directed their behavior and the results over the next year.

THE LEADER'S ROLE REGARDING MOTIVATION

So, what is the leader's role in motivation? Very broadly, I would say it is to hire people who are already motivated, to help illuminate their passions, dreams, and goals, to help align goals with the organization's needs, and try not to de-motivate them. That's easier said than done. How do we accomplish this? It starts with the hiring process. We need to hire the:

- Right personality profile. If we hire people who are going to be "swimming against the current" of their natural personality, they will be frustrated and de-motivated from the beginning.

Hire motivated people and try not to de-motivate them.

- Right talent and experience. Hire people with the talent and experience to do the job because they want to do the job and know how to do the job.

- People who want to make a difference – "cathedral builders." I had dinner with an old friend recently. I could tell he was really tired. When he explained his schedule of the last few weeks, I understood why. I thought he might be frustrated with his job and ready to quit. Yet, that wasn't the case at all. As I listened to him, it was clear he had a great vision for the impact he could have on the company and the quality of healthcare people were receiving. He was passionate about making a difference and was willing to push himself to the limits to achieve his goals.

> **I'd rather have people with a great vision of the difference they can make than just a good incentive package any day.**

Application

I. How much of what you do is based love of others versus just trying to make a living? What would you change?

II. Are you satisfying the desires of your heart? If not, what will you change?

III. Do you consider yourself highly motivated? Yes_____ No_____
    A. If not, why not?

_____

_____

_____

    B. What goals would you want to achieve with your life if you KNEW you couldn't fail?

_____

_____

_____

IV. Does your team seem highly motivated?

    A. List those who are:

_____

_____

_____

    B. List those who aren't:

_____

_____

_____

A. Do you understand why some are and some aren't?

Yes_____ No_____

B. Do you understand the dreams, passions, and goals of the people on each list?

Yes_____ No_____

C. What will you do about the list under B?

_____

_____

_____

V. Test your key team members below and answer Yes or No to each of the questions:

	<u>Yes</u>	<u>No</u>
1. Their personality profile fits their role?	_____	_____
2. They have the right talent and experience for their job?	_____	_____
3. They want to "make a difference" for other people?	_____	_____

If any of your answers above bother you, what will you do about it?

_____

_____

_____

By the way, answer these questions for yourself.
Do any of your answers bother you?

Chapter 20

EMPOWERMENT THROUGH HIGH EXPECTATIONS

Thought!
Have you ever considered how much of your team's
and organization's potential you are
sacrificing because of your low expectations?

"Then Jesus said to his disciples,
'If anyone wishes to come after me,
he must deny himself, take up his cross, and follow me.' "
Matthew 16:24

YOUR EXPECTATIONS HAVE A BIG INFLUENCE ON THE TEAM

Through the experience of having parents and being a parent, I know firsthand the impact of expectations on people. In my family, we were expected to work hard. We did, and it just seemed normal. In my wife's family, they did a lot of things to please and meet the expectations of other people. That thinking was so ingrained in her she still does it to this day. When I ask her why she's doing something, her response is often based on what somebody else expects. The expectations I had of my children has impacted them significantly. I talked in an earlier chapter about how I guided expectations of them in college based on their hardwiring.

In society, I see the impact of expectations on people. There are for-profit businesses and non-profit organizations that have cultures of high expectation. By contrast, there are those that have cultures of low expectation resulting in mediocrity.

Sadly, I see this in the church in North America. Many churches have cultures of low expectations. Frankly, the standard required to be involved in the social fraternity or sorority in college are higher than those required to be a member of many churches.

The importance of teacher expectations in facilitating student learning has long been recognized.[10] What you believe about people drives your attitude toward them. Your attitude drives your communications with them and your behavior toward them. That in turn drives their attitude and behavior. They start reacting to you through either positive or negative attitude and behavior. The first psychologist to systematically study this was a Harvard professor named Robert Rosenthal in an elementary school south of San Francisco.[11]

Self-Fulfilling Expectation

If you expect something to happen, you increase the chances of it happening. If you expect something good to happen, you tend to be optimistic, you look for opportunities, and you set goals. Over time, with this outlook of preparedness, chances greatly increase that something good _will_ happen.

Conversely, when you expect something bad to happen, you are pessimistic, you miss opportunities, and you behave in a way that generally does bring some disappointment to your life. This is true even in the area of health. The medical field established long ago that people with positive and expectant attitudes are healthier and live longer than those with negative and depressed attitudes.

Similar research has also been done with children. In Rosenthal's or similar studies, one group of teachers was told they had students with below average IQ's. The other teachers were told that their students had been tested and were gifted with very high IQ's. At the end of several months, all the students were given standard achievement tests. As expected, the first set of children did poorly, and the other set of children scored very high on the achievement tests. The teachers were told afterwards that all the students had been tested in both groups and they all had average IQ's.[12]

You tend to get what you expect.

POOR STUDENTS

So what was happening here? The teachers who thought they had below average students expected them to perform poorly. They never considered that their attitude, actions, and follow-up could be the problem because the students were already destined to perform poorly. Think about what probably happened in this classroom. The teachers did the minimum to inspire and encourage. The feedback was likely negative. Comments were likely made such as, "Will you pay attention?", "Are you ever going to learn this?", "Why can't you seem to get this right?", and "I give up. You'll never learn this."

GIFTED STUDENTS

Now think about the feedback and interaction from the teachers who thought they were dealing with gifted students. The teachers expected the students to do well and naturally assumed that if they didn't, it was their responsibility as the teacher. They worked harder themselves. They encouraged the students. The feedback was very different. They said things like "You can do it," "Let me explain this a better way," "You didn't understand that because I did not do a good job of explaining it," and "Let's spend some more time on this because I know you can get it."[13]

People tend to live up or down to your expectations.

I could go on and on with examples, but I think you get the point. What the teachers expected not only drove their attitudes and behaviors, but it had a significant impact on what the students were able to achieve.

I believed I had a great team at HCA.
Some people disagreed with me. That didn't matter.
What mattered most was that I believed it, and my team believed it.
That made the team better because *we believed it*.

FRANK'S STORY

I remember a story about a young boy who brought a Christmas present to school for his teacher, Mrs. Jones. She opened the gifts in front of the students. When she opened Frank's gift, the other kids laughed. It was a partially used bottle of perfume. Frank was obviously embarrassed because of the laughter of the other kids, but Mrs. Jones thanked him for it and made over it like it was a fine gift even though she didn't quite understand.

A bit later when none of the other students were around, Mrs. Jones asked Frank how he chose that particular gift. Tears came to his eyes as he explained that it was his mom's perfume. He had given it to his mom last Christmas because he knew it was her favorite perfume. His mom was very sick that Christmas, but she always wore it and thanked Frank for it. She passed away a few months later. Frank told Mrs. Jones that he hoped she liked it as much as his mom did and wanted her to have it so she would smell like his mom.

"Do not look out merely for your own interests.

Look out for the interests of others."

Philippians 2:4

Mrs. Jones then took a special interest in Frank. She found out about his home life which was tough. His father did the best he could but was poor and had to work long hours leaving Frank to fend for himself. Mrs. Jones began to look at Frank differently. She determined she would encourage, support, and love him. In the final half of his fourth-grade year, Frank went from being a poor student to a very good student. In the years that followed, Frank would always go by and see Mrs. Jones every year and tell her how he was doing. He was making "A's" every year. At some point, he moved away, and she didn't see him anymore.

Little things leaders do can make big differences in people's lives.

A few years later, she got a note from Frank. He had just graduated from high school with honors, and he wrote a note to Mrs. Jones thanking her for the difference she made it his life. Four years later, she got another note from Frank. He had just graduated from college at the top of his class. A few years later, she got another note thanking her for the impact the she had on his life. He had just finished medical school and was now a doctor.

You can change someone's life by taking an interest in them.

Leaders often underestimate the impact for both bad and good that they can have on the lives of people under their sphere of influence. When we take a personal interest in people, understand their background and challenges, and go the extra mile to meet some of their personal needs, the impact can leave a deep impression. Often, it doesn't take anything heroic to make a big difference and a deep impression on someone's life.

I remember the going-away party the team threw for me when I left the internal audit department at HCA for a different role. A grown man stood with tears in his eyes telling a story that I had long since forgotten. I began to remember some of the details as he told the story. I was on vacation and made a call to a hospital CEO to recommend this fellow for a CFO position which he got. That move was a stepping stone to other career moves that turned out really good for him. I thought nothing of it and had long since forgotten it. But because I took some time early in the morning while on vacation to help advance his career, it made a deep impression on this man. It required very little of me. I had forgotten about it, but it made a great difference to him.

INFLUENCING BEHAVIOR BY REINFORCING WHAT YOU EXPECT [14]

The carrot and the stick

In college, we studied the work of Pavlov and how he trained dogs. Positive and negative reinforcement is used in all animal training. Let's end the discussion of motivation on a positive note by talking about how to get the behavior you need from people. You may remember better by thinking of Pavlov and the slobbering dogs. All animal training is done using a simple approach. You give positive reinforcement to behaviors or actions you want to see repeated (carrot) and negative reinforcement to actions or behaviors you do not want to see repeated (stick/pain). When animals are trained, each movement in the right direction is rewarded with food. Over time, the animal must do more and more to receive their food.

People are not animals and shouldn't be treated like animals. But, positive and negative reinforcement can be used in organizational life to get the behaviors you want and to see that certain behaviors are avoided. That is, as long as it's done in the proper way with the right motivations. This is consistent with the biblical idea of accountability.

Let us look at some examples. Suppose you want to encourage teamwork among your employees. There are some on your team that like public recognition, but they tend to operate independently. If the leader acknowledges them in public when they contribute to a team effort in the appropriate way, those individuals will tend to repeat similar type behaviors to get the recognition. Be careful with this because not all people like public recognition. Some people most appreciate a pat on the back, a warm thank you or a personal note from the leader to repeat that behavior.

If you're trying to create a culture that follows the biblical instruction to "go the extra mile," every time people do something extra, reward them in some way that's meaningful to them. I found that often times a simple gift certificate for a meal will substantially impact employees' desires to look beyond just the immediate of what they have to do. I would add, however, to keep this in balance so that employees do not start neglecting the family or other important goals in life by responding to your positive reinforcement.

I remember Steve, the "straw boss" I worked for in the summer as a teenager. Each year, we hauled hay on the farm where Sydney worked. Sydney was pretty much a loner and didn't get much attention, but he was quite strong. Each day, he would come by and throw a few bales of hay. Steve would start bragging on him. The more Steve bragged, the harder Sydney would work until he was literally exhausted. And, Steve wasn't paying Sydney. He was doing it purely for the recognition. It is often amazing to me how badly people need attention and some positive reinforcement. I noticed over the course of my career that solid leaders who make a habit of positive reinforcement have lower turnover and much more loyal and contented employees. Positive reinforcement brings blessing to people's lives because it is such a strong need. This is an area where I had some good moments but a lot more that I'm not proud of. I missed a lot of opportunities to bless people by encouraging them.

Positively reinforce behavior you want repeated.

HOW ABOUT NEGATIVE REINFORCEMENT?

But, you may ask, what about negative reinforcement? You probably heard it said, "Praise in public, chew in private." Generally, I favor that approach. But, is it an absolute? When Jesus was telling his disciples what would happen to him, Peter argued with him. Jesus said in front of the other disciples, "Get behind me, Satan." That was a pretty strong rebuke, wouldn't you say? It would've been strong in private, but especially in front of the other disciples, it seemed very strong. Why did Jesus do that? Was it because he did not like or respect Peter? No, because another time he said to Peter, "You are the rock on which I will build my church." Jesus handpicked him to be the leader of the disciples when he was gone. Jesus' rebuke

Negatively reinforce behavior you want stopped.

was strong because Peter was making a huge spiritual mistake which Jesus did not want to see him repeat, nor did he want the other disciples to repeat it.

Another very strong example is seen in the early church. A couple, Ananias and Sapphira, made a contribution to the church. However, they represented that they had given more than they really had. When their dishonesty was revealed on separate occasions, they each dropped dead. In the church in North America, a lot of people would be safe on this since they don't give anything in the first place. Anyway, the point is that it was very critical to God that the purity and harmony of truth and actions be maintained in the early church. Therefore, this deception was rebuked severely and very publicly.

Public rebukes can be done at the wrong time, in the wrong way, and with the wrong motivation and can be very destructive to people. However, they can also be significant learning opportunities for the individual and others. So, negative reinforcement with love is also a part of the leader's playbook. In the home, psychologists often refer to this as "tough love." The form of negative reinforcement needs to fit the individuals who need to change their behavior.

Application

I. Write down the names of two or three people that have had a significant influence in your life.

Name

1. _____

2. _____

3. _____

What did they do for you? _____

_____

How did you thank them? _____

_____

II. Who is someone in your life you can have a significant influence on with a little extra effort?

_____

III. Do you have high expectations of your people and confidence in them? If not, why?

_____

_____

_____

What will you do about it?

_____

_____

_____

Notes

Chapter 21

EMPOWERMENT THROUGH EFFECTIVE DELEGATION

Thought:
How much better would your quality of work life be
if you could delegate anything you do to people
and be confident it would be done well?

"Moses' father-in-law said to him,
'The thing you're doing is not good.
You will surely wear out, both yourself and
these people who are with you,
for the task is too heavy for you; you cannot do it alone.'"
Exodus 18:17-18

What's the first decision any leader has to make? There are two approaches we learn from Moses and Jethro, his father-in-law. Moses kept all of the work to himself, and people were gathered all around him looking for answers. Jethro's approach, that Moses later adopted, was to delegate to capable leaders and handle only the harder cases himself.

In my experience, the three most simple keys to effective delegation are:

Explain <
- Be sure people understand the assignment.
- Be sure they know how to complete the assignment.

Then, Ensure →
- Be sure they want the assignment.

DO THEY UNDERSTAND?

It sounds so simple, doesn't it? You just tell people what to do. They are eager to please the boss, so they smile and nod. If you ask them if they understand, they are likely to say yes whether they do or not. They don't want you to think they are not smart, and they are hoping they can figure it out.

I just don't get this.

It has been my experience that the delegation process breaks down in telling people what you want them to do. Why is that? It's because it's a complicated process.

HOW DO YOU MAKE SURE THEY UNDERSTAND?

The internal audit department at HCA was staffed with young, bright, hard-working professionals. They were very eager to please. They were very hesitant about saying they did not understand. They normally would smile and say they understood. If they didn't understand, they would wait until I left and hope that a more experienced person on the team could explain it to them. After a few experiences, I learned to look deep into their eyes. I could discern a look of comprehension, or I would see what I called "a dazed or glazed" look. When I saw this, I knew they did not understand. Sometimes, I would say, "Tell me the first thing you will do to complete this assignment." Seldom did they know. Then, I would go over it again and sometimes again until I was confident they understood what they were to do. If they can explain to you the objective of the job and a general approach for accomplishing it, they likely understand.

Do They Know How?

Sometimes, people simply don't know how to do the task you are assigning. I faced this often in internal audit. The answer to this is simple: either do it yourself, give it to someone else, or train someone.

Do They Want This Assignment?

Sometimes, people know how to do something, but they simply don't have any interest in doing it—there's no passion.

If noone wants to do it, should you be doing it? - Maybe, but it's worth questioning

DELEGATION PITFALLS

When people complained, I tried to listen to what they thought should be changed or improved and gave projects to those individuals if I felt they had the competence. This did three things. First, it got the work done by someone who cared about it. Second, it stopped a lot of complaining. Third, it reinforced the culture of not complaining about something unless you're willing to fix it. It's important for people to do something they believe in and care about. Ecclesiastes says, "Whatever your hand finds to do, do it with all your might." This is an encouragement to work hard at whatever we do whether we like it or not. I don't consider myself an author, but I have thought of this Scripture many times as I wrote this book. Jesus said, "My yoke is easy and my burden is light." So how do these two ideas work together? The way it works is when leaders give people work assignments they have the talent, experience, and passion for versus giving them stuff that is drudgery for them. One business owner I know keeps giving people stuff to do they aren't even qualified for.

Though writing is not my favorite thing to do, God gave me years of experience and practice at doing it, and He gave me great passion for things I can do once this is written. What I will be doing in the future will be made much easier because God had me write this book.

Delegation is important. Without it, you can't grow your staff and organization or increase your span of control. But there are some pitfalls you need to be aware of or they can cause you some big problems. These problems arise from ignoring teachings of Scripture in this area:

- Know the condition of your flock — Proverbs 27:23

- Don't lord it over them — Matthew 20:20-28

- My yoke is easy and my burden is light — Matthew 11:28-30

- Whoever forces you to go one mile, go with him two — Matthew 5:41

KNOW THE CONDITION OF YOUR FLOCK

This certainly includes knowing the status of your organization or business. It also means to know what your people can handle. I have heard many leaders over the years describe what I consider a reckless approach to leadership. They say, "My approach is just to throw them in over their heads and let them sink or swim." I have seen leaders do that many times. The problem is sinking people tend to take others down with them, including the leader that threw them in.

I've seen the "throw them in over their head approach" used many times. The "I" and "I"/"D" personalities are most prone to doing this. When people are hired, or existing people receive a new assignment, often the leader just gives a free reign and lets people go do it. You say, "So what's wrong with that?" Well, you hire people believing they have a certain level of competence and motivation. But you've done absolutely nothing to validate or test it. The justification is "They are professional, and I pay them well. Therefore, I just need to trust them." And certainly, it's true that employees do need to feel like you have confidence in them.

It is also true their confidence is eroded, and they get frustrated with micromanagers that never really let go and give them autonomy. So which is best?

BALANCED APPROACH

You don't have to choose between throwing people in and seeing if they can swim or looking over someone's shoulder all the time. There is a third alternative which will get the best results. It is a balanced approach. You give them freedom after you know what they can do. One way to know this is by verified past experience. The other is by observing them. Employees need to be fully immersed in meeting the objectives of the organization. They need to be part of something where they maintain their distinctiveness but contribute fully to the organization. This requires them being fully immersed in the job you have given them but not in over their heads. In this approach, you give them responsibility and authority in smaller steps.

I hired someone recently to do some work at my house. He had recently hired someone who had represented his skills in a particular area of work that this subcontractor had never actually seen or observed his work. He "threw him in over his head" and sent him to my house unsupervised. The person messed up the job.

Using this third alternative, you avoid a lot of mistakes and save a lot of time correcting problems for the new employee and yourself. Consider the example I just gave. It cost this contractor considerable money to fix the problems caused by his employee. In addition, he risked not getting any future business from me, plus losing the potential for referrals that I would have given. This was a very costly mistake for the individual that easily could have been avoided. The cost of some additional supervisory time would have been minimal compared to what it cost him.

You make this transition as quickly as possible but not until you have a clear understanding of the capabilities of the new people. You avoid much of the frustration the new employees may feel of being micro-managed by explaining your approach. In doing so, the employees know your intent is to let go but not drop them in over their head. It's best to solicit the cooperation of the employees to make the transition as quickly as possible.

If you drop the new employees in over their head, they're going to take on some water that wasn't necessary. But when you walk them into the water up to their chin, they are fully immersed in the ownership of the project or task, but not drowning. This is the optimal place for the employers and the employees to be. It's like a river. A drop of water is completely a part of the river but retains its distinctiveness. Individuals need to be fully immersed in their role but maintain their uniqueness.

The approach above is consistent with how we see that Jesus led his disciples. First, he taught them. Then, he did things in their presence like healing people. Then, he sent them out in two's and had them come back and report on the results.

PERSONAL EXPERIENCE

In the last fifteen years of my career at HCA, I reported to thirteen different people. Therefore, I'm quite familiar with this process. I remember early in my career chafing over the engagement of my new manager. However, I noticed when new people reported to me, I insisted on a certain level of engagement. I went through the process just described.

I remember well reporting to a new manager and my CFO being extremely frustrated. He said, "Leon, we've been doing this for years, and we know what we're doing. Why can't they just leave us alone?" Then, I reminded him of the approach that we both used successfully over the years. I said, "We can make this process long and painful, or we can proactively engage with the new manager." The lights came on for the CFO and he said, "How quickly do you think we can do this?" I said, "If we really work at it, I think we can have him completely comfortable with us in the next thirty days, and then we will have substantial freedom just to go do our work." We worked hard at it and, in thirty days, we were given a great deal of autonomy.

DON'T LORD IT OVER THEM

I understand this command, telling us to avoid being abusive or overly controlling. People need and thrive on freedom when they are doing something they know how to do and have a passion for. When we are overly controlling, we limit people, we restrict their freedom, but we also restrict ours. It takes time and energy to look over someone's shoulder. When we don't empower people properly in the delegation process, we limit ourselves as well.

MY YOKE IS EASY AND MY BURDEN IS LIGHT

God never intended for people to be overloaded and burdened in their work. He doesn't intend for leaders to overburden people in their work either.

How many times do you find that people have more projects than they have time to complete? Do they put off one project and do the others? Or do they not spread the time they have among all the projects. What is the result? One project dies from neglect. Or all the projects suffer due to insufficient time and attention. The results can be devastating because all the projects could fail.

What's the better approach? Prioritize the projects. Are all equally time sensitive? Sometimes, they are not. Are all equally important? Generally, they are not. Then, the leaders and employees should mutually agree on which project gets deferred or dropped altogether. Otherwise, a high-priority project could die from neglect or multiple important projects could be done poorly due to insufficient time and attention.

DON'T OVERLOAD YOUR BEST PEOPLE

"For six days, the Lord made the heavens and the earth, the sea and all that is in them, and rested on the seventh day; therefore the Lord blessed the Sabbath day and made it holy."

Exodus 20:11

I can see two elements of delegation covered in this Scripture. One is that when people are doing work they were designed for, it tends to be easy for them to do. Coupled with the numerous commands in Scripture about rest, I also take this to mean that people should not be overloaded. This hurts individuals, but it also hurts the leaders. When leaders do this, they position themselves to get overly dependent on an individual or a few individuals. The unintended consequences of ignoring this Scripture can be significant.

In organizations, delegation is sometimes like water. It follows the path of least resistance. Some people are eager to take on more and more work. So what's the problem? It can get to the point that you are overly dependent on key individuals. This naturally tends to happen in small organizations but will also happen in larger ones if you are not careful.

I know of a businessman in Nashville who had a quite successful small business. He had one person responsible for his billing and accounts payable. That individual got sick. Customers were not being billed, so his cash flow was cut off. Vendors were not being paid and were upset. It caused a substantial disruption in his business for a period of time. The fact was if it had continued it could have ruined his business. I have heard a great many business owners, business leaders, and non-profit leaders make this very statement about one or more of their team.

One key rule of wise investing is diversification, i.e. don't put all your eggs in one basket. This applies to many aspects of organizational life, such as being overly dependent on one customer or supplier. It also applies to your people. Don't become overly dependent on a few key people. Mary, whom I talk about next, is a real person that I had experience with, but I have changed the name. In fact I have experienced more than one person like Mary.

Indispensible Person

Mary is great! I don't know what I would do without her.

It's not uncommon for leaders to brag on who they think are the very best people in the organization and the best fit for their job when, in fact, these people are dangerous to the long-term success of the organization. This is counterintuitive, so we need to unpack this one. Picture an employee that works hard, that does the work of two or three people, and that you count on enormously. Most leaders think that everything is right about the situation. In fact, they say, "I don't know what I would do without Mary." And that's the essence of the problem. What would you do without Mary?

The implication is quite simple. If something happens to Mary, you are in a real jam. But you say Mary isn't going anywhere. Does she never take vacation? Does she never get sick? Is she never going to retire? Is she not someday going to get promoted or transferred? If she's so good, is it not possible that someone would offer her a better package and hire her away from you? The reality is, it's not if you lose Mary, it's simply when or how. If you truly don't know what you would do without her, she is the most dangerous employee in your organization, and you need to start figuring out now what you would do when she is gone.

Jesus' work was too important to not be passed on or have a backup plan when something happened to one of his followers. His plan was the one Paul shared with Timothy.

"The things which you heard from me
in the presence of many witnesses,
entrust these to faithful men (people)
who will be able to teach others also."

2 Timothy 2:2

There are some alternatives. You can hire someone else and split up the work. This is difficult, particularly in small organizations. Another alternative is to train one or more people on everything like we did in internal audit. Then, you have a backup when something happens to Mary. Again, this is hard in a small organization. Another alternative is to have a documentation file on how Mary does her job. We did this in internal audit due to the high turnover. Then, at least someone can be trained using the documentation to fill the role more quickly.

Of course, the best solution is to plan and delegate in a way that avoids this problem from ever occurring. This is often easier said than done, especially in smaller organizations. Let's take a typical scenario and see how this occurs. The organization is having some success in its new business. Therefore, there is more work to do. Mary sees this as an opportunity to gain favor with the boss and have more impact and influence in the organization. Mary says, "I'll pick up the extra work." Mary does, and the boss is very appreciative. This keeps happening, and the boss starts thinking about adding a person. Mary wants to gain favor with the boss to have influence in the organization and to provide more financially for the family. She says, "Don't hire anybody else. I will just work more and you can pay me more." That sounds like a good deal to the boss. So that is what the boss does. As this continues over time, Mary truly does become the person the organization becomes too dependent upon.

OTHER PROBLEMS DEVELOP WITH MARY

Other than the fact that Mary will eventually be lost to the organization, other problems might develop as well. Once Mary understands how important she is to the organization, now she can make demands that may not be fair or reasonable to the leader or other employees. Mary can get inflexible, demanding, manipulative, and controlling. I've observed this happening many times when a leader gets overly dependent on one or a few people. What do you do? Your hands are tied, and you have let the rest of the organization down. In fact, you put the organization and the jobs of the other employees at risk. This does not bring balance and fairness to the workplace. It only jeopardizes it.

But, you say Mary would never be that way. Maybe that's right. Maybe she is so dedicated to you and the organization that she would never behave inappropriately. But knowing you can't do without her, does she feel the freedom to take off when she truly is sick? Would she stay at work when she should be going to her kids' functions? Would she ignore the health of her marriage for the sake of the organization? Would she continue to put the organization's needs ahead of her needs and her family? If she does, is that right? Is that fair? If you allow that as the leader, have you blessed Mary? Have you blessed her family? Have you blessed her friends? Have you blessed her peers? Have you protected and blessed the organization? Well, the obvious answer is no. So you see, sometimes a great, hard-working, loyal employee can be a risk to the organization and its long-term future.

My Experience with Marty

Let me tell you about Marty. This guy was a computer whiz. The company had an information technology department with hundreds of employees. I would ask them about the project for my department. They might say it would take six weeks. Marty could consistently do the project in two weeks. I was proud of Marty, bragged about Marty, and paid him well. I had begun to say, "I don't really know what I would do without him."

I realized I didn't know what I would do without Marty but one day I would have to.

Good Solution

Then, it dawned on me, someday somebody would see how good Marty really was and that somebody would hire him away from me. Then, what would I do? So we changed Marty's goals. Part of his goals was to write new programs. The other part of his goals related to documenting very well how to operate programs already written so that any programmer could come in and maintain, improve, or change those programs. This served us very well when this function grew. We hired someone else. They were able to carry on and even expand on the base of what we already had developed very quickly because of the documentation and the training that we had Marty do.

Non-profit example

I am familiar with one rather large non-profit ministry that had a multi-million dollar budget. They had grown substantially and so had their computer infrastructure. They had one person in charge of all the technology who did not like to document what he did, nor was he willing to train others. He made some mistakes that will have substantial negative effects on the organization for a long time. Nothing had been done about the situation because the organization didn't think they could do without him.

Go the extra mile

Organizations need people who are willing to go the extra mile. When is this not the case? When people do not agree with what needs to be done, or they do not know how to do the job. Why is this the case? Well, think about it. If you don't believe something is a good plan for the organization, how hard is it for you to put your best effort into the work? Also, if people are not qualified to do a particular project, what other choice do they have?

In complex organizational life, it's nearly impossible to tell people everything they have to do to complete complicated tasks. And even if you could, it takes too much time. When you find people only doing what you tell them to do, it's time to probe some more. Ask some questions to determine if they understand what you're asking them to do, if they simply don't have any interest in doing that work, or if they really disagree with the objectives of this particular project. I can't state how critical it is that people be assigned work not only that they are capable of doing but that they want to do. In Revelation 3:20, Jesus says "Behold I stand at the door and knock. If any man will open it, I will come in and eat with him." Here is my thought. If the creator and master of the universe does not force himself upon us, why do leaders think they have any right to force their will on other people?

I remember one time asking a manager to schedule an audit at a hospital. He really did not believe we should be doing that particular audit at that time. It takes some skill and effort to schedule an audit since people generally are not prepared or are not looking forward to one. Given that I knew his attitude, I should not have been surprised a few minutes later when he told me that he just couldn't get it scheduled. In complex organizational structures, it's hard to get things done that you want to get done and nearly impossible to get things done you really don't care about doing or don't even agree with.

So in the delegation process, watch out for people who are not going the extra mile. They may not have the talent to do the job or they may disagree with the plans.

Application

I. Do people tend to understand you when you delgate work to them? If not, why?

_____

_____

_____

II. Do your people know how to do the work you assign to them? If not, what will you change?

_____

_____

_____

III. How well do you know the capability of your people? What do you need to change?

_____

_____

_____

IV. In what ways do you "lord over your people?" What do you need to change?

_____

_____

_____

V. Who on your team are you tending to overload? What will you do about it?

_____

_____

_____

VI. Do you have a Marty on your team? What will you do about it?

_____

_____

_____

Chapter 22

CULTURE EMPOWERS PEOPLE OR FRUSTRATES THEM

> **Thought!**
> Have you considered how many people stay with
> your organization because they like the culture or
> how many may be leaving because they don't like it?

"Brethren, join in following my example, and observe those who walk

according to the pattern you have observed in us."

Philippians 3:17

An organization's culture is in essence the values of its top leaders put into action. The values of leaders are expressed through mission, vision, objectives and goals, policies, and procedures, but they are most clearly expressed by the attitudes and actions of the senior leadership team. The Apostle Paul encouraged people to follow the example he was setting for them. Since values are lived out by key leaders, let's look at examples of values.

Many years ago, I wrestled with the values needed for leading organizations. During my leadership of the internal audit department of HCA, I developed what I called the internal audit success profile. These were the five characteristics I saw in people within the audit function who got promoted or who went on to other parts of the organization and excelled. These five characteristics were service, innovation, teamwork, communication, and continuous learning.

Culture is values in action.

Over time, I noticed these weren't just the characteristics of successful individuals, but they were characteristics of successful departments and organizations. I refined and developed these into value statements. Later, I felt the need to add a sixth characteristic, integrity, to the list. In the internal audit function, integrity seemed to go without saying, but in other places, it needed to be said. I explain the values this way:

[1] Shouldn't people want to do their work according to chapter 21.

- **Integrity** — This means doing the right thing for the organization and other people regardless of your self-interest. It's doing what is right when nobody's looking. It's doing what is right just because it's the right thing. If people don't trust you to have their interests in mind or the organization doesn't trust you to have its interests in mind, why would or should you be trusted to serve in any capacity?

Vague

- **Service** — This is adding measurable value to the other person or the organization. There are two kinds of people in the organization: those who want power and want others to serve them as their primary aim, or those who want to add value to others and the organization. People seeking power make poor servants.

  I was able to predict the demise of several corporate initiatives because I saw the primary aim of the leadership in charge was to gain power. Invariably when that was the case versus serving the company, the initiative or function ultimately was disbanded. It usually took much longer for this to happen than it should.

- **Innovation** — Because things change and our expectations are always for something better in the future, we have to be creative to continue to provide higher levels of service. If we don't work at providing higher levels of service, someone else will, and we will become obsolete.

- **Teamwork** — There is an old saying, "None of us are as smart as all of us." The Proverbs say there is wisdom in many counselors. There is great value in avoiding mistakes through gaining the perspective of others. I found over many years that people working together are more creative and innovative for the organization than relying on only a handful of individuals.

  The Physician Services organization at HCA evolved over twelve years from a very narrow focus to many initiatives and functions. The ideas came from many individuals to help the organization evolve and improve. But no matter who had the initial idea, it was always improved upon by the team.

- **Communication** — When God wanted to halt the progress of mankind as they built the tower of Babel, He made them speak different languages so they could not communicate effectively. When teams are not committed to proactive communications, many problems arise. When I speak of communications, I don't simply mean talking. I mean proactive and meaningful communication where there is a meeting of the minds.

  Where there is not good communication, there cannot be good teamwork. Where there is not good teamwork, there cannot be good innovation. Where there is not good innovation, there cannot be improved service. In addition, where there is not good communication, your integrity can even be questioned.

- **Continuous learning** — To create a product or provide a service, everyone involved must bring some skill to the table. Given the rapid rate of change in the world, a commitment to lifelong learning is key to continuing to contribute to a high-performance team.

These became the values I tried to live by and incorporate into the value statements of each organization I led at HCA, and they served the team well in the healthcare business.

Here's a key question. Are the people in your culture more like fish in water or fish out of water? When my daughter Allyson was in college majoring in fashion design, she realized the work culture when she graduated would be very competitive. That did not fit her natural personality style nor was it what she wanted. She realized she would be a fish out of water in that culture and changed her major to get a degree in her area of strength that would allow her to work in a culture that suited her.

If you can't clearly articulate your values, they're not clear to the team.

DO YOU KNOW THE CULTURE YOU HAVE?

Different cultures may be needed based on the nature of the business organization. For example, technology organizations may need a more competitive internal culture, more accepting of some lone rangers because of their technical expertise. In certain healthcare situations, absolute teamwork is a required and necessary part of the culture.

These components—vision, priorities, accountability systems, policy and procedures, and the attitudes and actions of the top leaders—all make up the organization's culture. Often, cultures are not understood by leaders driving them. Very frequently, they don't appreciate the value it brings or the damage that typically occurs when the culture is not what it should be. Often the culture is not what the leaders think it is or want it to be. Their value statements and policies regarding people say one thing, such as "People are our most valuable asset; we value and respect our people." Yet, the leaders act differently. They may not treat people like they value them or respect them. They may think of them more as an expense item on the income statement and treat them that way versus a valued asset.

Or, the leaders may say things like they value families, yet work sixty to eighty hours a week themselves, expect it from others, and still think they really value family. It's not uncommon for

Culture attracts people to your organization or causes them to want to leave.

males to think because they work hard and provide well that it proves they value their family. However, it is time and involvement with family activities that make the spouse and children believe that they are valued. I have seen cultures that talk significantly about family values and say all the right things but model the opposite.

IS THE LEADERSHIP TEAM MODELING THE VALUES?

Sometimes, the leaders model the right behavior but include people on their senior leadership team that don't. I recall an example where the earnest desire of the senior leadership team was to treat people as valuable and with respect. However, one person was included on the senior leadership team that didn't buy into that value. That person treated people horribly. Everyone knew it and despised the person. The worst part, though, was the impact it had on the culture and on the credibility of the top leaders. It was seen as hypocritical and completely meaningless when the top leaders talked about how much they valued people and wanted people treated with dignity.

I regret to say that I've done this myself. I wanted a culture that was very heavily oriented toward teamwork. I had bright and hard-working technical people around me that I felt were needed to accomplish certain goals for the team. Yet, they didn't believe in teamwork, or at least view it the same way I did, and in the way others needed to experience it. No matter what I did, the culture

I wanted and the culture I was seeing were different until I made the hard decisions. I had to replace hard-working technical people with sometimes less talented, more team-focused people. Every time I made those concessions, though, we upped the morale and overall results of the team improved because of the synergy we got from everybody working together. They went the extra mile because they enjoyed what they were doing and the people they were doing it with.

Synergy
& Culture Driven

TWO EXTREMES IN CULTURES

Family culture

In family-oriented cultures, the owners or leaders typically see themselves as a father or a big brother figure. In relating to employees, they watch out for them and take care of them. They wish the best for them and are always looking out for their good, often times at sacrifice to themselves. I remember one time Dr. Frist, Jr., the CEO of HCA at the time, saying that he disciplined himself every day to have at least one idea for the betterment of the employees. This came from the mindset of a CEO with a very family-oriented view of the company.

In family-oriented cultures, leaders see their roles to protect and provide. They often take roles of instructing and guiding. They take pride in their employees, much like an adored child.

They coach and encourage them. They call out the uniqueness and their good qualities while either overlooking or compensating for weak areas. They expect the best out of them. They expect them to live up to the values of the culture just like a father expects children to live up to family values.

On family farms or in family businesses, everyone has a job and is expected to contribute. Good children don't do the job halfheartedly. The job is appropriate to their age and their ability, but over time growth and learning are expected.

I've seen all kinds of cultures. And as I said earlier, different cultures are required for different organizations. Sometimes, different cultures are even required for different seasons of the organization's life. As an employee, the culture I enjoyed most was that of a family atmosphere. Early in my work career, I had the opportunity to work in a very family-oriented culture even though it was a multi-billion dollar organization. So why do employees enjoy the family culture? The reasons are many.

Security is provided in this kind of environment. People don't want to leave. It's not uncommon for the children and relatives to want to go to work in a family culture. They attract friends who want to work in that culture. I've even seen people leave such cultures for more money or promotions in other roles and miss the family culture and eventually come back.

When Ross Perot hired a team that went into a foreign country to rescue his team members, he was playing the father figure. In this chaotic world where there is so much uncertainty, fear, and anxiety, it's hard to underestimate the positive impact of the security people feel in family-oriented cultures. And just to be clear, the most family-oriented culture I've ever seen was a multi-billion dollar business organization. I experienced it on the family farm, and I've seen it in small family-owned businesses. But I've experienced it also in a large business organization. It's difficult, but it is possible. Also, I think it's devastating when such cultures are established and over time removed.

It's not uncommon for businesses, churches, ministries, and non-profit organizations to start off with family-oriented cultures. Often, the further removed the original founder is from the leadership, the more that culture is lost to the detriment of the organization.

> **People feel secure in family-oriented cultures**

Fear-based culture

People tend not to leave family oriented cultures.

Some business, non-profit, and even church cultures are driven by fear. Great anxiety is a constant theme among the people in the organization. It limits the spontaneity and creativity of people. It kills morale. Over the long term, those environments cause literal sickness and even death. It's well established in the medical community that stress, which is caused by anxiety and fear, lowers the immune system and allows people to get cancer and other diseases.

SOME LEADERS USE FEAR AS A STYLE OF MANAGEMENT

If leaders tortured and killed people by other means, they would be prosecuted and put in prison. Yet, some leaders literally kill people in the organizations over many years by using a management style of fear.

The reason it is used so much is because it is quite effective at getting things done immediately. People who are afraid take significant action to relieve their fear and gain a sense of security. But, first of all, it's wrong. Secondly, a culture driven by fear is not a highly productive organization over the long term. So why do managers, not leaders, lead by fear? There are several reasons:

- Many have been fear-prone their whole life. Because fear is such a strong motivator, they worked hard, followed the rules, accomplished much, and were placed in management positions.

- Some are responding to upper-level management who are managing by fear.

- Some don't genuinely care about people and see it as an expedient way to get things done.

- Some like the feeling of power and control that managing by fear gives them.

- Some are just mean. I remember a portion of the movie *Good Morning Vietnam*. The colonel says to the radio station manager, "Dick, I've covered for you many times because I thought you were crazy, but you're not crazy; you're just mean." Unfortunately, we run into this in leadership in all types of organizations.

FEAR-PRONE MANAGERS

A lot of people in management roles have fear-prone personalities and things in their childhood and past experience that caused them to be motivated by fear themselves. Since they are motivated by fear, they do everything out of that motivation which spills into their management style.

I have to make a confession here. Too much of my style for too many years was based on being motivated by my own fears. I meant well. I masked the outcome of this under the guise of quality—doing the job right is important. I masked it under the biblical principle of "going the extra mile." I masked it under the principle of "luck is when preparedness meets opportunity."

The truth is quality is great, "going the extra mile" is great, and you do need to be prepared to capitalize on opportunity. But I realized that many times I pushed too hard, prepared too much, and tried to be too perfect because I was afraid. I was pushing hard to feel secure, not to be noble.

Being this way took its toll on me. It affected my health until I was able to learn to lighten up. But, what bothers me most is I know it had to affect other people. They seemed to appreciate my hard work, forward thinking and diligent preparation which served the team well many times. But, sometimes I pushed them too hard for too long in order to give me a sense of security.

When I taught people that quality was important, that was a virtue. When I taught on the biblical principle of the extra mile and modeled it, that was a virtue. When I taught them how to be well prepared to achieve success, that was a virtue. But, when I went too far because I was motivated by my own fears, I was wrong and not blessing their lives. Instead, I was causing unnecessary stress and anxiety. I was taking them away from their families and other important components of their life. I was wrong. I had no right to do that. And I'm really sorry I ever crossed that line.

It's hard to be afraid and creative at the same time.

IMPLICATIONS FOR THE ORGANIZATION OF FEAR-BASED LEADERSHIP

People leading out of fear are prone to violate the 80/20 rule. This causes inefficiencies and is not the highest stewardship of the organization's resources. People who are fear-prone tend to be perfectionists and will not follow priority management principles unless they are very consciously aware. This is something I was aware of and still struggled with in my leadership style. Often, because I was conscious of it, I was able to keep the balance. But sometimes, under significant pressure, I would violate these principles.

Safety as key to Creativity

Creativity and spontaneity disappear among teams that are managed by fear. People want to stay safe, so they don't take chances.

Fear causes us to limit some of our social interactions within organizations. This robs us of building alliances that will be key to the future. It also robs us of the simple pleasure of the positive interpersonal relationships we have a chance to establish in organizational life.

Fear causes leaders not to trust. Therefore, they don't delegate as much as they should or give as much freedom as they should unless they delegate. They over-control people and that leads to stifling them versus blessing them.

My Fear

Fear causes us to miss opportunities. It limits the organization and its people. I remember a small business owner in the healthcare field who asked for my help. I was willing to help him. But, he was so fear-prone he would not show me the depth and breadth of information I needed to help, so I never did. He missed out on the advantage of what could have come from our interaction and my help if he had not been so motivated by fear.

Otherwise good managers and supervisors take on the fear-based characteristics of their leaders and start using the same tactics. This creates an entire culture of fear in the organization. The morale of employees goes down. Health issues and interpersonal relationship issues with regard to teamwork and conflict go up. Turnover increases. More mistakes are made because of the tension and lack of teamwork and creativity. The experience for the employees is anything but a blessing. It's a toxic environment. We have too many of these in business, government, non-profit organizations, churches, and ministries.

FEAR/FAITH FORMULA

Talent/experience + effort + fear or faith + obedience = result

Most executives I know are extremely talented, have lots of experience, and work really hard. The key difference I see in long term results of their leadership and life is how much they are obedient in fear versus how much they are obedient in faith.

Scripture says it's impossible to please God without faith. Throughout Scripture, we see the devastating effects of fear. The children of Israel did not get to enter the Promised Land because of fear. We are told not to be fearful or to be anxious more times in the Bible than any other command. Scripture says the mind set on the spirit brings life, and the mind set on the flesh brings death. This is talking about spiritual life and spiritual death, but, as a practical matter, it has a broader application. The mind set on fear is worrisome and ages, which results in a

There is no trust in fear based cultures.

loss of health and in even physical death or an earlier physical death. The mind set on faith is optimistic, peaceful, encouraged, and is much healthier and typically lives longer. The mind set on fear sees the negative and loses opportunities, or in other words sees the death of opportunity. The mind set on faith is discerning and gives life to many opportunities. The mind set on fear sees the death of relationships. The mind set on faith sees the birth of many new relationships.

I'm familiar with a consulting firm that charges a large monthly retainer fee to executives. I spent two hours talking to them one day trying to understand what they did. They didn't seem to be organizational gurus or have any special technical area of expertise. Finally, I asked them, "So, what do you really do?" They said, "We help executives have the courage to act." I thought there had to be more to it than that. I thought executives simply wouldn't pay that much money every month for that one thing.

I later ran across a friend who was a client of this firm. I asked him about it, and he said these men had come along at a time when he was making very trying decisions, and they helped him through the process. He did, in fact, pay them to help him have the courage to act. As I thought more about this, I realized that much of my career one of my key motivators was reacting to my fears rather than to my faith. As I mentor and coach men, many are substantially hindered in realizing their potential and that of their organization because they are handicapped by fear. Again, "do not fear or be anxious" is one of the most common commands in Scripture for a reason.

So, what about you? Are you moving forward in faith, or are you being held back by your fears? It is impossible to please God without faith.

Fear is the opposite of faith and is something that stops risk-taking in organizations. We should remember that in the parable of the talents, God reprimanded the steward who took no risk with what he had been given. Appropriate risk-taking with resources in organizations is a key to making progress.

Application

I. Do you know for sure what the real culture is in your organization? Have you asked your team or had it objectively assessed?

II. Do you have the culture in your organization that you want? Yes___No___

    A. If no, what specifically do you want it to be?

_____

_____

_____

    B. What do you perceive are the barriers to the culture you want?

_____

_____

_____

    C. Are there people on your leadership team exhibiting behavior that doesn't align with your values and that are impacting the culture?

    If yes, what will you do?

_____

_____

_____

_____

III. Do you tend to be fearful as a leader? Yes_____ No_____

V. PROGRESS

God expects us to make progress . . .

*Be transformed from "firefighting" and playing the "blame game"
to realizing and sharing steady progress.*

*"A wise man will hear and increase in learning,
and a man of understanding will acquire wise counsel."
Proverbs 1:4-6*

*"Without consultation, plans are frustrated,
but with many counselors they succeed."
Proverbs 15:22*

*"Where there is no guidance the people fall,
but in abundance of counselors there is victory."
Proverbs 11:14*

*"Therefore bear fruit in keeping with repentance."
Matthew 3:8*

*"Now these things happened as examples for us,
so that we would not crave evil things as they also craved."
1 Corinthians 10:6*

*"When the apostles returned,
they gave an account to Him of all they had done."
Luke 9:10*

*"So then each one of us will give an account of himself to God."
Romans 14:12*

Questions to Ponder

- Do you find yourself always fighting fires?

- Are you always "swinging for the fences" trying to hit a grand slam in your organization?

- Would you be content and relieved to have steady reliable progress in your organization without the significant ups and downs?

- Do your people know how they and the organization are doing at regular intervals?

Issues Covered in this Section

- The importance of proper planning.

- Leading change effectively.

- The importance of documentation and training.

- The components and value of control systems.

- The value of the measurement and feedback.

Chapter 23

PLANNING

> **Thought!**
> If you don't know where you are
> going, any path will take you there.
> Do you strongly desire progress, but have no plan for it?

"Declaring the end from the beginning, and from ancient times
the things which have not been done, saying,
'My purpose will be established,
and I will accomplish all my good pleasure.'"
Isaiah 46:10

"Your eyes have seen my unformed substance;

and in your book were written all the days that were dreamed for me,

when as yet there was not one of them."

Psalm 139:16

You are not going to create positive change without a plan. God planned everything before He created anything. Scripture says He knew your days before there was one of them (Psalms 139:16). One of the best examples I can think of to illustrate an effective planning process is found in the book of Nehemiah in the Old Testament. Nehemiah got every aspect of the planning process right. Outlined below is the process he used. It worked for him. And when I have had the presence of mind to follow the same process, it has worked for me.

Problem/opportunity — We see that Nehemiah's planning process started with a burden or a problem and an opportunity.

"They said to me, the remnant there in the providence who survived captivity are in great distress and reproach, and the wall of Jerusalem was broken down and its gates are burned with fire."

Nehemiah 1: 3

The passion in people rises when something makes them mad, glad, or sad.[1] We are glad when we see a great opportunity and thus begin planning to capitalize on it. In Nehemiah's case, he was sad, and God revealed to him an opportunity to do something about the situation.

Prayer — Nehemiah 1:4-6, says that he, "Sat down and wept and mourned for days; and was fasting and praying before the God of heaven." In his prayer time, he got perfectly aligned with God. He confessed his own sins and those of his people. Then, he was prepared to hear God's plan for him. Regardless of religious affiliation or spiritual background, most people pray. Usually, it's not *if* they pray; it's simply when and how they pray. Most people tend to get in a jam following their own plans and then begin to pray asking God to help them out. There is a reason the Proverbs say, "And lean not on your own understanding."

Then, there are those who think they are being spiritual by praying earlier in the process. The problem is they have already made up their mind and then simply are praying for God to bless their plans. That's not how Nehemiah prayed. He had a burden after hearing about what had happened to his home city of Jerusalem and took his burden before the Lord.

Prayer is where God reveals His plan to us. We like to talk about vision in organizational life. For the Christian, vision is really God's revelation of His plan and our involvement. Nehemiah had a vision for rebuilding the wall in Jerusalem, but that plan came from God, and Nehemiah was to have a leadership role in it. He was clear about the vision, his role in it, and God's alignment with it before he did anything else.

Preparation — Nehemiah thought and made preparations for what would be required next and for the questions that would be asked of him. Prayer was also part of his preparation. In Nehemiah 1:11, he prayed that God would give the king compassion to help him. Let's not take the prayer time of Nehemiah as he prepared lightly either. People who served the king in that day and were sad in the presence of the king were subject to dismissal from their role or even death for being unhappy around the king. Nehemiah prayed for the king's favor and showed his sadness in Nehemiah 2:1-2, "Now I had not been sad in his presence." So they said to me, "Why is your face sad though you are not sick? This is nothing but sadness of heart." Nehemiah told him why. The king said to him, "What would you request?" This is where preparation in prayer and good administrative thinking came in. Nehemiah said, "If it please the King, and if your servant has found favor before you, send me to Judah, to the city of my father's tombs, that I may rebuild it." Next is where his administrative thinking in advance came into play. The king asked, "How long will your journey be, and when will you return?" So it pleased the king to send him, and he gave the king a definite time. There was a lot involved in rebuilding the walls in Jerusalem. Nehemiah must have spent hours thinking and figuring how long this massive endeavor would take. Therefore, when asked, he had a sure and ready answer.

I have seen leaders make many mistakes in this area over the years. And I made my share as well. The first mistake is not being able to answer basic questions about the cost and timeline when you're asking permission to do a big project. Another mistake is under-resourcing a project. There is a tendency to want to lowball the cost and time required to increase the chances of getting approval for a project. This usually comes back to bite you in the end when you have to go back and ask for more resources. It's harder to get them after you miss your initial estimates and don't live up to your commitments versus how hard it would've been to request more in the beginning.

I think the biggest single mistake I see people make in organizational life is the tendency to systemically over-promise and under-deliver. We had an initiative in Physician Services once where we had started small and spread the initiative through several hospitals and divisions. The concept had been sufficiently tested and proven so we were asking the CEO for funding to expand the initiative. We had worked for weeks on the business plan, and the team anticipated a $200 million measurable benefit over five years to the company. I looked at the business plans and thought the results were achievable if everything went right, but there was not much margin for error, and some of the results were based on what I considered soft measures. I asked the team to cut the measurable benefit in the projections to $100 million. The team asked me why. I said, "Let's think through this. If we promise $200 million in benefits and deliver $150 million, are you going to get an 'atta boy' for the $150 million or criticized for the $50 million miss? By contrast, if we promise a $100 million benefit and deliver $150 million in benefit, how do you think that will be received? Which position would you prefer to be in?" The team got the point and quickly agreed to make the changes.

The discussion didn't end there though. I explained there was more to my thinking. If I let the discussion stop there, they might have been left with the impression that the goal on an initiative is to "sandbag" the results. That wasn't my intent at all. I brought up several things that could happen and would be barriers to the $200 million projection and asked if we had contingency plans to fill gaps. I asked if anybody thought the soft numbers in the projections would be attacked by some of the senior executives in the boardroom when we went for approval. Scripture tells us to "build on the solid rock" (Matthew 7:24-27). I know the Scriptures are talking about building something solid spiritually. But I do think there is a practical application of that spiritual principle. Build on what is solid.

Take Note for the Sell

I've seen many times people going to meetings with seven justifications for a project. The first four are rock solid and what I call "no-brainers." The last three are potential benefits but more questionable with the last one being a bit of a stretch. Rather than going for the easy win, putting the four concrete justifications out and stopping at that for approval, I've seen many times where projects were not approved or were delayed because of the ensuing discussion over the less concrete benefits. I counseled the team to build on what was rock solid so that we did not risk losing credibility over things that could be seen by others as a bit of a stretch, even if we believed we were right.

You remember the principle from Scripture of "going the extra mile." This is where Jesus taught people to do more than what they were required by law to do. An extension of this foundational principle is doing more than what you promised to do. People who systemically over-promise and under-deliver are not seen as trustworthy, even though they may deliver some substantial results over time.

When we got to the boardroom on this initiative, the team was well prepared, and it went pretty much as we had anticipated. After substantial discussion with people trying to poke holes in the projections without success, the company CEO asked a question. He turned and looked me straight in the eye and said, "Leon, how sure are you about this $100 million in benefits?" Because the team had prepared so well and we had only left in the projections what we knew was solid, I was able to look him in the eye and say with a great deal of confidence, "I have a 95% confidence level in that number and the fact it is likely conservative. How many times in the past have I told you we could do something that we didn't deliver on or exceed?" He said, "$100 million over five years is enough for me. Does anybody else have any questions?" Of course, there were none, and our initiative was approved.

Anticipate obstacles — This is another important thing Nehemiah did that many leaders overlook. In Nehemiah 2:7-8, we see this. "And I said to the King, 'If it please the King, let letters be given me for the governors of the provinces beyond the river, that they may allow me to pass through until I come to Judah, and a letter to Asaph, the keeper of the King's forest, that he may give me timber to make beams for the gates of the fortress which is by the Temple, for the wall of the city and for the house to which I will go.'" Often, leaders make plans and do not anticipate issues that can arise from their decisions. Thus, they wind up spending enormous amounts of time solving unintended consequences they helped create by inadequate planning.

Establish priorities — Any good plan must have clear priorities. We see later in Nehemiah, Chapter 2, that he went out at night and inspected the wall. What was he doing? He was continuing his thinking and preparation process, and now he was thinking about priorities.

Engage the right people — I noticed that Nehemiah only took a few men with him. He said, "I did not tell anyone what God was putting into my mind to do for Jerusalem." He apparently only took a few men who were most trustworthy and could help the most in planning this massive project. Engaging the right people is critical for any leader. When Jethro was advising Moses to engage other leaders and share the load with them, he advised Moses to find trustworthy leaders, and he gave several criteria for what that entailed (Exodus 18:21). In First Kings 12:6, we see the young and new King Rehoboam as he consulted two groups of people. He asked the elders who had served his father, Solomon, what to do. They said "If you will be a servant to this people today, and will serve them and grant them their petition, and speak good words to them, then they will be your servant forever." Sadly for him, he did not listen to their counsel. Instead, he went to the young men who grew up with him. They asked him to make it even harder on people and to show his leadership by abusive strength and not by service or kindness. Because of his harsh response to people, most of them quit following him and rejected him as king. Engaging the right people and listening to them is a key characteristic of any successful leader.

Engage people properly — People's personality profiles are a huge driver in what they contribute to the team effort and in how to properly engage them. You may recall our discussion from Section II of this book about how to engage the various personality profiles. The dominant profile is going to speak quickly, make decisions quickly, and want to take control. Once a project is well planned, it's fine for that person to be the project coordinator. The influencer personalities are going to speak quickly and often and are willing to promote the project and care for the people aspects of the initiative. The steady personalities are going to be responsible for doing much of the work, they know how to do the work, and are great team members. They do not speak up as quickly. Therefore, you must create a comfortable forum to provide their input or ask for it directly and encourage them to share their perspective. The compliant or cautious personalities are going to think of detailed questions to ask and issues that could arise that nobody else is thinking about. They also are generally going to be hesitant to speak up. But it's critical that their insights be sought and listened to. A great number of mistakes can be avoided by listening to these people. Also, often times, they are able to improve upon already good ideas. Leaders without training or perspective on the unique personality profiles of their team are going to have a difficult time engaging people the right way.

Cast the vision — In Nehemiah 2: 17, he said, "You see the bad situation we are in, that Jerusalem is desolate and its gates burned by fire. Come, let us rebuild the wall of Jerusalem so that we will no longer be a reproach." You notice that Nehemiah said that they were in a bad situation. He could have talked from the perspective that the people were in a mess and he was there to save them. Yet, he did not elevate himself above the people or criticize them for their role in this situation. Before he left his great job to come help out, he had prayed, confessing his own sins and those of the people resulting in these circumstances. He opened up and shared his heart with the people. "I told them how the hand of my God had been favorable to me and also about the King's words which he had spoken to me" (Nehemiah 2:18). What is he doing here? He's encouraging the people that they have God's support and the king's support to undertake this great project.

Share the vision — In verse 18, we see the response of the people as they said, "Let us arise and build." It's critical that we do not miss the fact that this vision is not something Nehemiah dreamed up on his own. It was what God put in his heart to do. He did articulate the vision and encourage the people. But he did it in a way that inspired them, and it became a shared vision because they said "Let us arise and build." Many leaders would ride into town like a new sheriff calling attention to themselves, assigning blame and criticizing others, barking out orders, and expecting compliance. That was not Nehemiah's way at all. He came as a servant. He did not demand any of the rights he had as governor, and he shared the vision with the people in a way that they owned it and were excited about it.

Share the work — Nehemiah led the work, but people did the work. You notice, however, that people did the work they volunteered for and most wanted to do. Nehemiah was a very astute leader. We notice in Nehemiah Chapter 3 that most of the people rebuilt the wall in front of their house. When Nehemiah let people rebuild the wall in front of their house, they were doing the portion of the work that they actually cared about the most, and they did it with great care and enthusiasm.

Application

I. Does your planning process start with prayer?

_____

II. Do you look forward to anticipate unintended consequences?

_____

 III. Do you engage the right people in the planning process?

_____

IV. Do you engage them in the right way—considering their personality profiles?

_____

V. Is the final vision a shared vision?

_____

Notes

Chapter 24

YOU CAN'T MAKE PROGRESS "FIGHTING FIRES"

> **Thought!**
> Have you ever wondered how much you could get done
> if you weren't "putting out fires" all the time?

"Without consultation, plans are frustrated,

but with many counselors they succeed."

Proverbs 15:22

Right

Ask people if they like change. Some will say yes, others say no, and others will say it depends. Some personality styles tend to like change. Some are more comfortable with the status quo. But, we know that people want progress. They expect to do better next year than they did this year. How is that possible if the organization doesn't make progress? So, what are the keys to making progress?

AVOID "FIRE FIGHTING"

"Now these things happened as examples for us,

so that we would not crave evil things as they also craved."

1 Corinthians 10:6

One of the key things my internal audit experience taught me was the importance of anticipating and trying to eliminate problems. My experience is that really good control systems are proactive and offer early warnings so that more substantial problems are anticipated. Making progress in organizations is like making money in your investment portfolio. The first rule is: preserve capital. The second rule is: preserve capital. And, the third rule is: don't forget rules number one and two. Stated more plainly, the first rule of making money is to not lose money. Don't go backwards.

You will never make it to the top of the mountain if you keep stumbling and falling back down.

In organizations, it's like the picture of climbing a mountain. You can only get to the top if you don't stumble and fall to the bottom. It kind of reminds me of professional sports. So here's the question for you sports fans. How many professional games are won versus how many are lost? Here is what I mean. Sometimes, a team goes on the field and plays a superior game defeating an able opponent. They won! Yet, frequently games are decided by one team committing more fatal errors than the other. In football, you see excessive penalties that cause the loss of games. Sometimes, the penalties aren't even close to where the ball was and were completely unnecessary. Sometimes, it's a dropped pass that hits the receiver in the chest and should have been easily caught. Sometimes, it's a missed tackle that is basic. Sometimes, it's the missed field goal.

Sometimes, it's a busted play where the receiver turned in the wrong direction. Sometimes, it's a breakdown in the defense coverage. The list goes on and on. My point is, I've seen more professional football games lost due to fundamental errors than I have seen won due to superior playing.

Basic errors often cause teams to lose.

I see the same thing in basketball. I've seen national championship games lost because of a very low shooting percentage from the free-throw line. Games sometimes are decided by missed lay-ups, unnecessary fouls, or technical fouls due to unnecessary flaring tempers.

Consistency

You may say, "What does this have to do with organizations?" Everything! I see the same thing in business and other organizations. We tend to have a behavioral syndrome in organizations because of our high ego needs. Our goals seem to be oriented toward hitting a homerun, the grand slam versus consistently getting singles with no errors. How many times have we seen large, well-established businesses go bankrupt because of substantial errors? Their business models were not flawed. Their employees were good and talented. But someone, usually the leadership, makes a mistake that takes the company down.

Everyone hitting a single is going to win nearly every game. <u>Occasionally</u>, you may win because of a "grand slam."

The first key to getting ahead is: Don't go backwards. Avoiding errors, anticipating unintended consequences, and being proactive are the keys to not going backward.

The first key to making progress is don't go backward.

I dealt with a handful of turnaround situations in my career. I called these "firefighting" situations.

It's hard to get ahead in organizational life when you're fighting fires all the time.

The organizations spent so much time dealing with problems. The people worked extremely hard but couldn't make any progress. The natural tendency of leaders is just to work harder to put out the fires and try to eke out some progress. My approach was to triage the fires.

Metaphorically speaking, I first determined if it was a gas fire, wood fire, or brush fire. Gas fires cannot be put out by pouring water on them. Organizationally, these are the types of fires that don't go away with just more time and energy. They arise from systemic problems just like a gas fire has to be put out by cutting off the gas. The source of the problems has to be identified and stopped. This is one of the most important things a leader can do in a turn-around situation— identifying and stopping systemic problems.

Next, I identified the wood burning fires. These fires are very hot and will "burn the house down." They are worth the time and energy to put out in an organization and are a high priority.

The brush fires will burn themselves out without much damage if left alone. There are some problems in an organization that are isolated and will go away if left alone.

When I went into turnaround situations, I used a consistent approach to work through them. First, I distinguished between the small fires and the big fires. When you focus on priorities, you realize that some small fires will burn out, but the big fires will "burn the house down." I also learned some small fires will become big fires and "burn the house down." So, you focus on the root cause issues and take action on those things that are causing the big fires. It's always been my experience that it takes far less time to anticipate a problem than it does to fix a problem. Also, a lot of the problems in organizations are systemic. If you don't get to the root cause, they will happen repeatedly, consuming enormous time. My experience as an internal auditor taught me to look for systemic problems versus isolated ones.

Fixing the root cause on big problems is the first thing that will free up a lot of time in a "fire-fighting" organization. Then, you take time and put out the smaller fires that have the potential to become really big fires—wood burning fires. That saves another big block of time down the road. Understand that in the meantime, some of the smaller fires will have burned out by themselves—brush fires.

After the fires are extinguished, you can take that time and spend it on something productive and move the organization forward.

When I went to Physician Services, the first year was spent taking action to prevent big fires and putting out the major fires. It was the second year when we began to make progress.

Many otherwise good leaders significantly underestimate the importance of anticipating outcomes and avoiding unintended consequences. Look at the big oil company, British Petroleum (BP). A problem that never should have occurred and would have cost very little to have avoided cost the company billions of dollars. Or look at Exxon with the Valdez spill. This was a completely avoidable problem that caused the organization billions of dollars to solve.

So much focus is put on moving ahead that sometimes little attention is paid to those things that will move us backward. Let's think about some practical areas where we overlook opportunities to anticipate problems.

THE MOST COMMON AREAS WHERE LEADERS NEED TO ANTICIPATE PROBLEMS

#1 Personnel selection

Having the right people in place is critical to the success of an organization. Yet, many organizations have poor hiring practices. Many leaders are not well trained in handling the interview process. Often, candidates are not vetted well enough. It's not uncommon for organizations to hire people, have problems with them, and find out the same problems existed with previous employers. It would have cost the organization far less to find that out on the front end and not hire the person than discovering the same information later.

*"Furthermore, you shall select
out of all the people able men who fear God,
men of truth, those who hate dishonest gain;
and you shall place these over them as leaders."
Exodus 18:21*

Many organizations do not use personality profiles as a tool to understand the strengths and weaknesses of candidates they are looking at. Because they won't spend the time or money on perfectly good tools, they don't hire the best people for the job. Maybe the people do not fail, but they're not the best match for the job. There is still an opportunity cost involved.

Not taking the time in the recruiting process to get the best people is a very common area where organizations fail to avoid serious problems.

#2 Communications

Have the courage to call

The second biggest problem I see repeated, especially in larger organizations, is the failure to communicate proactively. And, it's so easy for this to happen. You're really busy. Your gut tells you that you should call certain individuals and give them a heads up or see what they think before you take action. But you think "It's my decision to make, and I don't have time." You move forward and people are upset or a mistake is made. The phone call to inform people or ask a question usually would have taken only 10-25% the amount of time it takes to smooth this over now that it's a problem. You multiply this several times a day, and you see the impact of failure to be good at proactive communications.

#3 Mismatched goals

Alignment of the goals between individuals in the organization and between departments/functions in the organization is key to progress. When the organization has one set of goals and the individuals have different goals, what happens? The individual goals win out in the short-term and may hurt the overall organization.

"For he who is not against us is for us."

Mark 9:40

"Choose for yourselves today whom ye will serve..."

Joshua 24:15

Individuals pursuing their own goals is not something that should be a surprise to leaders. Following our human nature, we are inherently self-focused. As the preachers say, there's an "I" in the middle of sin. It's something that you can count on.

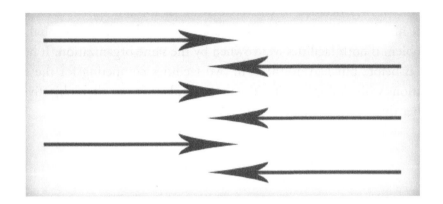

Organizational Goals   Individual Goals

We don't seem to be going in the same direction.

To ensure right fit, communication must be consistent

Aligning people with the mission, values, vision, priorities, and accountability is key. [2] Any time this is not done well, individuals are going to pursue their own goals. That's why this exercise on an annual basis is so critical. It's also why checking priorities between the leaders and employees throughout the year is critical to see that they're aligned.

When individuals don't agree with the goals of the organization, at a minimum they don't pursue them aggressively. At the extreme, they work consciously or maybe subconsciously against them.

People need to be working toward a common goal for the cooperation and success in organizational life.

COMPETITION WITHIN YOUR OWN TEAM

Even in facilities owned by the same company, there is often competition versus cooperation. I remember a hospital system that owned several hospitals in a major market. One of the hospitals had 90% of the obstetrics (OB) market share. Another hospital nearby decided this was a good, profitable business. They decided to convert existing space and started an OB program. After some time, the first hospital had 50% of the market share. The second hospital had 40% market share. The problem is both facilities were owned by the same organization. It had the same 90% market share as before but had overhead in two facilities competing for the same patients. In large organizations with multiple units, it takes good planning to align objectives so that entities cooperate rather than compete with one another.

RECRUITING PHYSICIANS

When I led Physician Services at HCA, we created regional recruiting offices. One of the benefits of the regional offices was the ability to plan the recruiting efforts with the maximum opportunity to sign a physician in our system while minimizing the expense. Information was gathered regarding the physicians' geographic preferences, and they were sometimes flown to an area with five company-owned hospitals. They might have had an interest in opportunities available in three different HCA-owned hospitals. With one trip, the company was able to let the physician evaluate three different openings and align them with the one that best suited them. This increased the chances of being able to recruit the physician to an HCA hospital, and it minimized expenses by accomplishing three interviews in one trip.

Before this system was created, the three hospitals with physician needs might use different recruiting firms to meet their recruiting needs. Therefore, a physician was flown in by the recruiting firm to visit one hospital. Sometimes, the recruiting firms used also recruited for the competition. There could be times when the physician visited an HCA hospital and that of a competitor with HCA paying the expenses. The new model eliminated all that. So, you would think everyone would be delighted.

Yet, there was a fair amount of conflict at times over this model. Hospital "A" didn't care about the needs of hospital "B." They didn't care that hospital "B" might be the best fit for that physician, upping the chances of signing the physician and keeping him for the long-term. They were interested in signing the physician at their facility. You see, the goals were not sufficiently aligned within a market to encourage cooperation among hospitals versus competition. In large organizations, there is competition among departments, operating units, and individuals all the time. It takes great diligence in the planning process to minimize it.

CONFLICTING GOALS BETWEEN THE CORPORATE DEPARTMENTS AND THE OPERATING FACILITIES

I remember a particular time when the company went through a major computer conversion. The information technology teams were incentivized based on the number of conversions accomplished during the year. I was in internal audit at the time and raised questions about the quality of conversions. I believed if conversions were not handled well, it would impact the revenue cycle and increase bad debts. The company had just been through a major merger, and the individuals making these monumental decisions had never seen computer conversions on that scale. I wasn't able to get my message across.

After six months, the revenue cycle had been so impacted and bad debts had increased so much in converted facilities, it was impacting the results for the entire company, and the conversions were halted until the quality dimensions could be covered. It is very common in large organizations for departments and operating units to have goals not well thought out that can hurt the operating units and even the entire company. It often takes better planning than exists in even sophisticated organizations to make sure there's well thought out alignment among goals to limit sub-optimization.

I have a friend who buys distressed companies, turns them around, and eventually sells them. Frequently, these are subsidiaries within larger companies. Many times these subsidiaries are not doing well because they do not receive the appropriate focus and attention. Their goals are not aligned with that of the bigger organization enough to make a meaningful contribution. Therefore, it is better for the organization to spin them out than to keep them.

> **Bless the team through aligning goals.**

Employees can have a great deal of fun and fulfillment in organizations where goals are clear, consistent with their talents and passions, and well aligned. This blesses the employees and brings productivity to the organization. When this doesn't exist, employees are stressed, confused, non-productive, and uncommitted. If you want to bless employees and have a productive organization, make sure goals are aligned.

> **Realign goals with accountability systems when change occurs.**

It is easy, especially in large organizations, to set up financial incentive systems and be too slow to change them as the environment changes. In the healthcare system, the ability to measure the quality of the care and the payment mechanisms to incentivize hospitals for improving quality of care began changing. This particular system had many incentives for their leaders based on the financial results for the year. In meetings and speeches, the CEO kept focusing on quality results. Professionals were hired to help improve quality of care. But, things seemed to change very little. The year this organization changed its financial incentives for all its leaders to include improvement in the quality scores at the hospitals, there was a marked improvement.

This is a great reminder to leaders. When the environment changes, you have to change the accountability structure for your team in order to get a different result. Simply talking about it, saying you want to see something different, criticizing people for not changing, and even threatening to do something if there's no change, doesn't do anything. When you change the accountability system to line up with the goals, behavior starts to change quickly.

The Key to Avoiding a "Firefighting" Culture – Listening

It's obvious that not going backward is critical in organizational life. So, how do we make sure we don't go backward? Listening to other people is key in this process.

> *"Without consultation, plans are frustrated,*
>
> *but with many counselors, they succeed."*
>
> *Proverbs 15:22*

Different personality profiles see different slices of the world. Some tend to see the opportunities. Some tend to see the impact on people. Others tend to be implementers and see the practical steps to make something work. They will also see when something will not work. Some personalities will tend to see the pitfalls. They will also tend to improve upon the idea. When you get all these perspectives involved in solving the problem or creating a plan, you have much greater chances of moving forward without creating more problems to be solved down the road. One of the challenges in organizations is that the aggressive, risk-taking personalities don't like to seek and listen to the advice of the more process-oriented personalities that could help them avoid pitfalls. This is exacerbated by the fact that the people who understand the process best and are most capable of improving it tend not to speak up until asked. The aggressive types often dismiss the wise counsel of these individuals should they volunteer advice.

THE CEO WHO LISTENED

I'm thinking of different CEOs I've seen in operation. One had the best vision and was perhaps the most gifted intellectually that I had ever encountered. I can think of numerous times when people offered dissenting views, but he was right. Yet, there were a couple of areas where people tried to give him counsel, and he refused to listen.

> *"Before destruction the heart of man is haughty,*
>
> *but humility goes before honor."*
>
> *Proverbs 18:12*

They were pretty fundamental areas, but he continued down the same path. He eventually lost his job as CEO. This man was no doubt the hardest working CEO I had ever met. He was also one of the smartest people I've ever met. Yet, he lost his job primarily because he reached a point where he no longer valued other people's perspectives.

I contrast this CEO with another CEO. He was also exceptionally talented. Yet, for important decisions, he consulted more people than anyone I've ever experienced. Also, when he wasn't solving problems, he still asked people he met in the organization for their perspective. From the executive suite to the boiler room in the basement, he asked for people's opinions and really listened to them. His knowledge was so strengthened by multiple perspectives that there was never a big mistake made on his watch.

INDIVIDUAL APPLICATION

Anticipating problems is critical in leaders' personal lives as well as their organization. In fact, many organizational problems result from poor personal choices. What are some of the areas that cause individuals problems that shipwreck careers and affect organizations? Just like King David's affair affected the kingdom of Israel, affairs in organizational life cause leaders to fail and affect their organizations negatively.

Another example is excessive drinking or drugs. A number of careers of up-and-coming executives have been derailed by getting drunk at the wrong function or by becoming addicted and causing a crash in their personal life, also diminishing their career.

Another example is being a workaholic. Family is ignored, resulting in divorce which impacts the person's whole life, including the organization. Often, in smaller privately owned organizations, a divorce can ruin the business.

Application

I. What are the three potential problems that could cause your organization to fail?

1._____
2._____
3._____

II. What do you struggle with personally that could cause you to fail?

1._____
2._____
3._____

III. Do you do a good job:

- Selecting people?

- Communicating proactively?

What do you need to change?

_____
_____
_____
_____

IV. Are there departments or teams in your organization that tend to compete or fight with each other vs. cooperating with each other?

Are their goals and incentives aligned? Yes_____ No_____

If no, what will you change?

_____

_____

_____

_____

V. Do you get the perspective of others before making major decisions? Yes_____ No_____

If no, what will you do in the future?

_____

_____

_____

_____

Notes

Chapter 25

YOU CAN'T MAKE PROGRESS STANDING STILL!

> Thought!
> What potential are you giving up by not
> being proactive in leading change?

" . . . but one thing I do:

forgetting what lies behind

and reaching forward to what lies ahead."

Philippians 3:13

Vision Def.

Dick Wells, author of *Sixteen Stones*, says the difference between your present position and your vision is the change that is necessary to achieve your desired future. One thing we all deal with in organizational life is change. My experience has been that the initial reaction to change is either skepticism or outright resistance unless people are already clamoring for change. Some leaders avoid making changes until they have to because of the tendency of some people not to like change.

Auditors tend to be more comfortable with the status quo. I would get some resistance every year when we did our plans and plotted changes. I would ask, "Do you want a year with no change?" Most of them said yes. I said "Are you sure?" And they said, "Yes." I said, "Let me remind you, no change means no compensation increases, or promotions." They quickly said, "No, we want *those* changes."

The Reason to grow profits

I applied the idea to the broader company showing that if we didn't change anything to continue to grow profits, there would not be money for merit or promotional increases. When the team understood that change was necessary for progress, they were open to the change.

LEADER'S ROLE IN CHANGE PROCESS

A critical role of leadership in an organization is to lead the change efforts. It can be frustrating because it's not easy. It tends to cause tension, and many times the improvement sought is not achieved. So, why is there so much tension and resistance if change is necessary for progress, and people tend to want progress?

CHANGE IS UNCOMFORTABLE AND INEFFICIENT

Change isn't comfortable for many people. It's especially uncomfortable for certain personality types that do a lot of the work in organizations. Plus, change is initially inefficient. You may ask how change can lead to progress if it's inefficient. Change is like taking one step backward and two steps forward. In fact, that would be the picture of a successful change. An unsuccessful change would be two steps backward and one step forward. A neutral change would be one step backward and one step forward.

1 step back and 2 forward = Good change

1 step back and 1 forward = Neutral

2 steps back and 1 forward = Bad change

Leaders often have new ideas for improvement. It's very clear to them that the change will be an improvement over the old way of doing things. They get excited about the impact of their new idea. It's such a good idea that they actually forget some people tend not to like change. Then, when people *don't* wholeheartedly embrace the change, they get upset.

Leaders need to remember that even good changes take a while for people to adapt to. Remember the children of Israel in the Bible. Moses led them out of slavery, and they were now free people. What did they do almost immediately? They began to complain. There were aspects of their enslaved lives that they remembered and missed. Even though the change was positive, living through the change seemed hard.

It's common to see this related to computer conversions. People will beg and almost cry for better technology. The new software is implemented. Now, the screens and reports don't look the same. Even though they may be better, it takes longer to do what the employees used to do. It's not long before people are literally crying and wishing they had the old system back.

DON'T SEE THE NEED

Often, leaders simply don't see the need for change. I remember as an auditor asking questions about how things were done at various operating units. One of the most common responses was, "Well, we've always done it that way." Consultants hear that a lot. "We've always done it that way and its worked fine so far, so why should we change it?"

The reason it should be changed is because it can be a lot better, but that is often hard to see. When we create things and refine them over time, we tend to think that we've made it as good as it can be. It takes a fresh look to see things from a different perspective. I learned this when I got opportunities to lead new departments or functions at HCA. I looked and asked questions and saw certain potential changes for improvement. They were just obvious to me. I did not create any of the processes. I had not hired any of the people. So I could just see things very objectively and spot needed changes.

My ability to see opportunities for improvement only lasted one or two years though. After that period of time, I had created and refined enough things and formed an affinity to the team so that it was hard for me to see what needed to change. Then, I would have to get the perspective of other people through paid consultants or the advice of other people in the company further removed from what I was doing.

I use the analogy of people standing next to their house with their noses pressed against the window. When you're in that position, you can't tell what the front of the house looks like or see if there are bricks falling off the house. Yet, perfect strangers who know nothing about your house and have never seen it before can stand in the driveway and have a broader view. They can spot obvious things that you're unable to see from your perspective. Sometimes, organizations need consultants for their specialized expertise. However, often consultants simply come in with an objective perspective and gather information objectively that the leader did not have time to gather, summarize, and give to the leadership.

But is objectivity the ideal?

I could see things much more objectively when I was given the opportunity to lead new functions. I did not know the history of the people. I had not implemented processes, policies, or procedures. I was able to look at everything without any emotional attachment. But, after a year or two, I would lose my objectivity.

There is a great tendency for leaders in large matrix organizations to want to own and control their own back-office functions. I remember having this mentality. Then one day, my boss wisely asked me the question, "Is the time and energy you spend on these back-office functions worth that much of your attention versus the strategic decisions you need to be making?" I quickly said no and began the process of turning those functions over to the matrixed organization.

There is a great benefit to making small strategic changes over time. There is less risk of failure in making the change. But sometimes the biggest risk is not making a big change. Sometimes, big opportunities come along or the big problem shows up and small changes are not enough. Sometimes, we are faced with making a major change for a strategic opportunity that will not present itself again or solving a problem that has the potential to severely damage the organization.

FEAR OF FAILURE

Often, leaders hesitate to make strategic changes they believe will be beneficial for the future of their organization, but since there is the risk of immediate failure and criticism, they will defer making a change until they feel they have no choice. I have personally hesitated to make tough personnel changes and other changes I knew needed to be made because I was not feeling any pressure with the status quo and knew there was risk of criticism if I made a change and was wrong or didn't execute it well. We shouldn't underestimate the fear and doubt that leaders often experience in making changes of substance. It didn't get easier with time or experience for me. The more success we have, the more it seems we are unwilling to risk any of our reputation on making an important but risky change when we have another choice.

HOW NOT TO LEAD CHANGE

First, let me tell you what doesn't work. Early in my career, I had just assumed leadership responsibilities for the internal audit department at HCA. The culture, the processes, and the results all needed to change. The department needed to gain more credibility, and it needed to happen within the next year. I locked myself away in my office for a few days, including some weekend time. I came up with goals that I saw as critical to what we needed to accomplish in the next year.

I called a meeting of my direct reports and proudly laid out the goals and initiatives that we would need to accomplish. I waited for my team to respond, expecting them to be impressed with the thoroughness of my work, the soundness of the plans, and have a great deal of appreciation for the fact that I figured all this out for the team without making them do it. It seems so foolish now, but I was genuinely surprised at their near rebellion. It wasn't that they didn't think the plans were good; they were simply overwhelmed by them. Being a new leader, I did the only thing I could think of. I retreated!

OK, I'd like to hear your ideas now.

I asked them what they thought were the most important changes we needed to make. They told me. I asked them what we could get done in the next month. We wrote them down and agreed. I asked which of those changes we could make in the next week. We wrote those down and agreed. We did this every week for a month and, at the end of the month, had accomplished more than we thought we could do that first month.

A Good Weekly Meeting

We went through the process for another month. We made plans weekly and monitored progress. At the end of the second month, we had accomplished more that we had targeted for the month.

Now I could see the team was getting momentum. So, we tried the same process, but this time we set goals for the next three months. We monitored progress monthly. At the end of three months, we had exceeded the goals we set. We continued to do this for the balance of the year. At the end of the year, we had accomplished more than the goals and initiatives that I had initially outlined.

THE KEYS TO LEADING CHANGE

Involve the team

One of the first keys is that people like to have a say in change that affects them. We all know that from our own personal experience. They're much more accepting of change they help plan. Nehemiah was masterful at this. When they have input and involvement in making the plans and setting the deadlines, people feel ownership and commitment that doesn't exist when plans are simply announced. Plus, you usually avoid a lot of unintended consequences, or you get better ideas by having them involved. Remember, the "S" and "C" temperaments are going to see unintended consequences that the "D" and "I" temperaments don't.

We can take a cue from Jesus. He wants to change our life and change it radically. Yet, in Revelation 3:20, we read, "Behold I stand at the door and knock. If any man will open it, I will come in…" Think about this. If the creator of our universe waits for an invitation to come in and change us, shouldn't we think long and hard about forcing people to change? It's much better to invite and lead change than to force it.

Goals the team believes are achievable

The next key was to set goals that everyone thought were achievable. The team was simply overwhelmed with the goals that I laid out for the year. By contrast, Nehemiah only asked the people to build the wall six inches per day.[3] Time proved that my plans were achievable because we achieved even more. But it was more than the team could absorb at the time. People's experiences and personality profiles determine the timeframes in which new changes need to be accomplished. Some personalities can get overwhelmed. Others tend to set goals too high. Some leaders, knowing that people tend to fight change, assume the only way or best way to make it is to force it and get it over with. That does work sometimes, but you always pay a price for it, and it's very risky. You don't know how people will respond. Sometimes, a forced change at work is the "straw that broke the camel's back." They have accumulated a lot of baggage and pent up emotions. When team members respond differently than usual to any pressure or even perceived threat to them, it's wise to quickly sit with them and try to understand what else is going on in their lives. Most of the time, I found their behavior or attitude was driven by something else going on in their lives other than the work circumstances. By understanding that, we can avoid damaging some relationships and downstream problems in our organization.

Share the credit

I noticed in the eighth chapter of Nehemiah that after the project was completed, he called a great gathering of the people. Yet, unlike many leaders who would call such a gathering and take credit for success and maybe share some of the credit with their key leaders, Nehemiah brought no attention to himself at all. Rather, he put the priests in charge of the event. They celebrated their success. Nehemiah acknowledged the work of every group of people. He didn't brag on the top performers. He acknowledged the amount of work they did, and he didn't criticize the ones who did the least. Rather, he acknowledged what they did to contribute to the success of the whole project. Nehemiah didn't take any of the credit. He didn't seek the approval or accolades of the people. He only asked for one thing. He asked God to remember his service and sacrifice.

THE MUSTARD SEED AND LEAVEN (YEAST) APPROACH TO CHANGE

God's approach to making change is quite simple. From the parable of the mustard seed, in Matthew 13:31, we see the importance of starting small and letting something grow over time. From the parable of the leaven, in Matthew 13:34, we see the importance of growth or change at a steady, measured pace. Remember Nehemiah again. He only asked the people to build six inches of wall per day.

WHY DON'T LEADERS START SMALL AND GROW AT A MEASURED PACE?

It seemed like such a simple principle. So why don't people do it? Well, there are several reasons:

1. Pride

Politicians could make dramatic changes over five, ten, and fifteen year periods if they used a biblical approach to change. So, why don't they? It's very simple. Pride! Politicians want to be known for some spectacular bill so that they can go down in history and maybe have something named

I'm not for off...

II

after them. Working with the team to accomplish smaller results over a longer period of time that don't draw any fanfare is not attractive to them.

"Before destruction, the heart of man is haughty,

but humility goes before honor."

Proverbs 18:12

Even as I write this book, our nation is in a terrible mess. The politicians hold to their extreme positions to please voters and, therefore, take no action. There are many things that both political parties could agree upon that would be good for the nation and could be enacted immediately. Yet, they refuse to compromise and take a measured approach.

There is an old saying, "It's amazing what you can get accomplished when you don't care who gets the credit." We can see the truth of this in politics for certain. And it's true in business too. Corporate departments work against each other based on pride and ego rather than for the good of the whole organization because they want to control what happens and be able to take credit.

Churches, ministries, and non-profit organizations aren't exempt from this either. Seldom do they try to make small changes. Instead, they create big initiatives and programs. Often, the motives are pure, but not always. Sometimes, the leaders are seeking recognition.

2. Fear

A long-time, very successful executive coach recently told me that the greatest barrier to success he saw in the life of executives was having the courage to act. They knew what they should do but were afraid to do it. This really struck a chord with me. I can think of numerous times that I knew what to do but didn't act or delayed taking action because of fear. I see the same thing often in others. They know what's right but want to play it politically safe versus speaking up and taking the lead in something that won't be popular. By the way, we talked about pride first and then fear. They are actually two sides of the same coin. Our pride causes us not to take risk because we fear failure and loss of reputation and status in our organizations.

3. Procrastination

Let's face it; leaders have enough going on every day. Often, they find themselves just trying to keep up. The thought of doing more, the resistance they will deal with, the risk of failing with change, and so on makes procrastination very easy. So what happens? Because changes are not planned and implemented systematically through the year, leaders find themselves responding to crisis situations where big changes have to be tried quickly.

4. Lack of planning/clear priorities

Implementing change by starting small and growing at a measured pace requires clear priorities and constant planning. Leaders who aren't committed to progressive change and always leading change programs will get distracted and find themselves in crisis situations implementing major changes quickly.

5. Hurry

Some leaders are just in a hurry. They are anxious and impatient. When they decide they want something done, they want it done right then. They tend to like big initiatives. So they don't slow down and plan incremental changes. They force change through their organizations and make people feel they're drinking out of a water hydrant. They are impatient and can't see the details and potential problems that can occur.

BENEFITS OF STARTING SMALL AND GROWING SLOWLY

Starting small allows us to do pilot testing and float "trial balloons" before making a larger commitment. Also, we tend to get less push back from people more comfortable with the status quo. We observe businesses doing this all the time. HCA piloted new computer software before large scale rollouts. Restaurants pilot new menus in key markets before making nationwide changes.

Starting small

George Barna wrote a book, *The Frog in the Kettle*. He explained how you can put a frog in a kettle of water and turn the heat on. Because the water warms up slowly, the frog will not jump out of the kettle and will boil to death. Barna makes this application to the impact of changing societal values.

Let's take a simple example. If I had a 300-page book and asked people to read it, many would feel overwhelmed. They would begin to explain how busy they were and how it would be near impossible for them to read the book with everything else going on. If I gave them the same book and asked if they could take ten minutes and read ten pages that day or evening, most people would say yes. If I did that for thirty days, they would have read the 300-page book. I have actually used this approach to get feedback on this book as I have written it. I have asked people to read a section at a time and give feedback vs. reading the whole book at one time.

Often, the reason for procrastination is people feel overwhelmed at the size of the project. That's why it is so important to take big projects and break them into small pieces. Remember my example earlier of leading the audit team? When the team worked together to take big initiatives and break them into the small projects, there was no pushback to moving forward.

The TV industry has used a gradual approach to impact our culture and society significantly, though I don't think in a positive way. When I had children and started watching reruns of programs from when I was a kid and then watched network TV, I was struck at the change in the language, the violence, the sexual innuendos, and the overall values from thirty years earlier. If the programming we watched today had been aired thirty years ago in this nation, there would have been a rebellion and families would have turned off their TVs. But, because the change in programming was done gradually, it never reached that tipping point in a given year so that people rebelled and quit watching.

Pilot testing

This principle works in computer conversions. After computer software is changed, it is implemented in a pilot. It stays in the pilot until all the bugs are worked out. It saves considerable time and cost to pilot new software versus implementing it on a broad scale. Imagine the time and costs required to fix computer bugs at multiple locations. HCA went through a major computer conversion one time. We operated over three hundred hospitals. We went through the process of pilot testing of the new system and made numerous modifications. Imagine the time, cost, and disruption to the operations and the resistance to change if we had implemented the new software in three hundred facilities versus doing a pilot in one. Pilot projects are designed so that they are not overwhelming.

Starting small, "pilot testing," increases efficiency over the long run because problems are avoided. When national restaurant chains want to change their menu, what do they do? They take a restaurant or a market and pilot the change. They see the reaction to the change. They make any needed modifications and re-test. Then, they begin to roll it out to all their restaurants. If the change is not successful, they haven't failed in three thousand restaurants. They've failed in one restaurant or in one market. Any changes needed are made in the pilot and not three thousand restaurants.

Let's assume they were changing three menu items. They do it in one restaurant and change one menu. Two of the items are very successful, and the third isn't. They change the menu to include only two items. It costs much less to do this one restaurant versus three thousand restaurants.

LEADING CHANGE IN PHYSICIAN SERVICES

In leading Physician Services, we used the principles of the mustard seed and yeast to expand our initiatives significantly over several years. One example was the recruiting function for physicians. We took one market where there was a desire to consolidate the recruiting efforts for the market. Our team did that with good success. We built on that success and went to other markets in that division. The division was having better success than other divisions in that group. They went to another division within the group and had good results. After some time, we had implemented in all divisions in that group.

Then we went to another group and showed them the results. There was one division within that group that wanted to pilot the program. We implemented with good results. The other divisions followed within the group until we were running the program in all divisions in that group.

Over three to four years, we implemented the program across the entire company. If we had tried to implement that program as one big initiative, it would have never gotten national level support and would have never happened.

We implemented a hospitalist initiative by working with one group president. He put an individual on his payroll, and we performed the management oversight. The results were very good at the hospitals in his group. Then, we were able to put the manager on our payroll and promote the initiative on a broader basis. Success always breeds more success. We would go to hospitals who wanted to implement the initiative. We communicated the successful results, and other hospitals wanted the program. We began managing all the contracted vendors for hospitalists. If this had been presented as a national initiative from the beginning, it would have never gotten the support.

We did a similar thing, but in a different way, with a hospital-based anesthesia initiative. I believed we were paying too much in anesthesia subsidies because we did not have enough expertise at the local level in many situations. We found an individual who was very qualified but couldn't get the approval to put that individual on the payroll. I talked to one division president who was always good to work with and had a big opportunity in this area. I asked him if he would do a pilot where we contracted with this person to do the anesthesia contracting and negotiation as a consultant. I said that Physician Services would pay half if his division would pay half. We had enough room in the budget for the consulting fee but couldn't get approval for an added person on the payroll.

We ran the pilot for six months and saved so much money in anesthesia subsidies that we were able to get approval to hire the person full-time. We did a lot of work and that division showed substantial results. Then, we went to other divisions within that group with great results. Over three years, we developed an extensive team and did work throughout the company with many millions of dollars in savings. Without a creative low risk approach, this initiative would not have gotten started.

Over twelve years, we added a number of service lines and major initiatives within the Physician Services function. They all had a national influence, but every one was started as a pilot and implemented throughout the company gradually. There's not a single one that we could have sold as a national initiative from the beginning.

Another thing that was very important was giving other people the credit at every opportunity. We were most effective when pointing to an operational success that we were part of rather than trying to take the credit for an initiative. After a successful pilot, we would point to operations and give them all the credit.

"Do not claim honor in the presence of the King,

and do not stand in the place of great men."

Proverbs 25:6

Our role in the process was always ultimately revealed, and we were given the opportunity to help the next set of operators. Small pilots became very large initiatives over time using this approach.

APPLICATION IN YOUR PERSONAL LIFE

I remember years ago when I wanted to run for my health and weight control. About a mile into the run, there was a long uphill grade. I would grit my teeth and try to make it all the way. I would tense up and try harder the further I ran but could never make it. Then, I set lower goals. My goal was to get to the next mailbox. Each time I got tired, I looked no further than the next mailbox and asked myself if I could just run that much further. Each time I did. The very first time I used this approach to running that incline, I made it to the top and kept running.

Over the years, I found the hardest part of exercising is putting on my shoes. In other words, once I make a commitment to do something, put my shoes on, and get moving, it is easier and I do more than I thought I would. I used to think I had to run or walk a certain number of miles. Just thinking about it some days was overwhelming. So, I quit thinking about it. I put on my shoes and decided to walk only one mile, which seemed easy. Yet, there was never a time that I only walked one mile. By the time I walked a mile, I felt better and wanted to walk a second mile. Often, I would do a third or fourth mile. Getting started is part of the battle, and that's easier to do when you set the goals lower.

WHAT'S THE CHALLENGE WITH SMALL MEASURED CHANGES?

It's a great way to lower risk and gain acceptance of the team, but it's not always possible. Sometimes, there is a crisis or a big time-sensitive opportunity, and you have to act quickly. Certain changes don't lend themselves to the slower approach. Corporate mergers and acquisitions are an example. Enough comes at you in this complex business society you can't deal with on a small scale that it's even more important that you be diligent about leading smaller change programs for things you do have control over.

The world changes quickly and often competitive landscapes in the business world change very quickly. Sometimes, making small improvements and changes to what you are already doing just aren't the right answer. Operating managers like to be efficient, and small, gradual change is the most efficient form of change. But we need to be effective to be successful over the long term also. Around the year 1900, the most efficient buggy whip maker was the last to go out of business. The effective businesses changed their model and were making leather for car seats. Sometimes, radical change is in starting something brand new, or totally remaking something is required to face the future. Again, I think of the executive coach who said the biggest barrier to success that he had seen over the years in leaders was the courage to act, to make change.

Leaders are sometimes hesitant to make these radical changes because of the risk of failure and the resistance they feel they'll face. Yet, by not making significant changes when the situation warrants, they guarantee their longer term failure. Sometimes, the biggest long term risks we take are in not taking the current risk we face.

WARNING – IDEA OF THE WEEK LEADERS

Some leaders see themselves as change agents when, in fact, they are simply "idea of the week" leaders. Most organizations of any size have one somewhere. They go by different names, but this is a common one. Change for the sake of change without a clear plan and use of "pilots" to monitor success are not the ways to implement change.

Some leaders say that the process or people are not working out, and they begin making changes without the counsel of others and without a plan. This often results in no improvement or in the situation getting even worse. Too much change, change not well planned, or change that the team has not been involved in is usually going to yield poor results.

Entrepreneurial leaders in for-profit and non-profit organizations can do this a lot. They are often creative in nature, get bored easily, and make change for the sake of change. There are certain personality profiles that are highly creative and have problems with the status quo. Sometimes, they will make unnecessary changes. There is a difference in leading continual change programs toward a "vision" versus creative leaders who are often referred to as "idea of the week" or "idea of the month" leaders.

Application

I. Are you proactively leading changes for your organization? What are the three most
   important changes you are implementing this year?

1._____
2._____
3._____

II. Are you going to pilot your changes? Yes_____ No_____

   Can you accept the risk if it fails and you didn't pilot it?

II. When your plan changes, do you get genuine input of your team,
    especially the more analytical and probing temperaments? Yes____No____

III. What important changes are you putting off?

1._____
2._____
3._____

IV. What changes do you need make in your personal life?

1._____
2._____
3._____

Notes

Chapter 26

PROGRESS THROUGH DOCUMENTATION AND TRAINING

Thought!
Have you considered how much time
you could save if what you knew was
well documented and people were trained?

"Now these things happened as examples for us,

so that we would not crave evil things as they also craved."

1 Corinthians 10:6

If you look back over history, when did mankind start making its most significant progress? Most people would agree it was after we learned to write. Dr. Frist, Sr. used to make this point frequently. In fact, there was a significant change in the progress of mankind after the invention of the printing press. Being able to document what we have learned so that each generation doesn't have to "reinvent the wheel" has been significant to the process of mankind. One reason God had men write the Bible was so that we could learn from the lives and mistakes of others and wouldn't have to learn everything based on our own experience. This is what I Corinthians 10:6 above is talking about.

We see the same thing in organizations. When I led the internal audit department, one of the things we dealt with was turnover. Even though it improved, it was still high compared to other corporate functions. That was the nature of the internal audit department because it was used as a training ground and promotional opportunity for many professionals. As we tried to add value to the company through our work, I began to hire specialists in certain areas. They would do great work and take our capabilities to new levels.

They would normally stay about two years before someone else in the company hired them because of their specialized knowledge. Then, it felt like we would start all over again with someone new.

Then, I made the commitment that we would have heavy documentation of all that our specialists knew. We created detailed audit programs. We added supplements to the audit programs that explained in detail the thought process and best methods for completing each step. We designed preprinted work papers to facilitate the consistent gathering of information. Once we did this, we did not lose all the expertise of the person that moved somewhere else in the company. In fact, the replacement was able to get up to speed very quickly and usually improved on what we had already developed.

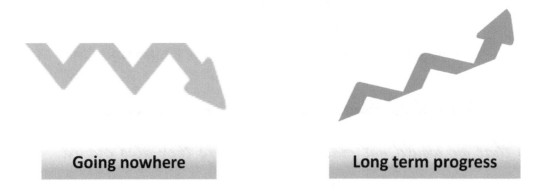

Going nowhere   **Long term progress**

Following this protocol helped us avoid the peaks and valleys in the quality of our work. Over time, our expertise grew and we performed at higher levels. As our department grew more, we also added staff and multiple trained individuals, which was also important for the retention of knowledge. Without good documentation and training, organizations cannot maintain a consistent standard of performance or grow its expertise.

Its Tedious but it creates Stability

This is one of the reasons why small organizations stay small. Everything is known by a few people, and the organization can't grow beyond what they personally know and oversee. Documentation allows an organization to develop and learn from best practices, to continue to improve, and to efficiently train and engage others in the process so that the organization grows. This is one thing that makes franchise models so successful.

When documentation and training are done properly, the new job holders don't start from scratch. They begin with the documented knowledge of the previous job holders and often are able to add their unique perspective and experience to improve the results. It's much quicker and more efficient to bring people up to speed with good documents.

Developing the human capital of the organization should be one goal of any leader, especially in service organizations. This book deals with the five essentials that every leader should know to lead a successful organization. However, there is still much that managers and supervisors need to know to be most effective in organizational life. If you want a comprehensive management development course for your team, I recommend that you consider Model-Netics from Main Event Management. This course can be taught to people at every level of the organization. The use of models makes the material memorable and easier to use among a team that has had the training. Operating managers teach the course to their people so that it applies to their circumstances.

Application

I. Do you have good documentation for your:

A. Mission?

B. Values?

C. Vision?

D. Organizational objectives?

E. Organization chart?

F. Policies and procedures?

G. Control systems?

H. Exception reporting systems?

I. Information systems?

II. In what do you need to improve your documentation and training?

_____

_____

_____

_____

_____

Chapter 27

PROGRESS THROUGH ENABLING CONTROL SYSTEMS

Thought!
How much more could you relax if you had an easy way of knowing things in your organization were in control? If you had a system to keep things on track, how much time and energy would you save?

"So then each one of us will give an account of himself to God."

Romans 14:12

One of the great challenges many entrepreneurs face is empowering others and letting go appropriately. They do not know how to empower, yet keep control. The behavior I see ranges from the ultimate micromanagers where they "have their thumb in every pie" to the leaders who give instructions and never follow up on the end result.

GOD'S APPROACH TO CONTROL

If we are going to be godly leaders, we should look at how God handles this issue of control. In this area, I see two extremes in how people think about God. There are those who believe that God is an over-controlling, micromanager who does everything He can to make sure we do not enjoy life, punishes us every time we get off track, and wants to keep us from doing what we really want to do. Then, there are those who believe that God is uninterested and uninvolved and that everything that happens in life goes according to chance. One theme in the Forrest Gump movie was, "Life is like a box of chocolates. You never know what you're going to get."

Let's look at this through Scripture to see how God really empowers but also controls appropriately. The fact that God empowers is clear before the world was even formed. Before time, the Trinity existed as God the Father, God the Son, and God the Holy Spirit. God the Father did not handle creation himself but rather left that to Jesus who is the agent of creation (John 1:2).

After everything was created, Scripture says that God gave man dominion over the garden and every living creature (Genesis 1:28). That seems like a God who empowers. He lets go. He gives people freedom with His creation.

So what about control? In the beginning, God only had one rule. That was to not eat from the tree of the knowledge of good and evil (Genesis 2:17). In fact, God said of any tree and any plant in the garden Adam and Eve might eat, but not of that one single tree. That doesn't seem like micromanagement to me. There was only one rule. And what was the purpose of the rule? Was the purpose to restrict their freedom? Was the purpose to restrict their enjoyment of paradise? No! The only purpose was to protect them from what God knew would harm them. But, they did eat from the fruit of the tree. It changed their way of life and excluded them from life inside a beautiful garden.

Guess what people got next? God gave them more rules, which we know as the Ten Commandments. There were certain things that we are to be sure to do and things that we are not to do. What was the purpose of the Ten Commandments? Following them was to work for their good. All ten commandments were to protect and preserve the relationship with God and to enhance their relationship with others. God gave people these commands to protect them. They were to create more enjoyment and fulfillment in life, not less.

As time went on, God's people rebelled more, and God continued to give them direction through rules—always intended to guide and protect them. The rules were never controls for the sake of God exerting His power, showing His strength or limiting the people's freedom and enjoyment of life. They were always to guide and protect—to keep people from hurting themselves or one another and to maximize their enjoyment of life. Jesus said, "I came that you might have life and have it more abundantly." Some translations say "have it to the full" (John 10:10).

Have you noticed yet that every time people were not lined up with God's mission but followed their own plans, He had to implement more rules to protect them against themselves? In our organizations, the less people are aligned with the mission, vision, and values, the more rules we have to make. It would be far better to have greater alignment so we could have fewer rules.

THE LESSON OF THE RIVER

I think we learn a lot about God through nature. A river reminds me of how God works. I sometimes ask people what a river has that other bodies of water do not. They quickly come to the conclusion that river has a current that gives it movement. Then, they point out the river has banks to guide it.

A river is made up of millions of drops of water that fall during a rain, run into streams, then run into creeks, and finally join the mighty river. The water is in motion. The banks of the river do not micromanage each drop of water but rather gently guide the river.

Now think of how a good organization functions. People, tasks, or activities are not micromanaged. Rather, they are guided gently by the boundaries in place in the organization toward its vision. What in an organization creates the current or movement? The organization's vision and goals for each individual create the movement.

What creates the boundaries equivalent to the banks of river. There are several things that create boundaries: policies and procedures, operating manuals, standards for performance, training, accountability systems, and so on.

Why should these be created? To enable individuals to accomplish the mission and vision of the organization. When done properly, leadership will know the status of all the things that impact the vitality of the organization. Some people and certain personality types like control just for the sake of exercising control. After many years of being an auditor, I have a firm belief that control systems should never be about control just for the sake of control. Nor should they limit an individual's freedom unless it also protects people and is in the best interests of the organization.

SWAMP ANALOGY

If you took away the banks of a river, what would you have over time? It would resemble a swamp or become a swamp, wouldn't it? What is a swamp like? First of all, it stinks because the water has become stagnant. Next, it's very easy to get lost in a swamp because there is no flow of water or banks to give direction. Third, swamps are dangerous for human beings to try to live in. There are a lot of surprises in swamps, and almost none of them are positive.

Now, let's think about what an organizational swamp would look like. I've been in a number of them in my organizational career. First, the culture stinks because everything is stagnant. Next, there is no flow or direction because vision of the organization is not clear. And, finally, people are just trying to survive. They're lost and don't know how to get out but don't feel safe staying in.

So how do you turn organizational swamps into a river that has life, direction, and flow? Here is what I did in these situations. As a foundation, we created as a team clarity about why the organization existed—mission. Then, we discovered God's vision for what the organization should become. Next, we created strategies and tactics to accomplish the vision. Finally, those were broken into goals for individuals with an accountability system for achieving them. This created energy and current for the organization. Then, appropriate policies and procedures, operating manuals, training systems, and enabling control systems were put into place to guide people and activities.

ORGANIZATIONAL FLOODING

We just saw what happens if the river banks get too wide—an organizational swamp is created. Now let's look at what happens if the banks get too narrow. If you had a big river that was a mile wide and suddenly narrowed the banks down to one half mile, what would happen? That's right, flooding! Where there is too much water and the banks are too narrow, water moves outside the banks and creates damage in surrounding areas.

Water = Change

How does flooding in organizations occur? Usually, large amounts of change are created that cannot be accommodated by the existing boundaries of the organization. When the boundaries are too narrow for the changes occurring, people, trying to achieve their goals, work around the existing boundaries, seeing them as barriers. Now instead of having control, the organization has lost total control. I've seen this happen many times, and it's dangerous to the organization.

This issue of setting the boundaries and vision for the organization is very important. Remember, Scripture says where there is no vision, the people perish. In organizational life, if there is not a clear vision and the boundaries are too broad, it becomes an organizational swamp. By contrast, if there's a clear vision and a lot of movement and change but the boundaries are not set appropriately, you have organizational flooding where people work around existing boundaries and all control is lost. *I create Flooding in groups*

EMPOWERING WHILE HAVING CONTROL

Finally, this brings up an important question in terms of how you empower and set boundaries. Do you empower people and never follow up and hold them accountable? In Lee

Iacocca's book, he describes his turnaround efforts at Chrysler. One thing he did was quarterly reviews or accountability sessions with each of his vice presidents. This is a practice I adapted and with good results. Using this method properly, it's not possible to go more than ninety days with your direct reports being off-track toward their annual goals without you knowing it. Of course, I had more frequent contact and follow-up, but these quarterly reviews were comprehensive in nature. At the end of the year, they had already had the three reviews with me regarding their progress. Therefore, the annual review was easy to accomplish, and there were no surprises.

Finally, let's talk about how you set the boundaries. Who do you engage in setting the boundaries and what is your attitude and motive? This brings us back to the People section of the book where we looked at personality profiles. The "D" profile likes to feel in control but doesn't like getting into details and will tend to delegate the establishment of policies and procedures, operating manuals, and controls. The "I" personality doesn't like getting into the details and tends to feel controls are abusive. The "S" personality is good at developing operating manuals, knowing how things are done, and will appropriately engage in the development of manuals, policies procedures, and controls. The "C" personality will tend to be more detail-oriented, risk-averse, and will design very tight controls. In many larger organizations, the "C" personality will create the boundaries and will volunteer for that work. The problem is when you don't have all four personality profiles involved, you will tend to get boundaries too narrow and the flow of the organization will actually be restricted. Then, people simply comply and are not creative and proactive, or they rebel, work around the system, and you have less control.

It is a given that you can over-control and hinder progress. We have already discussed that. However, good and well-balanced control systems help detect problems early before they get too big, and they help keep us on track toward meaningful progress. What does a control system look like? From my experience, the simpler, the better. HCA had operating indicator reports that showed the standard, actual, and variance. Varying degrees of follow-up were initiated base on the degree of variance and its impact.

WHY EXPECTATIONS ARE NOT MET

Some things are easy to express in a measurable standard, and some are a bit harder. The most common reasons expectations are not met are:

- The expectation is not clear, or the employee did not understand the expectation or how it would be measured.

- There are too many expectations, and some do not get the focus.

- The expectation gap is not followed up on in a timely manner by the leader.

Follow-up in a reasonable timeframe is a helpful key in making sure expectations are clear. Any gap in understanding can be resolved so that you do not go for an extended period of time with an important expectation not being met. One of the biggest issues in not getting the expected results is leaders who do not follow up to ensure that the expectation is met or some plan of action is created.

CHURCH EXAMPLE

Though it's been over ten years, my kids still delight in telling the story where they claim I kicked the ministers at church out of a management development class. My recollection of the story is different. I was teaching a management development class. I thought I had been clear about the expectations. My role as teacher was to show up on time, to be prepared, and to let them out on time. Their role was to come to class on time, to take detailed notes, and to study for each class session.

We were in the third week of the course. As we reviewed the prior week's material, it was clear that nobody had studied and had almost no recollection of what was taught the prior week. When I realized they had not studied, I said, "I assume you've had a busy week and have not been able to study. It's not beneficial to you to have another class until you have time to catch up. So, class is dismissed, and I'll be prepared to teach when you learn the material from last week."

Well, what do you suppose happened the next week? A few people didn't show up. They wanted nothing else to do with class. That was fine. They weren't learning anything anyway. But the ones who did show up knew the material and knew it well.

I had previously done a class at a church but didn't follow this approach. People fell behind and didn't know the material from the prior week, and I just let it go. It was no doubt the weakest class that I ever taught. I wasted my time, and they wasted theirs.

In the second class at church, when I dismissed class and made it clear that people were to show up having learned the material from the prior week, everyone who came kept up. Yes, a few dropped out. That's okay because it wouldn't have been beneficial to them anyway because they had not studied. If they had stayed or been allowed to stay without being prepared, they would have adversely affected the rest of the class. They would have thought it was acceptable to come to class unprepared. As it worked out, the best got better and the weakest links in the chain were plenty strong.

This became one of the best classes I ever taught. And most of the people in that class got promoted one or more times in the next ten years.

HOW DO PEOPLE JUDGE WHAT YOU EXPECT?

I once had a boss that had a new idea every week on something we should do. If I thought it was a good idea, I did it immediately. If not, I waited. If he mentioned it again and it was an okay idea, I worked it in. If I thought it was a bad idea, I waited for him to mention it a third time before

I discussed it with him and acted on it. Most of the ideas were never acted on because he never mentioned them twice or followed up.

Some leaders are strong advocates of the idea that people will do what you expect. I agree with that, and I've seen it many times. Other leaders believe people do what you *inspect*. I agree with that, and I've seen it many times. So, how can I believe two different things at the same time? They aren't really two different things. People tend to judge your true expectations by what you follow-up on and put a focus on. Having a lot of expectations without clear consistent follow-up that is appropriate for the circumstances and individual will generally result in less effectiveness in meeting expectations.

DOES MEASURING GUARANTEE PROGRESS?

Because we measure something doesn't necessarily guarantee progress toward the objective. I learned by experience that just measuring without follow-up and accountability doesn't produce a result.

A common mistake leaders make is having too many expectations. Therefore, they don't focus on the deviations and don't require follow-up. If I focused on the variances and required written action plans to close the gap, substantial improvement occurred. In fact, often all I had to do was say we needed to pay attention to a particular issue or the next step would be written action plans. People hated to write action plans. Many times, they would take action to close the gap before we got to that step.

Application

I. Are you careful to make sure your expectations are understood when you delegate? Yes_____ No_____

II. Would your employees agree? Yes_____ No_____

III. Do you follow-up at reasonable intervals on your expectations? Yes_____ No_____

IV. What changes do you need to make based on the discussion of this chapter?

_____

_____

_____

_____

Chapter 28

PROGRESS THROUGH MEASUREMENT

Thought!
How much easier would your work be
and how much more in control would you feel if
you had a few measurable indicators telling you
what you need to know?

"Immediately the one who had received the five talents

went and traded them, and gained five more."

Matthew 25:16

We like to keep score. We can't go to a kids T-ball game, where the scores are not officially kept, and not try to keep up with it in our head. Keeping score gives us a sense of accomplishment. Would you keep playing golf if you couldn't keep score? Would you keep watching sports if scores weren't kept? Of course not. We have this innate need to create and be productive. Keeping score lets us know how we're doing. Measuring and reporting the right things can have substantial impact on the progress of an organization. Measuring the wrong things can hurt an organization.

Jack Welch once said at an HCA leadership conference, "If you can't measure it, you can't manage it." It's true when you start measuring things in the organization. It impacts people if those measures are communicated and followed up. So the key is what do you measure? The simple answer is you measure the high priorities—those things that move the needle.

Scripture says that God numbers the hairs on my head. We are enough like our Creator that built within us is the desire to keep score. I know some people in ministry who give the impression that keeping score is not good. Yet, these people are like all the other parents at the kids' T-ball games. T-ball is for the very young kids where the coaches don't keep score. Yet, every parent there, including the ministers, know if their team won. It's just built into us. We like to keep score. Imagine playing a round of golf and not keeping score. Imagine going to a football game or basketball game and not keeping score. How much fun would any of the sports activities be if scores were not kept? Have you noticed how frequently the score of the game is displayed on the TV screen?

Some would say spiritually that score keeping is wrong, and I will be the first to acknowledge that keeping score can be done wrong and do damage. Yet, in the parable of the talents, score was kept and the stewards were rewarded for multiplying their investments. Peter asked Jesus what he and others would get for forsaking all and following him. Jesus did not rebuke him. Instead, he said Peter would receive a hundred times what he had given up. If we are keeping score only to show that we beat someone else, perhaps that is unhealthy competition. But in Scripture, accomplishment is commanded, commended, and rewarded.

So, how do we keep score in organizations? An organization has measures it tracks daily, weekly, monthly, and annually. It knows exactly where it stands against expectations for those timeframes. How about the employees? Do they know how they're doing within defined time intervals? If you don't keep score and provide feedback, they are likely to experience some anxiety or insecurity that is not necessary if they are doing well.

You may say, "We can't measure everything we want the employee to accomplish." This is particularly true in certain complex leadership roles. You can, however, give feedback on as much objective data as possible, as well as your perspective on performance against your expectations. Lee Iacocca did this quarterly with his vice president team when he turned Chrysler around.

Not subjective?

I adopted the same approach at the vice president level in my organizations and believed it added to the focus, accomplishment, and lack of surprises or disappointments in the annual review process. The frequency really depends on the role, concrete data that may be available, and the personality of the individual. Some people like broad measures over longer periods of time. Others tend to need more frequent feedback and affirmation.

WHAT SHOULD WE TRY TO IMPACT?

The key to what we should try to impact is tied directly to the mission, values, vision, and priorities of the organization. We should measure those things that directly relate to these, and special focus should be placed on the priorities that have been agreed upon for the next year. When establishing measures, keep in mind what really "moves the needle." You're far better off having a few key measures to narrow the focus of what contributes most toward your vision. Think about how a river works. The narrower the banks are, the faster the water flows.

One mistake leaders sometimes make is not having balanced measures. If we measure quantity but not quality, we tend to produce poor quality goods or services. If we only measure quality but not quantity, we tend to be less productive. If our focus is only on cost and trying to reduce it, we may negatively impact quality.

I've seen numerous examples of new initiatives in organizations where measures are not kept in balance. One company did a massive computer conversion where the information technology department was incentivized based on the number of conversions, but not the quality or the downstream costs to the revenue cycle of a poor conversion.

In Physician Services, as we rolled out new service lines, one of the things we had to keep in balance was how quickly we rolled something out versus maintaining the quality of the program. There were times when hospital or division operators wanted something done very quickly. Responding to those requests and doing things more quickly than we knew was prudent always caused problems that we had to fix. In the end, it took longer than doing it right in the first place.

Often, our leadership in Physician Services found themselves working hard to put the brakes on programs so we could implement them at a speed that would not create additional problems.

MICRO-MANAGERS VERSUS CONTROL SYSTEMS

Leaders of small organizations tend to limit themselves to what they can personally oversee.

One reason they want to be so personally engaged is to have a sense of control. Yet, a clearly established measurable standard and a reporting system to identify progress and exceptions give leaders much more control than just what they can see. That doesn't mean that "management by walking around" isn't a good idea. It is.

Leaders walking around and observing are also informal acts of measurement. Plus, there are benefits to the leaders being engaged beyond the measurement and control system aspect.

THE CHAIN IS NO STRONGER THAN ITS WEAKEST LINK

I saw this principle applied at HCA one time in the area of accounts receivable. As a company, the days of accounts receivable were just too high. It seems like the average for the company may have been in the seventy to eighty range. Leadership thought fifty-five was a reasonable standard. So, what did they do? Simply announce that fifty-five was the standard? What would that change? They did do some promotion and fanfare. They printed stickers and created banners that said, *"Stay alive at 55."* But what began to change things was the publishing of results and comparison of the operating units. Now that there was a contest, about 10% of the business office managers in the company wanted to have the lowest days of accounts receivable. So, they started working on ways to improve the results. And they did. After eighteen months, the top business office managers had their days of accounts receivable average less than forty.

What about the others? Well, some of those business office managers began to learn from those who had better results. So, their days in accounts receivable went down. In some divisions, training programs were implemented and several of the business office managers improved their results. In some cases, business office managers were not able to learn enough from others or the training programs to improve the results. Some looked for easier jobs, and others were asked to leave.

Here was the dynamic I observed. When the worst days in receivable in a division were ninety, the office manager at eighty or eighty-five was comfortable. When the worst came down to their level, they got really busy looking for ways to improve. The end result after eighteen months was that the worst hospital was at fifty-five days, and the company average was about forty-seven.

So let's make application to organizational life. Who sets the performance standard? Most operating managers would quickly say management does. I ask, "How?" They say, "We set the performance goals and standards." I ask, "Are they always met?" Rarely does anyone ever say yes. So I ask again, "Then, who is setting the standard?" The real answer is the "weakest link in the chain."

It is the people known to have the lowest level of performance that continue to keep their job in the organization. The reason is because as long as everyone else can look at those people and know they're doing better, they feel safe. And that is fine as long as those people's levels of performance are acceptable.

The bottom line is: to get improvement, do these things:

- Measure and publish results;

- Create a contest where the top performers can compete;

- Create opportunities for the lowest performers to learn from others;

- Offer training to help people meet the performance standards; and

- Make a change in personnel if people are not qualified for the job.

Application

I. Do you measure the things you want most to impact in your organization?

Yes_____ No_____

What are the five things you want to impact the most, and how would you measure them?

1._____

2._____

3._____

4._____

5._____

II. Do you share measures with the team so they can see how they are doing relative to their goals and relative to their peers?

Yes_____ No_____

VI. SUMMARY

Chapter 29

WHY SHOULD LEADERS CONTINUE LEADING?

Thought!
Have you ever considered how much joy you are missing
in life by not leading as a servant leader?

"...who for the joy set before him endured the cross..."

Hebrews 12:2

WE LEAD FOR THE POTENTIAL JOY

When we think about leadership, joy is not one of the common terms that come to mind. We often think about power, control, perks, and money. But we don't think about joy. How often have you heard the expression, "Leadership or management would be fun if it weren't for the people?" Or, "Business would be fun if it weren't for the people." I'm the first to admit that a lot of the key challenges in organizations relate to the people aspect. However, I can also tell you that when you do it right, nearly all the joy comes from the people aspect.

JESUS

It was Jesus who said, "For the joy set before me." In essence, Jesus left the throne room of heaven. He left equality with God, absolute power, absolute control, complete knowledge and an existence without limits. He was not limited by either time or space. He left all that to take on the limits and pain of the physical body and to be misunderstood, betrayed, falsely accused, beaten and finally crucified. Why? For the joy set before him. And what was that joy? It was the opportunity to love, to serve, to sacrifice for others, to suffer for others and to create a family for a relationship of complete love and fellowship.

NEHEMIAH

We see something similar in the Old Testament character of Nehemiah. He was the king's cup bearer. This made him the most trusted and indirectly powerful man in the kingdom. Yet, we see him crying over the troubles of his people. He cried because the walls of their city, which represented their heritage and protection, were broken down. He cried because they felt defeated and without purpose. He cried because they had not reached the potential God intended for them. And because he cared about the people, he did something that was brave and very risky. He showed his sadness in the presence of the king, which in that day could have resulted in his immediate execution.

He went further by asking the king to send him to Jerusalem to rebuild the walls. He also took one other step by asking the king for the provisions needed to rebuild the walls. Why? Out of love and devotion for his people. Nehemiah lived in absolute comfort. He had absolute, almost unlimited provisions. He had significant power and influence within the kingdom where he served. But he left it. I believe it was for the joy set before him.

OUR CALL

And this is the true call of leadership—to serve others, to sacrifice, and at times to suffer for others. Dr. Bill Stevens preached a sermon from Romans on presenting yourself as a living sacrifice. He said, "Sometimes, dying for your faith is easier than living out your faith." He said, "The problem with living sacrifices is they keep crawling off the altar." I think being a true leader calls for us to be a living sacrifice. And I will admit that I have crawled on and off the altar many times. When I think deeply about it, as difficult as it can be at times, I believe being called to be a leader is a real privilege and can bring great joy to the leader if approached with the right heart and mind.

I hope and pray you will find great joy in your leadership, and your team will find great joy in following you. I hope something in this book sparked an idea that will make it easier and more productive for you to live and lead with greater joy and impact.

Application

I. Can you honestly say that you take joy in your leadership?

Yes_____ No_____

II. Do you consider it a joy to serve others?

Yes_____ No_____

III. Do you get any joy out of sacrificing for others?

Yes_____ No_____

What changes do you need to make to create a perspective of joy in your leadership?

_____

_____

_____

_____

_____

_____

Chapter 30

The BOTTOM LINE

Thought!
Do leadership concepts and their application
sometimes seem blurry and confusing?
Would you like a simple summary of your role as leader?

"Let all things be done decently and in order."

1 Corinthians 14:40

There are only two kinds of people reading this chapter. One is those folks who are real troopers. You read the entire book, glad it's finally almost over, but would like a simple summary of how it works together to give the book some context. The other kind is those folks like me, who like to read the last chapter and know the ending before they commit to reading the book. They're interested in the CliffsNotes and may or may not read the rest of the book. I welcome both of you to this chapter on the bottom line.

The essence of the message in this book is that if God called you to be a leader, it's because He wants you to bless the lives of the people in your organization and all those people your organization touches. It doesn't matter if you're in business, ministry, church, or a non-profit organization. God wants you to bless the people you touch as a leader. So, the key is how do you bless people through your leadership role? How does the leader continue to bless the team they lead and the organization they serve? There are five essentials to a healthy organization that blesses the team and the people it touches. The leader is responsible for many decisions and activities every day. But, you must always keep these five essentials in mind and make them your overriding priority. The five essentials are purpose, people, priorities, power and progress.

5 P's

People have five key needs we discussed throughout this book that relate directly to these five essentials. People must have:

- An understanding of their calling—purpose for being;

- Meaningful work where they can express their unique personality, pursue their passion, and use their life experience and training;

- A clear set of priorities to focus their attention and energies;

- Empowerment through a clear vision, set of goals, and freedom to operate within an enabling set of boundaries; and

- The ability to make progress and receive feedback on how much they are contributing.

PURPOSE

↓ Def.

People everywhere are searching for meaning in life. They desperately need to know they matter. They search for organizations and roles in organizations which they believe will help make a difference and be important. Purpose in organizational life is expressed in its mission. It gives a foundation for the existence of the organization. It can also give people a strong sense of connection to something bigger than themselves which gives meaning and expression to their efforts.

People need a vision—a hope for the future.

There is another aspect of purpose which relates to the future. People need a sense of direction. The most common question I was asked in interviews or team meetings related to direction. Where are we going? People desperately need clear "vision" in their life. The vision gives a sense of direction and hope which people desperately need.

I recently heard a state homeland security employee talk about people who go on shooting sprees in their workplace. He said one of the warning signs to look for in people who might do this is despair. When people have no sense of meaning in life and have no vision or hope for the future, it leads to despair. As leaders, we may be adding to a sense of hopelessness and despair, or we may be relieving it for our people.

The leaders are responsible to ensure the organization's mission is clear and the organization does not stray from it or forget it. Once you are clear about your organization's mission, you are in a position to create a compelling vision that will attract and excite other people to join you. You are also responsible to see that the vision is clear and compelling enough that it attracts the right people to the organization and repels or identifies the people who do not fit.

People in many organizations cannot articulate the mission or vision or how they fit into either. This is a sign of an organization not reaching its full potential. In a chaotic and confusing world, people search for and need an organization where there is order and structure. They need to know how they fit into that structure. A highly functional organization has a clear mission, set of compelling values, a vision for its future, clear priorities for at least the next year, goals for each individual, and an accountability system with the potential for discipline and performance incentives, financial or non-financial, meaningful to those individuals.

Key

It seems to me that a lot of leaders are not clear themselves about the organization's mission and vision. They want to make progress. So they make one change after another, confusing the team about the real priorities. Being clear about your organization's mission and always casting a compelling vision are very time-consuming and, frankly, some of the hardest work you will do in organizational life. That's why some leaders don't take the time and energy to do it. They think, "I have great people, great process, and I'm a change agent. I'll be able to make things happen and make great progress." Let's ask ourselves a serious question here. How much progress do you want to make if you're going in the wrong direction or if you're going in circles? Aren't you at a minimum wearing yourself out and, worst-case, working against yourself? Does it matter if you have the best people in the world and great processes if you're going in the wrong direction or in circles?

> **Ken works in a small CPA firm. He just sat for the CPA exam and hopes to pass so he can find a job with a different firm. The partners in his firm don't have a clear mission or vision for the future. They often disagree and argue. Their primary vision tends to be taking business from another firm because they're mad at the lead partner. Ken is not committed to the mission nor compelled by the vision of the organization because neither is clear. The vision he is committed to is finding and joining another firm![1]**

MEANINGFUL WORK

Meaningful work is a blessing to people.

People need meaningful work to be able to express their unique personalities. After God put Adam and Eve in the Garden of Eden, the first thing He did was give them meaningful work. God could have tended the garden himself but, out of love, let Adam and Eve share in His work. When my son was three years old, he wanted to help me in the yard. I didn't need his help, but he would become incredibly upset if I did not let him help. He thought what Dad was doing was important, and he could be important by helping me do that work. God built into human beings the need to do work they believe is important. Work was and still is a blessing from God. Sometimes, it doesn't seem like that because work became much harder since the fall of man. Sometimes, it's hard to see that until you see a person that doesn't have meaningful work to do. I still remember my dad crying when he hurt his foot and couldn't milk the cows.

When an organization's mission and vision is clear, the leaders are ready to select the right people who agree with its mission, embrace its values, and are excited about its vision and the role they can play in helping achieve it. Leaders attract people to the organization that can be themselves, exercise their passions, and achieve their goals while also helping the organization achieve its vision. When there is perfect alignment, the individuals would do the work for free if money were not an object to them. I was recently speaking to a friend about his son who works eighteen hours a day. Why? He loves what he is doing. He is 100% in his element, living out his passions, and achieving his goals. He was also voted best in the state in his particular job. He loves it, works hard at it, and is excellent at it. He is what we would have called a cathedral builder in Chapter 3.

Many organizations recruit for talent and experience. Unfortunately, some organizations don't even get that much. Some leaders in business, non-profit, and ministry organizations hire their friends or people they feel comfortable with or, even worse, people they feel like they can control. Every leader is responsible to attract people to the organization whose calling/purpose, values, passions, talents, and experience match the role they are being asked to play. In other words, can these people do what they want to do, what they're best at, and what they really enjoy doing, while also helping the organization achieve its mission and vision?

> Ken doesn't really fit the firm he is with. He is really people- and team-oriented. He hates conflict and confusion. The environment of this CPA firm is toxic to Ken's natural personality profile. Ken needs to work for a small firm with a participative managing partner where there is no conflict and a clear set of procedures for him to follow. There is no alignment between Ken and this organization other than he needs a job, and they need a "bricklayer" type employee. Ken will leave for any opportunity for better alignment.

CLEAR PRIORITIES

People need a clear sense of priorities to focus their attention and energies. Health professionals are well aware of the fact that when people have too many priorities, their attention is diverted, they experience more stress, their confidence and energy goes down, and their physical health is negatively affected. It causes them to accomplish less than if they had a few very clear priorities. It's hard for people to feel they are contributing when the priorities always change in an organization. Good leaders maintain a consistent focus on priorities. It is so easy to begin the year with a plan based on well-written priorities for the organization and goals for each individual. Then, things change and the leaders start reacting. In the midst of the stress and pressure, it's easy for the leaders to forget about the mission, vision, and priorities for the year. They come up with new projects and start changing direction. The individuals who had a clear set of goals are now whipsawed, responding to the leaders.

You get more accomplished by doing less.

Remember my London example? When I was in London, I decided to walk through Hyde Park, five hundred acres, to get back to my hotel. I asked individuals along the way about the directions to South Kensington. One person sent me in one direction, the next person sent me in another direction, and so forth. I finally got to my hotel in South Kensington and realized I had zigzagged across the park. I had walked twice as far as necessary to get to my destination. When leaders do not maintain a clear and, very importantly, consistent focus on priorities, they cause their people to zigzag, spending twice as much time and effort to reach the goal as should be required. Often, this is such a distraction the goal is never reached. Leaders are helpful when they keep a clear, consistent focus on the priorities. They bring great chaos and confusion into an organization when they are inconsistent or not clear regarding priorities for the organization and their team.

Leaders bring chaos, confusion and frustration when they are not clear or consistent with priorities.

Great leaders understand that "less is more" when it comes to making progress. Many leaders think the more initiatives and projects, the better. Yet, when people get spread too thin, they get their priorities out of order. They work too many hours messing up other areas of their life. Or, they are less effective on the projects they work on and may do important projects poorly. The effective leaders know how to discern the high priority projects in order to keep focus and actually get more done through their team working on fewer high-impact projects versus tackling too many initiatives. People are energized when they feel like they're making significant progress on high priority projects. They feel confused, unimportant, and frustrated when they're working on low priority projects or changing priorities. The focus and energy the organization should be giving is lost, and a sense of vision and hope for the future is also lost. You may recall the story from Chapter 1 about ditch diggers who would not work for double the hourly rate because they did not see the purpose in repeatedly digging and filling in the same ditch. Leaders with constantly changing priorities give their teams the same feeling. Remember, clear priorities serve like the banks of a river. The banks do not micro-manage each drop of water, but they do guide the flow. If the river banks narrow, the current of the river speeds up. When the list of priorities is narrowed, things move faster, and more is accomplished in less time.

> **Ken doesn't have a clear set of goals where he works. The partner he reports to shouts instructions at him that often are unclear. Ken's personality is such that he needs clear specific instructions from this partner. Yet, the priorities are never clear and are constantly changing. Ken hates this environment, and his top priority is to pass the CPA exam so that he can work for another firm.**

EMPOWERMENT

People need empowerment and freedom. They need to feel as though they own a piece of the mission and vision of the organization. A key decision you must make is whether you're going to lead like Moses when he started out with all the people gathered around him waiting for answers and direction. Or, are you going to distribute power like Jethro suggested and delegate authority to dependable people? In other words, are you going to run a "mom and pop" type operation, or are you going to lead it more like a franchise operation where you distribute power and authority to capable leaders?

On the family farm, I fed the calves. This was more involved than feeding the pigs because the milk had to be mixed properly, and each calf had to be fed individually. Daddy taught me how to

Empowered people feel more freedom and contribute more to the organization's results.

do it and entrusted me with it. If I had not done it well, the calves would not have grown, and Daddy would have inspected. But, he had trained me well. I was conscientious about it, and I thoroughly enjoyed doing it. I felt like I owned a piece of the farm. I was empowered. Not only that and I didn't expect it, but Daddy gave me a piece of the profits. When we sold the calves, Daddy gave me the money from one of them. That really helped me feel like I owned a piece of the farm.

When you properly empower people, you give them great freedom, coupled with corresponding accountability. Done properly, people feel like they own a piece of the vision of the organization. They feel like they own their piece of the organization because they have freedom to act and are compensated according to their contribution. The leader ensures there are policies and procedures to give guidance and direction without over-controlling. Operating manuals exist to illustrate best practices. Enabling control systems provide early warning signs and indicators when adjustments are needed. Training is provided when needed so the team members feel competent and confident in their role. People who are empowered properly have higher self-esteem, make a more significant contribution to the organization, and are more committed to the long-term success of the organization.

> **Ken has no sense of empowerment where he works. He is given work piecemeal from a partner with very little explanation of how this work is related to the bigger project. In fact, Ken often feels his work is a waste of time and doesn't really matter.**

PROGRESS

People have a real need to know that they are making progress. The first command that God gave to man was to be fruitful and multiply. Progress is expected. It is implied in the parable of the talents where the stewards multiplied what the master had given them. God built within us the expectation and the need to make progress.

The leader positions the team to make progress. Some of you may be thinking, "Finally, we get to talk about progress." There is a reason this book is written in the order it is. As much as you type "A" folks want to jump in and begin doing things to make progress, it just can't happen without the appropriate preparation. If you do not have a clear mission and vision, why does progress matter? If you're going in circles or going in the wrong direction, does it matter that you do it faster? You want great people on your team. You can't attract or keep the great people without a compelling mission and vision for the organization. If your organization has a lot of dysfunction, the best people will leave.

Let's assume you have a clear mission and vision for the organization. If you don't take the time to choose the right people whose passion, calling, talents, and experience match what you need them to do, do you think you are going to make progress? If you have constant turnover because you're not good at choosing the right people, do you think your organization can make progress? If you have people in the wrong spot because of poor initial selection or because things changed, they no longer fit and you don't know how to deal with it or are unwilling to deal with it, do you think you'll be able to make progress?

Now let's assume that you have a clear mission and vision and great people. But, you're not good at focusing on clear priorities, day-to-day, that help achieve the mission and vision of your organization. You're not good at keeping people focused on the most important priorities. In fact, once the plans are set for the year, you start changing directions frequently. If you change directions a few times during the year, think about the cost of that to your organization. If, because of changing priorities, you spend twice the time and energy to reach your final destination, you may be so inefficient organizationally that your competitors become a more attractive option for your best people, and you lose them. Without the ability to stay focused on clear and important priorities, do you think you can make progress?

Now, let's assume you have a clear mission and vision and have great people and you maintain a great focus on high priorities. If you choose to use the mom-and-pop approach discussed in Chapter 16 to run an organization, your ability to grow it will max out pretty soon. If you do not use the franchise approach and truly empower people so they have a sense of owning a piece of the vision and contributing clearly to the vision of the organization, do you think they will stay highly motivated? Do you think you'll be able to keep them long-term? So, if you don't rightly empower people, you are not yet ready to begin making progress. And, frankly, you'll never have any freedom without the ability to empower others.

Now that we've discussed the necessary preparations to allow progress, we're ready to talk about the five key things leaders do to help make progress in organizational life.

First, they create a plan based on prayer and engage the right people using the right methods. They listen and engage the whole team, and often outside experts, to ensure they are not blind-sided by problems. It's hard to make progress in a firefighting organization. Firefighting organizations continually deal with problems rather than doing what's necessary to prevent them.

Second, the leader encourages the never-ending process of high-impact change programs. Change for the sake of change is tiring and frustrating to the team. Well thought out plans, which the team helps create and that start small and grow over time to achieve an impactful result, raise the energy level and excitement of the team.

Third, documentation and training materials are created which help employees do the job better and do it more independently versus having to get one-on-one instruction from their supervisors. These allow for efficient and progressive improvement in an organization and its results.

Fourth, the leaders help create enabling control systems. Control systems generally have a nega-tive connotation. That's because sometimes control systems are stifling versus enabling. Enabling control systems give early warning indicators of issues that can be avoided and let the team know where there is an issue to be addressed before it gets more important. Environments where people know whether they are in bounds are actually less stressful than those where people don't know where they stand. However, over-controlling is stifling and detrimental to progress. When the banks of a river get too narrow, water gets outside the banks and you have flooding—no control. This happens in organizations all the time. When controls are too restrictive, people work outside the system, and you have less control, not more.

Fifth and finally, effective leaders create measurement of high priority activities tied to priorities of the organization and provide feedback to the team. How excited and interested would people on a ball team be if they were never allowed to know the score? Would they really do their best? Would they give their all to achieve a result when they don't really know how they're doing? People would not play or watch a sport very long if they didn't know the score. Why do you expect people in organizational life to be engaged and do their best if they don't know the score? It's so discouraging for people and causes great fear when they don't truly know how they're doing or how they are contributing to the organization's success. Do your people know how the organization is doing? Do they know how they are doing relative to what's expected of them? Do they know how they contributed to the mission and vision of the organization? If they don't, their lives are not being blessed by your leadership.

> **Throughout this chapter, we have talked about Ken. He is miserable in his job. Why wouldn't he be? The mission of the firm is not clear. It has no vision for the future to excite and retain him. The values of the partners are clearly different than his values. The culture of the firm does not fit his personality profile. Priorities are either non-existent or confusing to him. Everything is given to him piecemeal with no explanation. Therefore, he doesn't feel empowered to achieve something of significance. Change is handled in a reactionary mode, and firefighting occurs all the time. There is not good documentation and training to help instruct him in how to go about his work. He always has to ask for explanations from a partner who's in a hurry and doesn't explain things well anyway. There is no objective measure of his progress or contribution to the firm.**

Many of you reading this may say the above is a hypothetical example of a small organization where everything is done wrong. The truth is, this is a real example. Yet, there are many small businesses, non-profit organizations, churches, and ministries that have a similar set of circumstances. There are medium-sized and large organizations that have some or even a good deal of this kind of dysfunction. People are not blessed in these kinds of environments. They cause great stress and anxiety for people and, frankly, they don't serve their customers and constituents as well either. I've seen ministries where employees and volunteers were challenged in their faith because the environment they worked in is so similar to Ken's.

What about your organization? Does any of what Ken experienced exist in your organization? If you see small crevices in your organization, people like Ken will see mostly gorges and huge valleys. Leadership and organizational life are an ongoing challenge.

How Not to Lead

In your organization, if your goal was to frustrate, confuse, and ruin people's health by stressing them out, or if you wanted to decimate their sense of humanity, how would you do it? You would do it by doing the opposite of what we talked about in this book. The organization's mission would be kept a secret. They would not be allowed to know under any circumstances the vision or future plans of the organization. You would put them in a job exactly opposite of that suited for their personality profile. You would be sure to give them something that they have no passion for or interest in. You would continually frustrate them by low expectations and a culture of fear. You would be unclear about the priorities and change them frequently so they would be sure to stay confused. People would have no authority to do anything without receiving your permission first. You would make sure they see no correlation between what they do and how they are disciplined or compensated. You would never let them feel like the organization was making progress or that they contributed to it in any way. The culture would be characterized by firefighting. All change would be reactionary. There would be no training or documentation on how to do the job. You would make sure they never knew where they stood in terms of performance, and fear would be a constant for them.

You may think, "This is ridiculous. No organization is this bad." Actually, too many are. The question you need to ask yourself is whether any of these things are even partially true for your organization. If so, these are areas where you're hurting people and not blessing them. I personally have been guilty of too many of these too many times. It's my prayer for you that you would not do any of these things to your people.

Finally, I need to say that the principles of good leadership can be laid out and made to seem so simple. I can tell you from personal experience of working hard at this and seeing other talented people work really hard that this is not easy. It's easier to lead a dysfunctional organization than to lead one to bless people. It's hard work, and it takes constant vigilance. But, it is a real blessing to be in a position to be a "big brother" like we discussed in the Introduction and to help other people if God gives you that opportunity through a leadership position.

Now that you know what an organization looks like under the "Good King" and "Bad King" models, you have to decide which one you will be. Let's end by talking about the five key choices a leader makes.

To serve or not to serve

People followed Hitler because they believed he had solutions to their problems and could make their life better. They started following him by choice. But after he got into power, they followed him by force. When you're in a position of leadership and authority over people's lives, the first choice you have to make is whether you are going to serve people. Will you have an influence or power that lasts, or are you going to assume the position of having the upper hand and control and manipulate people?

Choice # 1 -- Are you willing to serve people?

Power is the possibility to influence the actions of people.[2] In the context of Christian leadership, we want to influence other people positively to serve God's kingdom and for the good of the individual. In this context, having power is good if we truly serve people. We get real lasting power, the ability to influence people, by serving them. Dale Carnegie once said, "You can have anything you want in life if you're willing to help enough other people get what they want." I have found this to be true. But, I would be quick to say that the purest form of service is when we do it out of love of God and our fellow man, regardless of what comes back to us in return.

Power achieved or maintained by force is temporary power. People only respond to that as long as the threat is there. Since the key to leadership and having continuing influence on people is service, it seems like it would be a no-brainer that every leader, and especially every Christian leader, would take that stance. But it's not that simple. You have to have the heart to serve. Remember the story of the young man with the red car that his big brother had bought him? Do you remember the little boy saying he wished he could be a big brother like that? The little boy had a heart to serve. We can only serve purely, completely, and consistently when we have that heart.

I spent a lot of years bouncing between head and heart on this issue and was inconsistent. When my heart got more aligned and more pure, my service was more pure, and the impact on people in a positive way was much better.

Promoted – now what?

In organizational life and when you serve well in leadership roles, you are most likely going to get promoted and hold positions with more and more "positional power." Positional power is the power and authority that goes with the role. As President of Physician Services for HCA, I had a certain amount of power and authority that went with the job. I can remember sometimes my team being frustrated because they wrestled with an issue for weeks, and I would get involved when they escalated it. Sometimes, it would take as little as fifteen to thirty minutes to solve the problem. They would say, "Leon, what have I done wrong? I worked on this for weeks." I would say, "If you had it to do over, you would probably have called me a lot sooner." This particular issue had nothing to do with what you said, how you said it, or what you did or didn't do. I was able to get this resolved because I held the position of President of Physician Services.

There's nothing wrong with positional power. It's needed in organizations. The problem comes when you have a lot and start to abuse it versus stewarding it wisely. Remember the story from Chapter 16 where I made the pigs dance? When you're in a position of power and your heart is not right, you tend to control, manipulate, and use people versus serving them. So, your second choice has to do with what you do when you get positional power.

Choice # 2 -- When you get positional power, will you continue to serve?

POWER – KEEP IT OR DISTRIBUTE IT?

Power achieved or maintained by force is temporary.

Our society has numerous organizations in business, the non-profit sector, and ministries. There are organizations of all sizes from huge conglomerates and franchises to medium-sized operations to small, sole proprietor type organizations. There are two ways to lead an organization. One is the mom-and-pop approach where the founders, owners, or leaders retain all the power. You put an automatic ceiling on how large your organization can be and how many people you can touch and bless with this approach. The other approach is what large organizations and franchises use. Power is distributed by delegating, using agreed-upon goals to provide direction, policies and procedures, operating manuals, training, and enabling control systems that guide but don't stifle people as they go about doing their work. The support around them is like the banks of a river that guides people and activity toward an ultimate objective or destiny but doesn't micromanage. People feel empowered. They feel a sense of freedom. And they feel a sense of ownership. The next choice deals with how you handle power. Are you going to keep it all to yourself as Moses did before Jethro, his father-in-law, came along and told him that what he was doing was not good, that the burden was too heavy for him to carry, and that he would wear himself and the people out? Or will you distribute the power by delegation and use the approach of large or franchise type organizations to empower people?

Choice # 3 -- How will you handle power? Will you keep it or distribute it?

YOUR VIEW FROM THE ORGANIZATION CHART

When you look at the organization chart and your place in it, what do you see?

Most people see boxes connected by lines. Organization charts are good. They bring structure and order to the organization that is needed. So please don't misunderstand some of the things I'm going to say next as suggesting that organization charts aren't needed because they are. What I want to discuss next is what we *see* when we look at our placement in the organization chart. What is our view of our place in the organization? If we view ourselves from the perspective of the "box," there are some things we need to be aware of:

- The box can begin to define us. It can limit us and the services we provide if we operate within its perceived limits. If I had allowed my box on the organization chart to define me, I would have had a hard time seeing myself as anything different than an internal auditor since I spent so many years in that role with HCA. Or, if I had seen the role of the President of Physician Services as what defined me, I would never have had the freedom to do what I'm doing now.

- We can begin to relate to other people through our box versus our unique personality. We may think we are more powerful, but we will be less unique and less human and, over time, much less effective in this approach.

- The boxes on organization charts can be seen as sources of power and control. We can start depending on that box for power or influence.

- There is a real temptation when we view an organization from the position of the box that we start trying to control the other boxes.

At some point my career, I chose a different view. In my mind, I knocked the sides and top out of the box and was left with only a platform for service.

PLATFORM

Choice #4 -- Will you view your position in the organization through the lens of the box or as a platform for service?

Viewing the organization this way gave me a sense of freedom. My view was that I was there to serve the organization and the people in it, and that I should be a good steward of any opportunity to serve. I think it's that view that allowed me to have the opportunities to lead multiple corporate functions at the same time. This view made it easier for me to transition from one role to another without letting the box define or limit me. When we serve well on our platform, we need to be careful that it doesn't become a pedestal for us. According to Proverbs, pride precedes a fall. The higher the pedestal, the harder the fall.

I believe this principle is more important than most people understand. If the box starts to define you, it becomes your identity. When it becomes your identity, you become less than God created you to be. Work, although important, is not the totality of your life, but your role in an organization chart can begin to define your identity. If it does, when you no longer have the position, you've lost your sense of identity, which is very dramatic.

I can tell you firsthand that after spending many years leading internal audit that I did have a great deal of my sense of identity in that role. When I left Physician Services after twelve years, I realized a lot of my identity was tied to that role. When I left HCA after thirty-one years, I realized how much of my identity was tied to being an executive at HCA.

You feel freer and serve better from platforms than boxes.

Anytime we let anything other than our identity in Christ define us, we are limiting the abundant life or full life that Christ gives us. Anytime we find our identity or security in anything or anyone other than God, we have just formed an idol in our life.

I can tell you this. If you view your role in any organization from the perspective of a platform for service, you will feel freer, serve more, serve better, and have more impact than if you see it as a box. The truth is, if you see your role as a box, it will make you less than who God created you to be. Conversely, if you see your role through the lens of a platform, you would tend to expand the box.

I thought a lot about why human beings in our society have such a fascination with the boxes on organization charts. People tend to ask you questions when you're an executive, wanting to find your reporting relationship relative to the president or CEO of the organization. They want to know how high up you are in an organization.

I think it becomes very important to us because when we are perceived or perceive ourselves in an important role, we think that makes us important. I spoke to a large group of young professionals recently and asked them if they felt special. Some raised their hands. I asked them if they would feel special if they had their senior vice president's job. More raised their hands. I asked them if they would feel more special if they had the president of the company's job. Several raised their hands.

If the department they were in promoted from within and they were the last choice, they would have one in over one hundred chances to be senior vice president. If the company promoted from within and they were the last choice, they would have one in 150,000 chances of being the president. But here's a truth we don't often think of. Shortly after we were a gleam in our father's eye, we each faced the fiercest competition we would face for a spot in this world. Scientists tell us there are between four hundred million and 1.2 billion cells that could have united with your mother's embryo. There were likely over one billion chances of someone else being born instead of you. Jeremiah 1:5 says, "Before you were formed in your mother's womb, I knew you." I believe that God picked you before your mother and father were ever born and before He ever created this Earth. He had a unique plan, design, purpose, and destiny for you. Scientists tell us that no two snowflakes that ever fall are exactly alike. The human being is the most complex of all God's creation and the height of God's creation. We are genuinely unique. No one ever has or ever will be created just like you. No one ever has or will be created to have the impact on human history and the kingdom of God that you were created for. So, why do we look for a position on an organization chart to make us feel special?

John Candy was in a movie about a Jamaican bobsled team. He was the coach of the team. It seems that years earlier, he had coached a team and won a gold medal. Later, he coached a team and cheated to win another medal. When his Jamaican team asked about it, his answer was predictable. He said, "After you win one, you feel like you just have to keep on winning to get the next one." Then, he said something along these lines: "But I realized if you're not enough without the medal, you will never be enough with the medal."

I don't look to John Candy or movies for my theology, but there was a lot of truth in that. Think about it. If you don't feel special, and you're not enough without the position, will it be enough for you? I can remember thinking that if I could just become assistant vice president, I would have arrived. Then, I wanted to be vice president. Then, I wanted to be senior vice president. God allowed me to have all that and more, but He did help me realize that if His love for me and my identity in Christ wasn't enough, there was no position that would ever be enough. If you're not enough without the car, without the house, without the title or position, and without the money, you'll never be enough with it. If Jesus isn't enough for you, nothing the "world" offers you as a substitute will ever be enough for you either.

The truth is, the only thing you can do to be any more special than you were the day you were born is to simply become more and more of who God intended you to be. All the things people do to feel special makes them less special and less unique. I see three key ways that people become less special. They try to:

- Fit a position on an organizational chart to make them feel good about themselves and make them feel powerful versus just seeing it as a platform to serve other people and the organization well. When we seek a position on the organization chart to make us feel special and conform to that box, it can make us less of who God intended us to be and cause us to have less impact with our life than He intended by just becoming more of ourselves.

- Conform to the expectations of other people. Proverbs 29:25 says that fear of man and conforming to their expectations will prove to be a snare. But, fear of God is the beginning of wisdom. We always become less than God's ideal when we conform to the expectations of others out of fear versus honoring who God wants us to be.

  The only way you can become more special is to become more of who God created you to be.

- Be like a person they admire versus the person God created them to be. It's great to admire people. It's great to want to be like other people in terms of character and spiritual strength. But it is unfair, unreasonable, and wrong for us to have the unique hardwiring that God gave us and, rather than appreciating it and living out our unique personality, wanting to have someone else's. That only leads to dissatisfaction and disappointment. It keeps us from growing into the person and being the person that God designed us to be.

> ### Choice # 5 -- Are you willing to serve in small ways?

DO LITTLE THINGS MATTER?

One of the reasons our politicians don't seem to be able to serve us well in Washington is because they all want some big initiative to be remembered for. It seems that people want a bridge, road, building, or something named after them. But, Jesus didn't build roads and buildings or bridges. He touched people, often one life at a time. So here's the question for you. Do seemingly small things matter to you? In my last three or four years with HCA, God gave me the opportunity to help start a hospitalist initiative. This initiative hit at the core of many things important to a hospital company. It improved the quality of care, reduced cost, and often created a much better patient experience through the timeliness and care of the hospitalists. In four years, we built this one initiative to five hundred employees with a $50 million budget. Nobody ever has or ever will get tears in their eyes when they remember that program.

But, I can tell you a couple times when people did. I remember Bill speaking when I transitioned out of the internal audit department. He was a grown man with tears in his eyes talking about the time I helped him get a job as a CFO in a hospital. That didn't seem like a big thing to me. I had helped many people get those jobs. Even as he told the story, I only vaguely remembered it. It seems I had been on vacation and gotten up early one morning and called a hospital CEO promoting Bill for the position. It only took about fifteen minutes of my time, but it made a big difference in Bill's life. He remembered it to the point it brought tears to his eyes when he mentioned it. It was a small thing to me, but it was a big thing to him.

I remember Larry from Physician Services. Larry moved two to three times for the company. He worked really hard. One day, I sat down and wrote a handwritten note to Larry thanking him for the sacrifices he made and how he served the company. When Larry retired, he said with tears in his eyes, "I was almost sixty years old when I got that note. Nobody had ever written me a note thanking me for anything in my life." It may have taken twenty minutes for me to write that note. It didn't seem like a big thing to me, but it was to Larry.

I suspect most of you have heard the story of the starfish. There had been a big storm, and thousands of starfish washed up on the shore. A man was walking along, throwing them back in the ocean. Another gentleman came along and questioned why he was doing that. He said, "There so many thousands of these. You'll never make a difference." The man simply picked up another starfish, threw it in, and replied "I made a difference to that one."

We so badly want to be part of a big initiative to make us feel important without realizing that our biggest opportunities may be those simple touches of service that impact individuals deeply. Jesus said in Matthew 10:42, "If you offer even a cup of water to a little one in my name you will not lose your reward." So often we're trying to change the tide in our organization without offering the cups of water to the little ones and receiving our rewards.

I'm still thinking about the starfish and the statement that it makes a difference to this one. That's true, but it is not the whole truth. By saving that one starfish, it had the opportunity to mate with another and create other starfish that would create others and that would create others. In saving one starfish, that man may have actually been responsible for the lives of millions of starfish. Likewise, when we touch one individual in a deep and meaningful way, there's no way the touch stopped with only one. Only in eternity will we know the difference the small things we did, good or bad, will have.

Brilliant

Creating Legacy vs. Saving the World

GOOD KING / BAD KING

So, here are the five key choices of a leader:

Choice # 1 – **Are you willing to serve people?**

Choice # 2 – **When you get positional power, will you continue to serve?**

Choice # 3 – **How will you handle power? Will you keep it or distribute it?**

Choice # 4 – **Will you view your position in the organization through the lens of the box or as a platform for service?**

Choice #5 – **Are you willing to serve in small ways?**

Choose Wisely

I remember a movie where Harrison Ford played Indiana Jones and was searching for the Holy Grail. Some bad guys were also searching for it, believing if they drank water from it, they would have "life eternal." After enduring many trials and tests, the final one was in the presence of an old knight who had lived seven hundred years guarding the Holy Grail. The problem was there were several cups on the table. The bad guy got there first and chose a cup that belonged to a king. It was made out of pure gold. He poured the water in and drank it. In a few seconds, his body disintegrated and he disappeared. The old knight said, "He chose poorly."

As Indiana Jones thought about the choice, he realized that the cup of Christ would not have been like that of an earthly king made of pure gold. He realized it would be the wooden cup representing humility and service. He drank out of the wooden cup, and his body didn't disintegrate. The old knight said, "You chose wisely."

Again, I don't look to the movies for my theology or truth, but I did recognize truth presented in that movie. We do have choices. We can follow what the world teaches about the importance of wealth, fame, and power by force, or we can believe what God says about humility, service, and sacrifice. Make no mistake about it; we make choices every day about which cup we will drink from. When we drink from the golden cup, our work will be judged, and it will be burned up according to 1 Corinthians 3:13. But when we make the choice to drink from the cup of Christ, our works last and they will be rewarded in eternity, and we have "life eternal."

Have you made that destiny changing, life altering choice? If you don't have the heart of the little boy that would like to be the big brother and do something for somebody else or you're not becoming more and more like that, maybe you have never drunk from the cup God offers, and maybe you don't have Him or eternal life. If so, you might want to listen to a message from Andy Stanley, the pastor of NorthPoint Community Church. If you are at all interested, please go to www.NorthPoint.org/messages/uncomplicating-Christmas. He can help you understand how to drink from that cup.

If you know that you've given your life to Christ but have a hard time living it out, you may want to read Romans 7 to find some comfort in the trouble that the great Apostle Paul had in living out who he wanted to be. In other words, if you feel like a "bad king" at times and you hate it, I do not say give up. I say welcome to the club. There were a couple of times early in my career when I made people cry by how I handled things. Later in my career, it seems I cried a lot. I cried over how I had hurt people and the opportunities I had missed to really bless people. I think I cried most over the gap between how I wanted to relate to people and how I really did at times. Then, I remembered the Apostle Paul's struggle. I also remembered that God called King David "a man after his own heart" even after he had a man murdered.

I do want to encourage you that by the power of the Holy Spirit, God can change you. It may be fast for some of you or slow for many of you like it was for me. If you desire it with all your heart, you can depend on God to help you become the servant leader and have the impact He planned for you before He created the world. Let the river of the Holy Spirit fill you up and overflow through you. He will give you strength like the current of the mighty river. He will create tipping points in your life like a mighty waterfall and create great power through you. Finally, He will lead you to your ultimate destiny through the hazards of life just like maneuvering a rocky white water mountain stream. Journey on, my friend, journey on! Lasting rewards await you.

It's your choice. Will you be a good king or bad king?

Choose Wisely!

Notes

Appendix 1

THE LESSONS OF THE RIVER

> **Thought!**
> Would you like your organization to have the strength and
> beauty of a mighty river, waterfall and stream? Would you like
> your personal life to have the same power and beauty?

"For since the creation of the world, His invisible attributes,

His eternal power and divine nature have been clearly seen,

being understood through what has been made,

so that they are without excuse."

Romans 12:1

Through nature, we see that God created everything with purpose, symmetry, and beauty. They reveal His power and His nature. A river is a great example of this. I see numerous analogies or lessons of the river for organizations and our personal lives.

Lesson #1 — Every river was created to serve a purpose. They fill the oceans, support wildlife, and provide transportation.

Your organization serves a purpose or mission in God's world and in society. Organizations that know their mission and are true to it are strong organizations. Mission creep dilutes most organizations past the first generation of leadership. Maintaining a strong focus on the mission and vision of the organization helps it achieve its purpose. A godly organization should show God's beauty and power and bring Him honor.

When you know your individual purpose in life, your life becomes more meaningful and more productive. The choices you make in life become clearer and easier. You have a greater sense of fulfillment and living out the role God has given you in His creation and in society. Your life will reveal God more and more.

Lesson #2 — Rivers have a direction and destiny. Not all rivers flow to the same place or in the same direction.

Organizations have a direction and destiny. A clear vision and priorities give the organization direction. When the vision is not clear or rightly connected to priorities, strategies, and goals, the direction becomes blurred, and the destiny may not be achieved.

Personally, your life has destiny and direction. Do you know what yours is? Your calling and goals give you direction. When you know your destiny in life, you're able to move forward with greater confidence, intensity, and endurance.

Lesson #3 — Rivers have twists and turns. They continue in the same general direction but have twists and turns. Water flows in the path of least resistance.

Effective organizations continue in the same general direction, but they do have twists and turns. Any organization that stubbornly plows straight ahead will miss some opportunities available on a slightly altered course or burn precious resources always forging straight ahead. Effective organizations will alter their original plans to pursue newly presented strategic opportunities that will move them toward their ultimate vision. They will also alter plans to avoid issues that consume too much of the organization's resources relative to the value.

Our individual lives take many twists and turns too. Wise individuals alter their courses to take advantage of opportunities that help them achieve their destiny in life. Also, they alter courses to avoid issues that can consume more time and energy than they're worth. I remember many times coaching people in the organizations I led to spend less mental and emotional time and energy on issues that were too difficult in the present. I encouraged them to spend most of their time and energy pursuing things with fewer barriers that would still lead to our mission and vision and their destiny.

Scripture says, "Man makes his plans, but God directs his steps." It's often hard for us to understand the twists and turns that God allows in our lives as we journey with Him. It is hard for us to understand in our Western culture that God is more interested in our character than either in our comfort or our career.

Lesson #4 — Rivers support life. Rivers have all kinds of wildlife. The river is a habitat and source of life for these creatures.

A good organization supports life, health, and well-being of those that are a part of it. This includes employees, volunteers, suppliers, and so on.

Your life should support the lives of others. Your contribution should make a difference to others. Your words should encourage and uplift others at times and correct them gently at other times. Scripture indicates that your words carry with them the power of life and death.

Lesson #5 — Rivers flow. If there is no flow, it may be a pond, lake, or ocean, but it is not a river.

Good organizations are a constant flow of activities, people, and results. Sometimes, the organization flows fast, and sometimes it's slower. It is not a circular flow but one with a destiny.

You minister out of the overflow of what God is doing in your own life. As you flow through life at the direction of God, your life will be engaged in many activities, impact many people, and produce substantial results for His kingdom.

Lesson #6 — Rivers have banks. Banks are boundaries to guide the flow of water but not direct each individual drop. Without banks, the river would not have a direction. It would not have a flow. It would be more like a pond, lake, or even swamp which sustains different forms of life and serves different purposes. If it rains too much and the water gets out of the banks, there is a flood which is destructive. The narrower the banks, the faster the flow of water.

Organizations have boundaries. Boundaries are created by control systems, policies and procedures, operating manuals, and training programs.. Where there are no boundaries in an organization, chaos and confusion ensue, and there is a lack of clarity for appropriate behavior. When the boundaries are too narrow, the flow and strength of the organization are hindered.

Individuals without boundaries are directionless. They make more mistakes and tend to be accountable to no one. The unaccountable life is one that's out of control and headed for a fall. Every organization needs boundaries and every individual needs boundaries. These give direction and provide safety and security.

Lesson #7 — Rivers often have waterfalls. These are tipping points where the water runs much faster and with great power and beauty.

Organizations reach tipping points where initiatives flow much faster and create much power and results with seemingly little effort. This is sometimes referred to as synergy.

The same happens in your personal life. After much time and energy is expended toward certain goals, things seem to move faster and come easier.

Lesson # 8 — Streams after the waterfalls have rocks and risk. Mountain streams are filled with rocks. Some are visible, and some aren't. The streams have great potential for danger and risk. They also have great potential for fun, such as kayaking or white-water rafting.

Organizational life is like mountain streams. There is great potential for fun and great potential for danger. You cannot be a player in organizational life without taking some risks. There are two mistakes many leaders make. One is they don't listen to the lawyers, accountants, auditors, and human resource people. The other mistake is they listen to them too much and let them run the organization and stall progress by not taking prudent God-ordained risks.

There are a lot of sayings that characterize the same principle in your personal life, like "no guts, no glory" or "nothing ventured, nothing gained." Ecclesiastes says, "He who always looks at the weather will never sow." To experience the maximum that God has for us in life, we will have to take some risks to continue toward our destiny. The Israelites had to cross the Red Sea, put their foot in the Jordon River, and fight to claim the Promised Land.

Lesson # 9 — Beavers are in the stream for their own purposes. Beavers are very hard-working and active little creatures that like to make their life off the stream. Yet, unlike the fish and other wildlife, they're not truly part of the stream. They don't flow with it. In fact, they block it and hinder the ultimate purpose of the stream.

Metaphorically speaking, organizations have beavers. These are people that are very hard-working, self-directed, and controlling, but most of all they are people that only use the stream for their own selfish interests. And, in doing so, they actually block the flow of the organization. In churches, they are often false prophets. Jesus said there would be those who would profess to be believers but would despise the cross he was to carry. They don't genuinely care about the organization, its mission or vision, but only about how they can use it for their purposes. The Apostle Paul talked about people who preached only for gain. Even if they know they're hurting the organization, they are quite content to continue doing so if it benefits them personally. If you were a pioneer and realized that beavers were building a dam blocking the flow of much needed water for your family and friends downstream, you would quickly destroy the dam and do whatever it took to remove the beavers. Yet, in organizations, life downstream for people is blocked because of these beaver-type people that are allowed to hinder the organization. Leaders should be zealous in identifying these people and tearing down the dams to the flow of the organization that have been created through unneeded policies, procedures, politics, and activities. They should remove these individuals in a Christ-like way from the organization.

In our individual lives, we need to be aware of people who act like beavers. They use us inappropriately for what they want and block the flow of our lives. They may be very industrious, but they do not care about the flow of our lives and will hinder our progress to the extent we let them.

Lesson #10 — Some fish are not suited for a river. God made all kinds of fish and rivers are a great habitat for some but not others. The beautiful marlin would not survive in a river.

Not all people are suited for your organization. Some can exist and thrive there; others won't. Some people are made for larger organizations, others for smaller organizations, and others for more stagnant organizations that are more like a pond or lake. It's critical that you find people that fit the culture of your organization.

In your personal life, it's important that you align with organizations that you fit. Don't be a fish out of water. Don't be a fish swimming upstream. Understand the kind of organization that you fit. Some people like to be a big fish in a small pond. Some people like to be a bigger fish in an ocean. There's not a right or wrong answer other than following your unique destiny and living out the calling that God gave you.

Lesson #11 — There's great beauty in the river, waterfall, and stream. The river goes beyond just its practical value to show the beauty and grandeur of the creator.

While organizations should all serve a practical purpose, there should be a beauty that you observe from a distance in how it operates. The beauty of our Creator should be seen in a godly organization.

Our individual lives are about much more than just the work we do and what we produce. There should be a beauty about the life of an individual that shows the glory of our Creator. Legalists never show this beauty or even experience this beauty in their lives because they are so focused on "doing" that they cover up the beauty of the spirit-led life.

Lesson # 12 — Rivers are created from a series of streams. Numerous streams and creeks come together to create the mighty river. Streams flow into the river and become part of the river.

In organizational life, you may run a department or a division. If you do, remember it's not about your department. It's not about your division. It's about the organization. Everything you do should bring life and health for the organization and bring honor to God.

In your personal life, your stream intersects many other people's lives. But, it's not all about you. It's about the greater flow and purpose of what God is doing in his created universe. Your life should point people to God and honor Him.

Application

I. Which of these lessons have you learned?

_____

_____

_____

_____

_____

II. Which ones do you need to work on?

_____

_____

_____

_____

_____

Appendix 2

SIGNS OF A GREAT ORGANIZATION

> Thought!
> Have you ever thought about what your organization is like
> compared to what it could be? What does the ideal look like for you?
> How big is the gap between what could be
> and what is in your organization?

"Let all things be done decently and in order."

1 Corinthians 14:40

For those of you who have made it this far, God bless you. You're troopers! As I reflect on the journey of our discussion, I thought about what the ideal organization, career, or life would be like. Here's what I see.

ORGANIZATIONAL LIFE

God made everything on purpose and for a purpose. A great organization has a clear purpose/mission and vision. It creates a needed or viable product or service for the good of mankind and society. The mission and vision of the organization attracts the right people like a magnet.

The people in the organization can live out their calling in life by doing what the organization needs them to do to create its product or service and serve its customers/constituents well. The people feel privileged to be part of the organization and its mission. They share its values, and they are excited about its vision.

They clearly understand their role in achieving the mission, vision, and priorities of the organization. They believe what they do contributes in a meaningful way that brings them fulfillment and joy. When you ask them about their role they say, "I was made—created—to do this. If money weren't a factor, I would do this anyway and work hard at it." Other people comment on how well I'm suited for this role.

The leadership and team would be clear about the priorities daily, weekly, monthly, and annually. There would not be confusion over the real priorities, too many priorities, or constantly changing priorities. The organization's priorities and team priorities would be the same.

The leaders would empower people to do their jobs. The people could count on their leaders to help and support them when needed, but they would not become dependent on the leaders for the bulk of their job. The expectations would be like those of a family—high but achievable and appropriate to each individual. People would feel as if they owned an important functional piece of the organization. They would feel fairly and generously recognized and rewarded for their contribution. The team would work hard but would have fun together.

The leaders and team would work together to ensure measurable progress. They would plan and anticipate obstacles, create constructive change programs, and pilot projects for improvement, all of which would be the norm. Change would be innovative and steady versus reactionary.

There would be strong documentation to facilitate ongoing training in order to develop the potential of each individual. It would be a culture of continuous learning, continuous innovation and increasing delight in the product/service by the customers/constituencies.

Control systems would be supportive of progress and help send early warning signals of issues that could hinder progress. They would not be onerous or obstructive.

Measures of key contributions to the mission, vision, and priorities of the organization would be made and shared in a meaningful way so that people felt a sense of accomplishment routinely.

It would be an organization that people were proud to be associated with and would have a hard time thinking about leaving.

Application

I. Does this describe your organization? Yes_____ No_____

II. Identify the gaps.

_____

_____

_____

_____

III. What do you believe are the root causes of the gaps?

_____

_____

_____

_____

IV. What actions will you take to close the gaps?

_____

_____

_____

_____

V. What are the three most important things you can begin doing now to help improve your organization?

_____

_____

_____

_____

Appendix 3

MASLOW'S HIERARCHY

Thought!
Have you ever considered how much more productive
and happy your people might be if you knew their
real needs and were able to help meet them?

"I came that you might have life and have it to the full."

John 10:10

I think you see clearly now how goals drive behavior. The question now becomes how to understand people's goals and begin to influence behavior in a positive way. One way is a thorough understanding of Maslow's hierarchy of needs (which I learned about in college). Many leaders have a surface and somewhat shallow understanding and application of Maslow's hierarchy for their organization. Maslow's hierarchy says that people tend to satisfy their most basic needs first and then satisfy their higher needs. Maslow said people's needs are:

- **Physical** — food, clothing and shelter

- **Security** — the continued provisions of food (clothing and shelter for the long term)

- **Social** — positive interrelationships with other people

- **Esteem** — to be thought well of or valued

- **Self-actualization/self-realization** — becoming all we were created to be

- **Transcendence** — being part of something larger than ourselves

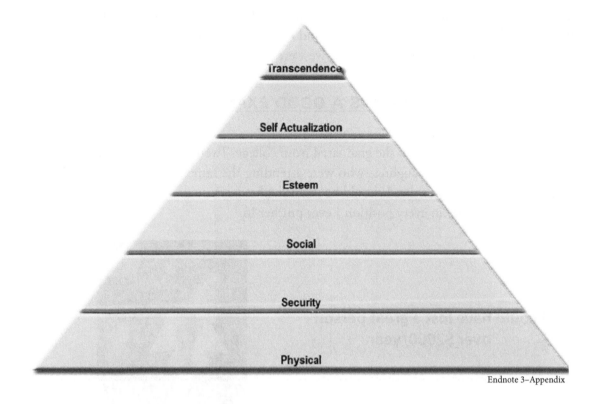

Endnote 3–Appendix

I've had some successes and enough blunders in all these areas that have deepened my understanding in the areas above. Scripture is clear that we are to build others up according to their needs. We should not withhold something that people need when it's in our power to act. This means, in being a good steward for organization, is it within our power to give the people what they need? If so, we should do that. Let's unpack each area of Maslow's hierarchy, and I will share some of my mistakes and things I learned along the way.

PHYSICAL

Early in my career, I made mistakes on the first step of the hierarchy—physical. I interviewed a lot of young accountants for positions in the internal audit department. My approach was to sell them on the wonderful career opportunities available for them over the long run in such great company. We offered fair and competitive salaries. When someone wanted to haggle over $1000 or $2000 in salary, I would get very frustrated because I thought they were missing the bigger picture of the opportunities ahead. I'm embarrassed to admit that sometimes I didn't hire really good candidates because of this frustration.

When I began to understand Maslow's hierarchy better, I realized that it didn't matter to the candidate as much what the future was until they were comfortable and could pay for their apartment, car, food, and clothing. My perspective changed. If another $1000 or $2000 really made a difference to them, was still in the pay range, and I thought they were worth it, I would hire them and tell them I expected them to earn what we were paying.

LISA IS A GOOD EXAMPLE

I hired Lisa just a few years after she graduated from college. Twenty-five years later, we were having lunch introducing our daughters who were attending the same college. Lisa thanked me for hiring her. My response was that I should be thanking her because she was such a good employee and helped enormously in every position I ever put her in.

I could have lost a great person over $2000/year

She reminded me of our first interview. She wanted $2000 more dollars than I initially offered. I thought she was an outstanding candidate and quickly gave her the $2000 and finalized the offer. I told her I expected she would earn the extra money. Her first project was rather complicated, and she did an outstanding job. Within six months, we paid a special one-time bonus to everyone on the team including Lisa for their good work. The $2000 and extra bonus cost very little from the company's perspective, but we got a truly outstanding employee who worked for the company for many years and in several positions. I shudder to think of the lost opportunities for the company if I had been shortsighted in this situation over the starting salary.

Career potential doesn't matter to people who can't pay their bills today.

This doesn't mean that I paid all candidates what they asked for in an interview. I only did that for truly outstanding candidates who were operating on step one of Maslow's hierarchy.

SECURITY

A lot of organizations' understanding of the security aspect of Maslow's hierarchy are restricted to the retirement, healthcare, and other benefits portions of the total compensation package. For way too much of my career, I did not understand the depth of the security issue. It includes retirement benefits, healthcare, and other perks. But it goes deeper. The deeper aspects for people are:

- How secure are they in their job?

- How secure are they in their relationship with you as their leader?

- Do they know where they stand with you?

- Do they believe you are for them?

- Do they believe that you have their back?

CALL FROM AN OLD FRIEND NEEDING ASSURANCE

I got a call from a friend. She had not worked for me for a long time. She was getting a new boss and was really nervous. She was putting a lot of pressure on herself trying to ensure she had the perfect first day. She wanted me to help her think of anything she may have forgotten. She told me what she had done to prepare, which was more than adequate. So, did I rack my brain trying to think of anything else she could've done? No, she was already very prepared. What she needed was not a longer list of prepared items. She needed confidence. She needed a sense of security.

Employees asking what else they can do are often seeking affirmation and security.

So what did I do? I gave her confidence and security. I reminded her that she was the best person in her role that I knew from a very long career. I reminded her of the background the new leader was coming from and that she was better than anything he'd ever been used to. I told her that if there was anything else he wanted, she would be more qualified to get it quickly than anyone else. By the time I finished explaining to her the confidence I had in her and how well-prepared she was, she was very calm and settled. Had I simply added to her list, she would've been even more prepared but still anxious and insecure. People are more creative and do a better job when they are calm and secure. They make mistakes when they are nervous and scared.

Sometimes, when employees ask you if there's anything else they can do for you, they are not always asking or volunteering for more work. Often they are seeking affirmation and security. If you have hired good employees, you have put yourself in the perfect position always to be affirming from the heart when employees feel insecure. And it is very critical in affirming employees that you be genuine. The best employees can spot a fake affirmation from a long distance.

BEING POSITIONED TO HONESTLY GIVE ASSURANCE

One of the ways to ensure that you can continually give employees the affirmation they need is to hire great people. When you take shortcuts in the interview process or hire somebody just to fill a position quickly, you are not confident that you have the right person. If you make a poor choice in hiring or in delegating a particular project, you will start to have doubts about the person's ability to get the job done. When you have doubts, you cannot maintain your integrity and give employees assurances that they can do the job.

Hire great people and you can give affirmation easily

Do they believe you are for them?

To feel secure, employees need to know that you are for them. You may ask who I would be for. Well, unfortunately, many are watching out for "number one." There are just too many leaders quick to take credit for anything good and quick to place blame on employees when things don't work out. Do you really think there's any security among employees under that kind of leadership?

"Do not look out merely for your own interests.

Look out for the interests of others."

Philippians 2:4

"... Give preference to one another in honor."

Romans 12:10

Unless employees simply can't pay the bills with a different job, they will leave those leaders quickly for more security. The key here is, do your employees believe you have their best interests in mind? Are you watching out for them? Do you really care about them? Or is your only concern the organization and perhaps yourself? When people know you are for them, they feel more secure and they are more loyal. That does not mean that you are not to be a good steward of the organization's resources. It does not mean that you say employees are right when you know they are wrong. It simply means that you know you have good employees and that you are an advocate for them, keeping in balance the good of the total organization and fairness to others.

Do they believe you have their back?

I never considered myself an easy leader to work with. I tended to have really high expectations of myself and others. When I left HCA, I had a great team. I really thought and feared they might be relieved to see me leave, hoping they would have an easier time with another leader. That's not what I saw as I made the transition. I sensed they considered my leaving a loss for them personally. I was curious about that. I asked them about that six months later and then a year later.

People need to know you "have their back."

I told them I knew I was not easy to work with, and I asked was the loss they expressed real and if so, why? Several reasons were given but the one they were all adamant about was "Yes, you were tough, but we knew you cared about us and that you always had our back. Because you had our back, we were free to go do our work without fear. We knew that you could and would take care of us." I asked them, "Isn't that what other leaders do?" They said, "Not consistently and not adamantly. We knew you would go to the mat for us." I asked all my direct reports, "And that really makes that kind of difference to you?" Every single person said, "Absolutely." After being a professional leader in a big organization for thirty-one years, I missed the depth of how important this issue is to people.

THE SUBCONTRACTOR

I had a guy doing some work around my house. He seemed troubled one day. So, I asked if something was wrong. He just had two customers file bankruptcy and would not receive payment from them. He started asking me for business advice. I inquired about what that meant to him financially. After discussion, I told him if he got in a jam on his cash flow that I would make him a loan. I told him that I knew he was good for it. He never asked for a loan and was able to work everything out over time, as I expected he would.

What I did not realize at the time was the impact this simple offer had on him. He mentioned this at least three or four times over the next few years and cited it as a real turning point for him. He always cited the fact that, since he knew I had his back, he could quit worrying and just work on improving the situation. He said that without this assurance, he might have continued worrying and not done all that was necessary to make his business successful.

This again reminded me of the importance of people feeling secure, knowing someone has their back, and being able to do their best work. Think about it. It's hard to put your full attention and energy into your work and look over your shoulder at the same time, isn't it? He started out asking me for business advice. And I could have simply given him some advice and moved on. But the advice alone would not have helped him that much. What he needed most was security and the confidence that he was going to be okay. I gave him that, and he has said many times since that it made a difference at that point in his life.

FEAR AS A MOTIVATOR

It's hard to be creative and do your best work when you are scared.

Fear is a powerful motivator. Some people manage by fear. It feels so productive. People are responsive because they are so motivated by fear. Yet, this does not produce the most productive organization over time. People operating in cultures of fear do not take risks. They don't tend to be creative except in how to relieve their own fears. Their primary focus is on how to do what the boss wants without getting in trouble. It is not on how to make the organization the best it can be.

SOCIAL

We are social creatures. We were designed for relationships with others. I realized that relationships were important. But being more task-oriented, I think I underestimated the value of relationships in organizational life. Plus, I underestimated the role they play in bringing joy to your life when you give them the right focus. A lawyer once asked Jesus to sum up the teachings of the Old Testament. The answer was, "Love the Lord your God with all your heart and soul and mind and your neighbor as yourself." Human beings quite simply were designed for relationships with God and others. Yes, some people are quiet and even withdrawn. That doesn't mean they don't need relationships. In fact, sometimes people with these personality profiles make the most loyal friends.

This point is proven by major firms who do employee attitude surveys for companies. A question that shows up in all the best surveys is "Do you have a best friend at work?" The surveys ask this question because it is a well-established fact that when people have a best friend at work, they are much happier and less likely to leave than those who answer no to this question.

People who work together and have fun together want to stay together. Some leaders think "nose to the grindstone" teams are the most productive. I have never seen that to be true. The most productive teams are those who work together, play together, and enjoy each other's company. There's greater trust among the team members, which deals with people's need for security. It's very hard to optimize the output of the team without high levels of trust. When people know each other personally and have fun together, trust tends to be built.

When I left HCA to form Vision Leadership, there were a number of things I missed. The thing I missed most, and without a close second, was the relationships I had with people. That's something I knew I would miss. But frankly, I didn't fully realize how much of my social life and friendships were tied to HCA. I didn't socialize outside of work with these people. My sense of professional boundaries and decorum kept me from doing that. But I was surprised to realize just how much fun, social interaction, and friendship had been built over the years.

Organizations that provide forums for employees to have fun together, socialize, and develop deeper friendships will retain people longer. They will have higher morale and, in the long-term, be more productive if the other aspects of leadership are done well.

Jesus was not the dull, drab figure that many people picture. He went to weddings and feasts. He often went to social gatherings at people's houses. In fact, he was accused by his critics, the Pharisees, of drinking too much and hanging out with the wrong crowd. Jesus had a good social life, and he engaged his disciples in it.

I started my career at HCA in the internal audit department. The job required a lot of travel, extremely long hours, hard work, and being with the team fourteen to sixteen hours per day. We ate breakfast, lunch, and dinner together. We often went out after dinner if we were at a good location with fun activities. We literally lived together five days a week when we were on the road, which was most of the time. During this season of my life, I worked harder for less pay than any other season of my thirty-one years with HCA. I still remember these as the times I made some of my deepest, most long-lasting friends. These were the times I had the most fun.

I thoroughly enjoyed my last few years at HCA in Physician Services. We had built a team that liked one another and just enjoyed working together. I really miss those folks. We built something very special together.

**One bad apple
can spoil the basket.**

The times I mentioned above weren't 100% good. During the internal audit season, it only took one bad member of the team to mess up the whole social fabric and make what should've been a great time a miserable time for the team. Fortunately, we understood that and were pretty quick to move people on when they messed up the team dynamics. Dr. Frist, Sr., one of HCA's founders, used to say, "Good people beget good people, and bad people beget bad people." He knew well the impact that a bad apple can have on the team.

I remember the same thing in Physician Services. We had great individuals. They worked really hard, and they were extremely competent in their roles. The problem was there were two or three who did not like most of the team. They were critical, accusing, and generally disruptive. The whole synergy of the team was affected because there was no trust. The team didn't watch each other's back. People were pitted against each other. And while they were all incredibly smart, worked very hard, and accomplished a lot, it simply was not what it could have been and should have been. I knew I was responsible for that as the leader. So, I had to make hard choices and some changes. Candidly, I hired people with less experience and less technical competence but with good people skills and a proper attitude toward teamwork and a similar work ethic.

So what happened? The productivity of the entire team went up. Morale went up. People enjoyed working together. They enjoyed being in meetings and seeing each other. The entire culture changed. As the leader, I was responsible. I should have done something to have avoided the problems in the culture and certainly should have done something sooner to have addressed the culture.

ESTEEM

"Give preference to one another in honor."

Romans 12: 10

In our culture, we talk much about self-esteem. But we don't spend as much time talking about showing esteem to others. We like to be thought well of. We like to be valued. It's a basic need people have. And the Bible teaches that we should do it. It says, "To think of others more highly than yourself." Of course, all people of all ages need to be esteemed. I've noticed as people mature in professional life, being esteemed takes on more value.

> *Some people would be happier with less compensation and more esteem.*

As a practical matter, how do we do this? Really, it's quite simple. Hire people that are more gifted for their job than you would be, a job that they will enjoy. Then, you can appreciate their talent and their willingness to do work that you are not suited for and don't like doing.

The message of many corporate cultures expressed or implied is "If you can't get the job done, we will find somebody that can." This mindset doesn't place a value on past service or the value of a unique individual to the organization. It assumes that if the results aren't being achieved, it's the fault of the job holder, and a change is necessary if the results don't change. Sometimes that is the case, but often it's not.

I know people in various organizations who would trade blocks of their compensation package to be genuinely esteemed by the organization's leadership. The mistake we make in organizational life, and that I've made, is to show appreciation and esteem to people only when the results are good. We tend to show esteem most when people need it least. Think about it. People know they're doing well, and they feel good when the results are positive. It is when results are not positive that people need to be esteemed the most.

I remember a turnaround situation I was involved in. I was working my hardest, being the most creative, and doing some of the best work of my career. In most situations, a lot of hard work and good planning happen a long while before results turn. That's where I was. And the corporate bureaucrats, not the top leaders, constantly made life hard on me. That reminded me of the time on the family farm when I was carrying a one hundred pound feed sack, and my much smaller brother hit me at the knees. I went down, of course. You can't carry that much weight and be hit at the knees and stay on your feet. My little brother did not know or care about that at the time.

We expect better out of our leaders. But, we don't always get it. I don't mean to be overly critical of others. I admit to not doing any better myself at times.

It's Monday...

It's Wednesday...

I remember vividly how it felt to be carrying such heavy weight and how unfair it felt for others to be piling on. If I had been lazy or doing the wrong thing, their involvement and follow-up could have been constructive. That not being the case, it only took more time away from important activities, caused me to work longer hours under more stress than was necessary, and with far less respect for those who were choosing to make life hard.

"That I may be encouraged together with you while among you."

Romans 1:12

After many months of some of the hardest and best work I had ever done in my career, the results started to turn around. Then, people started bragging on me. They said glowing things about me. I was relieved due to the lack of pressure, but the accolades from "other people" meant nothing to me. They were not really esteeming me. They were happy over the results and giving me all the credit. I wasn't due all the credit any more than I was due all the blame earlier. When things smoothed out, I wasn't working nearly as hard, as smart, or as creatively as months earlier. But, I was bragged on more for my hard work and intelligence than any other time in my career.

So what's wrong with this picture? I'm doing my hardest and best work ever under constant criticism when I most need to be esteemed and feel some sense of security. When the results change and I'm feeling good and secure based on the results, unneeded flattery and praise are abundant.

The situation reminds me of an interview with Jeff Fisher who was coach of the Tennessee Titans football team. Two years earlier, the Titans had come up one yard short of winning the Super Bowl. This particular year, they were having a tough season, and the TV broadcasters and fans were giving Coach Fisher a hard time. He stared into the camera and simply said, "Listen, two years ago, we came up one yard short of winning the Super Bowl. We haven't forgotten how to coach." In the experience I described earlier, I had worked for the company for over seventeen years. It wasn't like they didn't know me, my capabilities, or my past contributions. The bureaucrats, not the top leaders, who unleashed on me, simply didn't care.

I have to be honest and admit that even after that experience, I found myself doing the same thing to others at times. When we are under pressure and trying to get things done and when we are focused on our own image and reputation, it's really easy to forget about what the other people need. Our default mode is always to tell people what we want and expect and to blame them when the results aren't there. We truly have to be in a mode of thinking about what other people need most in the circumstances. Often that requires us to do something or say something the opposite of what we feel like saying at the time. I'm not suggesting at all that you ever lie or mislead people about what you are thinking. I'm simply suggesting that sometimes we need to think more clearly. We give people an assignment because we think they can do it based on their past history. If they truly can't do it, we are most at fault for delegating it to them and should point the finger at ourselves first.

Brilliance and hard work precede good results, so should the praise and encouragement.

If we've done a good job delegating, we should believe in the people to whom we gave the assignment, give them reasonable freedom, and follow-up at reasonable intervals. Most importantly, when the assignment is really challenging, we should remember to encourage and show our esteem for them as a valuable member of the team.

THE PASTOR'S WIFE

All people need to be esteemed. Their role in life doesn't eliminate the need. It's pretty surprising, at times, people who don't receive the esteem they should from others. I know a story about a pastor's wife who had a birthday party. She and her husband had served faithfully in ministry their whole lives. They had served one church for twenty years. The lady was a widow and some church friends were throwing her an 80th birthday party. She happened to comment how much she appreciated the party. Her next comment wasn't stated negatively but was quite a surprise. She said she had never had a party or recognition just for her. Everything else in her life had been associated with her pastor husband or the church. She was genuinely touched because at eighty years old, her church friends had a birthday party just for her.

ROCK QUARRY EMPLOYEE PUTS ON SUIT FOR CHRISTMAS BARBECUE

Gizmo worked at the rock quarry. He wore steel-toe boots, a hard hat, and dusty clothes like everyone else who worked there. Every year, we had the Christmas barbecue lunch at the quarry. Everyone else wore their steel-toe boots, hard hats, and dusty clothes, but not Gizmo. Gizmo wore a suit and tie. As a college kid observing this for the first time, it struck me really odd. So I asked the foreman, "What's the deal with Gizmo?" He told me that one year Gizmo dressed up a little bit for the lunch. Jim, the manager of the rock quarry, bragged on him and commented on how good he looked. Every year since then, Gizmo put on a suit and tie for the Christmas barbecue. Gizmo needed to feel important. He needed to stand out. He very deeply needed to be esteemed. The comments he got at the Christmas lunch may have been the most significant time during the year when he felt esteemed.

GOOD WAYS TO ESTEEM OTHERS

One of the most impactful ways I discovered of showing esteem is to write a personal note or letter to people. It doesn't have to be long, but it needs to be sincere, personal, and specific to them. I remember a guy who worked for me for several years and moved twice in the process. I wrote him a personal handwritten letter thanking him for some specific contributions to the company. Years later, he talked about the letter in front of a group of people. He teared up as he said it was the first letter he ever received in his life thanking him for anything. The tragedy is he was in his mid to late 50's when I wrote the letter.

Have you ever thrown away a heartfelt note that showed you esteem?

I've seen two different men tear up from something I wrote. The first was when I was a young manager and had written a curt note on a report from an employee. I happened to walk by his office as he was reading the note and saw the hurt on his face. That was over thirty years ago. It was the first time I had ever written a note like that, and it was the last. I never want to be responsible for making someone feel that way again. The second man I saw tear up over something I wrote was the one I wrote the nice note to. When I saw that, I thought about how many years I had been a leader and how many opportunities I had missed to show esteem to others or to bring them joy.

Think about it. How many personal notes have you received in your life where someone showed you esteem? How many of them have you thrown away? I've never thrown any of mine away and don't plan to. That's the difference they make. It may be one of the easiest, the most highly impactful things leaders can do.

> *People never throw away any letters or notes that esteem them.*

SELF-ACTUALIZATION

Self-actualization is becoming all you were created to be. It means to realize your true purpose and calling. Organizations have a tendency to put people in a box they don't fit in, reward them for staying in it, and punish them for getting outside it. God did not create us to fit in boxes. He created us with the unique design to achieve the unique purpose that only we can achieve at our place and time in history. We need to help our people be all they can be and help them in the direction of their calling in life.

> *Leaders should quit trying to make people be what they want them to be and quit trying to make them something they're not.*

In the year 2000, the pastor of our church talked to me about quitting my job and taking the role of executive pastor. After much prayer, I didn't sense I was supposed to quit my job, but I did know I was supposed to help. I talked to my boss about taking some compensation concessions and having 25% of my time to devote to the church as a volunteer in this role. The leadership of the company supported my request. My performance goals were not lowered, but I was given the freedom to help my church. My loyalty to the company and its leadership went up. I did this for three years and life at the top of Maslow's hierarchy and my final commitment and service to the company only improved after that. They helped me self-actualize, and I will always be grateful to them for that.

TRANSCENDENCE

This means being part of something larger than ourselves. We were created to live at the apex of Maslow's hierarchy. Each of us has an invitation from the creator of the universe to join in His work of caring for the creation and for the redemption of mankind. In Dan Miller's recent book *Wisdom Meets Passion*, he draws attention to the fact that some young people today are rejecting the focus on themselves and meeting their needs first as Maslow's theory teaches. Instead, they are pursuing their calling and connecting to purposes beyond themselves. They are pursuing meaning in life and not money, possessions, or status.

SUMMARY

"Now he who supplies seed to the sower and bread for food

will supply and multiply your seed for sowing

and increase the harvest of your righteousness."

2 Corinthians 9:10

"And God is able to make all grace abound to you,

so that always having all sufficiency in everything,

you may have an abundance for every good deed."

2 Corinthians 8:14

God has already met and will continue to meet every need described in Maslow's hierarchy. He meets our physical needs. In Matthew, He tells us, "Seek ye first the kingdom of God and his righteousness, and all these other things will be added to you." One of his most frequent commands is, "Do not be afraid," or "Do not be anxious." He is in control of the universe and will take care of everything that concerns us and will work it for our good if we love him and are called according to his purpose. Therefore, we can feel secure. If we came close to following all the biblical instructions on relating to each other, we would have an incredible social life, and people would esteem us. We will especially be esteemed if we discover our purpose and calling in life and live it out to the best of our ability. Our uniqueness will be noticed, and

Are you moving your people up Maslow's Hierarchy or moving them down?

our contribution will be substantial. The esteem of others will naturally follow. Finally, when we are living out our purpose and calling in life, we are in fact self-actualizing.

God created us with the dream in mind of all people being able to self-actualize throughout their life. It is still God's plan.

COMMON QUESTIONS ABOUT MASLOW'S HIERARCHY

Trying to understand and apply Maslow's hierarchy to your team can be challenging. Questions that are sometimes raised by people I talk to are:

- Can a person be on more than one step at the same time?

- Can a person move backward down the hierarchy?

- How do I determine where a person is in the hierarchy?

- What is my role as a leader?

More than one step?

Yes, a person can be on more than one step in Maslow's hierarchy. In fact, people can and usually are on a couple of steps at the same time until they reach the top. For example, people who have a need for security also have social needs to be met. People who are focused on the social needs may also be at a point where being esteemed is very important to them. People being esteemed or needing esteem can also be moving toward self-actualization.

Can people move backward?

Yes. Unfortunately, in our complex society, moving back down the hierarchy happens with some frequency. A common example is in divorce or death of the spouse. People may be functioning toward the high end of the hierarchy and because of divorce or death of the spouse, they are back at the bottom focused on meeting the physical needs and perhaps worried about their individual security. I talked to a man this week in his later sixties who had retired early but is going back to work because of losses in the stock market.

Another example is a failure due to addiction. People may be quite successful in their career but begin to drink too much or use drugs or get involved in Internet pornography and fall prey to the addiction. That can result in a job being lost and a good career being derailed. In our culture, it is not uncommon for this to happen. People over-stimulate to fulfill their social needs and cause their own failure.

Another common occurrence is people who need to be esteemed but are not feeling valued and are turning to alcohol, drugs, or extramarital affairs to medicate that vacuum.

A leader may ask, "Can I stop people from moving backward on Maslow's hierarchy?" Perhaps the best way to look at this is "Am I doing anything that puts the team at risk of moving backward?" For example, "Am I creating a culture that encourages people to live unbalanced lifestyles? Does my culture reward workaholics?" If people have unbalanced lives, that may create anxiety which moves them to dependence on alcohol or drugs. If I create workaholics, these people are not giving their spouses or children the time they need which can contribute to divorce, to significant family problems, or to health issues down the road.

How do I determine where a person is in the hierarchy?

The best way to determine where people are in Maslow's hierarchy is simply to listen to them. You may have to do some of this during a relaxed time, such as a casual lunch. Maybe a chat session at the end of the business discussion is where they will loosen up. Listen for what they're worried about and listen to their goals. Listen for what irritates them and what excites them. These will lead you to where people are on the hierarchy.

What is my role as a leader?

Since God intended for all the needs of Maslow's hierarchy to be met in people's lives, the leaders should realize they are in a position to help fill some of these needs or to actually hinder the process.

Very simply, your role as leaders is to understand where people are in Maslow's hierarchy and to use your influence to meet their needs within the context of the goals and values of the organization. Also, great leaders will work to help people find their way to the top of Maslow's hierarchy. In essence, they help people realize their destiny and fulfill their calling in life. Remember the story of the brick layers earlier in the book. Your role is to move them from brick layers to builders to cathedral builders.

Application to non-profits

There is a general tendency in non-profit organizations to think they cannot be effective because they use volunteers and need more paid staff. From a logistical standpoint, there may be merit to this because of when and how much of their time is available. However, we should not underestimate the potential value of volunteers in our organizations. A paycheck addresses the physical and some of the security needs that individuals are motivated to work for. That leaves four other levels of needs that have nothing to do with money by which people can be motivated. People can become very highly motivated to meet these other needs. In fact, I think people are most motivated to reach the level of self-actualization. In other words, to become the people that God created them to become and to fulfill their destiny.

Application

I. Mark where you are on Maslow's hierarchy of needs. Write your name there.

II. Where is each key member of your team? Write their names there.

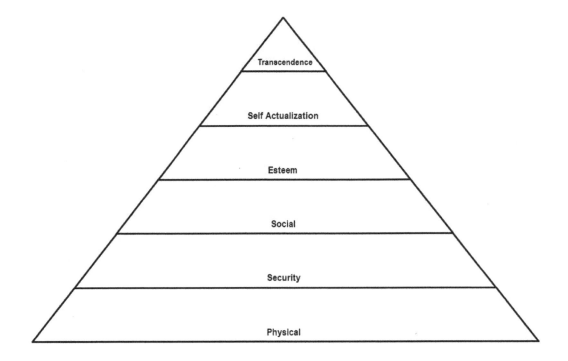

III. What do you need to change to help meet their needs and move them up the hierarchy?

Team Member

1. _____

   _____

   _____

2. _____

   _____

   _____

3. _____

   _____

   _____

4. _____

   _____

   _____

5. _____

   _____

   _____

Notes

Appendix 4

MOTIVATION HAZARDS

Thought:
How much would morale and productivity in your
organization improve if you could figure out
what derails motivation and avoid it?

"Do not covet your neighbor's house..."

Exodus 20:17

It seems like it should be so simple, doesn't it? First, motivate people and don't de-motivate them. But there are a lot of hazards that derail motivation. Let's discuss some.

Hazard # 1 – I Want More – The Basis for the Peter Principle

Wanting more often causes good people to be promoted to their level of in-competence – Peter Principle.

It seems inherent in human nature that we never have enough. No matter what we have, we want more. No matter how much we achieve, we want to do a little more. A reporter once asked a billionaire, "How much money is enough?" He said, "Just a little more." From a pure motivation standpoint, that has a positive aspect because people are driven to set goals and achieve more.

There are also some pitfalls though. Setting goals and achieving more for God and the good of others are great. But, setting goals that cause you to live beyond your strengths and talents aren't good. Have you ever noticed people in a job that fits them perfectly, but they are not content? It's a real tragedy to see people unhappy in a position that really fits them simply because they want more just for the sake of more. More what? Sometimes more power, recognition, or money, and sometimes all of these. So, what happens when this occurs? People don't have the satisfaction and joy in their work that they should have.

Ecclesiastes says, "There is nothing better under the sun than for a person to enjoy their labor." Sometimes, people make change for the sake of change. They ask for assignments they are not good at and experience unnecessary failure.

You may be familiar with the Peter Principle. This is "a management theory which suggests that organizations risk filling management roles with people who are incompetent if they promote those who are performing well at their current role." [4] A name was developed for this by Laurence J. Peter in his book *The Peter Principle* [5] because it happens so frequently in organizational life. Why? There are two practical reasons. The first is leaders not understanding the real skills, talents, and passions of their team. They take talented, gifted, hard workers who have done a good job, and they naturally assume the workers can do more without understanding their personality profile versus the profile required in the new role. Entrepreneurial leaders in startup organizations, for-profit and non-profit, often deal with limited staffing. Therefore, they often expect people to be better than they really are at certain things.

Somehow many leaders think the only fair thing to do is give good, loyal employees a promotion. Let's think about this. When it doesn't work out, have we really done those employees a favor? Usually, when the Peter Principle occurs, the position they once occupied and were successful in has already been filled. And even if it weren't, their ego wouldn't allow them to move back to it. People are most often lost to the organization. That's tragic for them and for the organization.

If you are going to bless people as a leader, you are going to give deserving employees promotions they desire that fit their talents, passions, and gifts. But, you are also going to encourage other people to stay where they fit. Encourage them to be content in roles that fit them rather than letting them be unsuccessful in a new position, or perhaps successful, but unhappy, because they don't fit the role. Sometimes, this seems counterintuitive or even unfair. But is it really? Which is best for the employees over the long term? So, why do leaders do this?

The second reason leaders do this is because employees expect it. Leaders want to accommodate good employees and sometimes feel the pressure to not disappoint them. This comes full circle to the point we were making. Because people tend to want more, they press their leaders/managers to put them in roles they don't fit, or that don't fit as well. "When they merely follow the dollar signs and can do it, but fail to acknowledge their unique personality style, they ultimately end up depressed, unproductive, or struggling in other areas of their lives."[6]

Hazard # 2 -- Expectations Not Met

I've seen many people develop unrealistic expectations and get disappointed. Sometimes, the least qualified individuals have the highest expectations. I have dealt many times in my career with people whom I was not even considering for promotion because their performance was average at best, but they thought they should be receiving a promotion. Sometimes, their expectations are reasonable, but things just didn't work out.

That's not what I expected!

Maybe they expected a promotion and they were qualified but someone else was more qualified, or they should've been chosen but were not. This leads to disappointment and usually a drop in productivity.

WHO MOVED MY CHEESE?[7]

Employees feel depressed when they experience a change from what they are accustomed to. The change could be any of a number of things. It could be a change in the benefits package. It could be the perks, privileges, bonus structure, equity participation, or salary. If any of that is reduced, they feel shorted.

We're not in Kansas anymore, Toto!

If you take away a benefit or a perk, people feel shorted... whether they have been or not.

Sometimes, organizations that have done very well and have very rich packages in all areas need to make reductions to stay competitive. Employees don't tend to view these changes in light of the bigger picture. They don't think about the fact that the company staying competitive is actually the best way for them to have long-term job security. Instead, they tend to look at what they're giving up and feel shorted. This is true even though what they have may be still at or above the norms for their industry. They don't typically think, "Well I'm glad the company is going to continue to be competitive and strong. I'm glad the package I have still beats the norm in the industry." Unfortunately, they typically look at what they gave up and feel shorted.

I have a friend who is a small business owner. He did many things over the years to be good to his employees. In fact, when he was doing well, they did very well. They were actually paid above industry norms for their roles. When the economy had its downturn, he needed to rightly adjust some pay scales to operate competitively. A leader would hope that employees would be appreciative for what they had received in the past, look at their overall compensation package relative to industry norms, understand the current business environment, and put the compensation change in perspective. His employees didn't. They felt shorted, even though that was not at all the case. My friend's experience is actually very typical in organizations, for-profit and non-profit.

So what do we do? We should design compensation packages, benefit packages, and other perks with the idea in mind that the competitive landscape changes and reducing any of these can cause employees to feel like they are getting shorted. I can remember times when I was able to do something beyond the norm for a particular employee. I was always careful to explain the circumstances. I explained that while I was able to do something more this year, it would not likely be the norm. I did this to manage future expectations so the employee did not feel shorted the next year when I could not do the same or more.

We see this played out in the automobile industry with unions. Take General Motors, for example. By any national or international standards, their employees had incredible health benefit packages. Yet, anytime the company would try to change any part of the benefits system to be more competitive, the unions treated it as unfair. This resulted in General Motors eventually going bankrupt. All the employees would have lost their jobs had it not been for a government bailout. Then, packages were changed to stay in business. And, guess what? The employees still felt like they had been shorted.

THOU SHALT NOT COVET

People tend to feel shorted when they look at what others have and think they deserve the same or more. This is where Jesus' command not to covet your neighbor is so important. Looking at what others have and thinking we deserve the same or more only leads to unhappiness when we don't get it. Actually, sometimes we are right. We do deserve more. Being unhappy about it won't change anything and will likely cause us to have attitudes and behaviors that reduce our chance for more in the future. Generally, however, we are not in a good position to objectively evaluate what we should have versus what other people have. And the comparison game only leads to misery.

"Don't covet."

Exodus 20:17

Recent college graduates tend to look at their raise relative to their peer group. Friends working hourly jobs tend to compare their hourly rate to that of their peers. They don't take into account the industry differences or how their particular company is positioned in the industry to be able to compensate their employees. Nor do they have any objective frame of reference for how they are doing relative to their peers. They just compare and become unhappy.

I remember doing this myself when I went to Physician Services. My predecessor was a doctor. He was a great guy. His skill set was different than mine. Looking back, there were things he could do that would have been impossible for me. But from the time I took the reins, there were administrative and organizational things I did that he couldn't or didn't do. Therefore, I concluded I was better at the job than he was and that I should be paid the same or more. That never happened. I'm embarrassed to admit that this bothered me for quite a period of time. I was very grateful to have the role. But, really, though I was grateful, I should have been more so. I made more than I did in previous roles. I was paid well for my background and experience. I would have been more grateful and happier had I not been making the comparison. We lose a lot of joy when we compare what we have to others and feel shorted.

JEALOUS COMPARISON GAMES

This whole motivation thing seems like it should be simple, doesn't it? We put people in the right spot and help them set productive goals. We think people should be happy, right? We all know it doesn't work that way. And much of that is because of what we've been talking about. People don't get what they expect and feel shorted. If you speak to one employee in the hallway but not others, they feel slighted. If you speak one day but not another, they feel slighted. In the smallest things you do as a leader, it is very easy for people to feel shorted.

I used to be so excited about giving people promotions. I never lost that excitement. But after some experience, I always approached promotions knowing that I would need to deal with the people who did not get promoted and how they felt about it. I always thought it was clear who deserved promotion and, ignorantly, assumed it would be clear to others as well. It never was. There were people I did not even consider for promotion that felt shorted because they weren't promoted. When people got moved from a cubicle to an office, it was the same routine. There were always those who thought they should have had the office.

When I ran the internal audit department, there were certain "plum" assignments. The audits in California were considered the best. People wanted to go to California and were excited when they got assigned. One year, there was a team going to Australia while another team went to California. You've already guessed it, haven't you? The team going to California was not as excited as in the past. They felt shorted because they weren't going to Australia.

Application

What are you doing that has hurt the motivation of your team? List specifics.

_____

_____

_____

_____

_____

_____

How will you correct these?

_____

_____

_____

_____

_____

_____

Image Credits

Image Credits:

Diana Rush–Organizational charts and DISC graphics
Clip art and photos are taken from Microsoft Word stock images, unless otherwise noted below or in the endnotes:

Page 28–Cathedral–Franco Di Meo/DepositPhotos.com/©2014
Page 64–Bridge–Thomas Lammeyer/DepositPhotos.com/©2014
Page 80–Presidents–Wikipedia, the free encyclopedia photos (NARA).
Page 104–Square peg–Santalucia Art, Inc./DepositPhotos.com/©2014
Page 104–Puzzle man–Dan Barbalata/DepositPhotos.com/©2014
Page 116–Astronaut–Lurli/DepositPhotos.com/©2014
Page 155–Checkerboard–Kritchamut Onmang/DepositPhotos.com/©2014
Page 157–Shotgun–Sergiy Palamarchuk/DepositPhotos.com/©2014
Page 282–Kettle–Jose Gelpi Diaz/DepositPhotos.com/©2014
Front Cover—/Crown–Sashkin–BigStockPhoto.com/©2014

ENDNOTES PART 1

Note #	Reference	Text Page
1	Nehemiah, Chapters 1-13	Page xx
2	*Module 7: Organizational Direction, Vision, Mission, Goals, Objectives,* McMonkey-McBean, page 2. Available from http://quizlet.com/11265967/module-7-organizational-direction-vision-mission-goals-objectives-flash-cards	Page xxi
3	*Mapping a Clear Organization Direction,* Triaxia Partners, Inc., page 1. Available from http://triaxiapartners.com/corp/strategy/articles/Mapping-Clear-Org-Figure	Page xxiv
4	Viktor E. Frankl, 1905-1997; Austrian neurologist, psychiatrist, and Holocaust survivor; quote attributed. Available from http://www.goodreads.com/author/quotes/2782.Viktor_E_Frankl	Page 4
5	Charles R. Swindoll, *Living the Psalms* (Brentwood, TN: Worthy Publishing, 2012), page 233.	Page 4
6	Viktor E. Frankl, *Man's Search for Meaning* (Boston: Beacon Press, 1959).	Page 6
7	Rick Warren, *The Purpose Driven Life,* (Grand Rapids, Michigan: Zondervan, 2002).	Page 6
8	Viktor E. Frankl, *Man's Search for Meaning* (Boston: Beacon Press, 1959).	Page 11
9	Rick Warren, *The Purpose Driven Life,* (Grand Rapids, Michigan: Zondervan, 2002).	Page 11
10	Charles R. Swindoll, *Living the Psalms* (Brentwood, TN: Worthy Publishing, 2012), page 26.	Page 12
11	Charles R. Swindoll, *Living the Psalms* (Brentwood, TN: Worthy Publishing, 2012), page 156.	Page 12
12	Charles R. Swindoll, *Living the Psalms* (Brentwood, TN: Worthy Publishing, 2012), pages 233 and 191.	Page 13
13	Charles R. Swindoll, *Living the Psalms* (Brentwood, TN: Worthy Publishing, 2012), page 277.	Page 13

14	Jim Collins, *Good to Great* (New York: HarperCollins, 2001).	Page 14
15	Robert Kiyosaki, *The Key to Hiring Right,* April 30, 2006. Available from Entrepreneur.com. http://www.entrepreneur.com/article/160158#	Page 20
16	*Mapping a Clear Organization Direction,* Triaxia Partners, Inc., page 1. Available from http://triaxiapartners.com/corp/strategy/articles/Mapping-Clear-Org-Figure	Page 20
17	*Mapping a Clear Organization Direction,* Triaxia Partners, Inc., page 1. Available from http://triaxiapartners.com/corp/strategy/articles/Mapping-Clear-Org-Figure	Page 22
18	Google Images, Earlsbusiness.wordpress.com, Part 1 – Strategic Planning Overview.	Page 22
	Google Images, ed.ac.uk, Strategic Plan 2012-2016.	
	Google Images, cognitivedesignsolutions.com, Planning Process.	
	Google Search, *Organizational Planning.*	
	Erica Olsen, *How to Write a Strategic Plan,* page 1.	
19	Erica Olsen, *How to Write a Strategic Plan,* May 11, 2010, page 1. Available from http://mystrategicplan.com/resources/how-to-write-a-strategic-plan	Page 23
20	David Grusenmeyer, *Mission, Vision, Values & Goals,* page 2. Available from https://www.msu.edu/~steind/estate%20Goals%20Mission%20Values%20Overview_ProDairy%2017pg.pdf	Page 23
21	David Grusenmeyer, *Mission, Vision, Values & Goals,* page 2. Available from https://www.msu.edu/~steind/estate%20Goals%20Mission%20Values%20Overview_ProDairy%2017pg.pdf	Page 23
22	Erica Olsen, *How to Write a Strategic Plan,* May 11, 2010, page 1. Available from http://mystrategicplan.com/resources/how-to-write-a-strategic-plan	Page 24
23	*Mapping a Clear Organization Direction,* Triaxia Partners, Inc., page 4. Available from http://triaxiapartners.com/corp/strategy/articles/Mapping-Clear-Org-Figure	Page 24

24	David Grusenmeyer, *Mission, Vision, Values & Goals,* page 2. Available from https://www.msu.edu/~steind/estate%20Goals%20Mission%20Values%20Overview_ProDairy%2017pg.pdf	Page 24
25	David Grusenmeyer, *Mission, Vision, Values & Goals,* page 2. Available from https://www.msu.edu/~steind/estate%20Goals%20Mission%20Values%20Overview_ProDairy%2017pg.pdf	Page 24
26	David Grusenmeyer, *Mission, Vision, Values & Goals,* pages 4 and 5. Available from https://www.msu.edu/~steind/estate%20Goals%20Mission%20Values%20Overview_ProDairy%2017pg.pdf	Page 24
27	*Mapping a Clear Organization Direction,* Triaxia Partners, Inc., page 3. Available from http://triaxiapartners.com/corp/strategy/articles/Mapping-Clear-Org-Figure	Page 24
28	Andy Stanley, *Visioneering* (New York: Doubleday Religious Publishing Group, 2005), page 41.	Page 25
29	Andy Stanley, *Visioneering* (New York: Doubleday Religious Publishing Group, 2005), page 12.	Page 25
30	Andy Stanley, *Visioneering* (New York: Doubleday Religious Publishing Group, 2005), page 25.	Page 25
31	Google Images, Earlsbusiness.wordpress.com, Part 1 – Strategic Planning Overview. Google Images, cognitivedesignsolutions.com, Planning Process *How to Write a Strategic Plan,* Erica Olsen, page 2.	Page 26
32	Greg Coker, *Building Cathedrals – The Power of Purpose* (Chicago Spectrum Press, 2012).	Page 28

33   Google Images, Earlsbusiness.wordpress.com, Part 1 – Strategic Planning Overview.   Page 36

Google Images, ed.ac.uk, Strategic Plan 2012-2016.

Google Images, cognitivedesignsolutions.com, Planning Process.

Google Search, *Organizational Planning.*

Erica Olsen, *How to Write a Strategic Plan,* page 1.

34   Jim Collins, *Good to Great* (New York: HarperCollins, 2001).   Page 45

ENDNOTES Part 2

1   Dan Miller, *No More Dreaded Mondays* (New York: Random House, 2009).   Page 56

2   Dan Miller, *No More Dreaded Mondays* (New York: Random House, 2009).   Page 60

3   Belle Learning System   Page 67

4   From the movie *Cool Hand Luke,* spoken by the prison warden.   Page 75

5   About.com, *Inspirational Quotes for Business: Team Building,* by Susan M. Heathfield, page 1. Available from   Page 90

http://humanresources.about.com/od/inspirationalquotations/a/quotes_team.htm

6   Robert Kiyosaki, *The Key to Hiring Right,* April 30, 2006. Available from Entrepreneur.com. http://www.entrepreneur.com/article/160158#   Page 90

7   Dick Wells, *16 Stones* (Franklin, TN: New Vantage Publishing Partners, 2012).   Page 92

8   Dan Miller, *No More Dreaded Mondays* (New York: Random House, 2009).   Page 95

9   Monster.com, *Management Skills:* How to Deal with Poor Employee Performance?   Page 104

Available from http://hiring.monster.com/hr/hr-best-practices/workforce-management/employee-performance-management/employee-performance-issues.aspx

10   Monster.com, *Management Skills:* How to Deal with Poor Employee Performance?   Page 106

Available from http://hiring.monster.com/hr/hr-best-practices/workforce-management/employee-performance-management/employee-performance-issues.aspx

11   Monster.com, *Management Skills:* How to Deal with Poor Employee Performance?   Page 111

Available from http://hiring.monster.com/hr/hr-best-practices/workforce-management/employee-performance-management/employee-performance-issues.aspx

12   TerminatingEmployees.org, *Terminating Employees with a Professional Attitude,* page 1.   Page 115

NYSSCPA.org, Ten Practical Suggestions for Terminating an Employee, by Chauncey M. DePree, Jr. and Rebecca K. Jude, pages 2 and 3.

Available from http://www.nysscpa.org/cpajournal/2007/807/essentials/p62.htm

13   TerminatingEmployees.org, *Terminating Employees with a Professional Attitude,* page 1.   Page 116

NYSSCPA.org, Ten Practical Suggestions for Terminating an Employee, by Chauncey M. DePree, Jr. and Rebecca K. Jude, pages 2 and 3.

Available from http://www.nysscpa.org/cpajournal/2007/807/essentials/p62.htm

14   Monster.com, *Management Skills: How to Deal with Poor Employee Performance?*   Page 116

Available from http://hiring.monster.com/hr/hr-best-practices/workforce-management/employee-performance-management/employee-performance-issues.aspx

ENDNOTES Part 3

1   Dan Miller, *No More Dreaded Mondays* (New York: Random House, 2009).   Page 144

2   Zig Ziglar and Tom Ziglar, *Born To Win—Find Your Success Code* (Dallas: SUCCESS Media, 2012), page 3.   Page 145

3   Dan Miller, *No More Dreaded Mondays* (New York: Random House, 2009).   Page 151

ENDNOTES Part 4

1.   Smallbusiness.chron.com, *5 Sources of Power in Organizations,* by Paul Merchant, page 1-7.   **Page 168**

Available at http://smallbusiness.chron.com/5-sources-power-organizations-14467.html

2.   Google.com, Positional Power definition, page 1.   **Page 171**

Available from https://www.google.com/#q=positional+power+definition

3.   Jim Collins, *Good to Great* (New York: HarperCollins, 2001).   **Page 172**

4.   Smallbusiness.chron.com, *5 Sources of Power in Organizations,* by Paul Merchant, page 1-7.   **Page 173**

Available at http://smallbusiness.chron.com/5-sources-power-organizations-14467.html

5.   Google.com, Positional Power definition, page 1.   **Page 176**

Available from https://www.google.com/#q=positional+power+definition

6.   Google.com, Positional Power definition, page 1.   **Page 176**

Available from https://www.google.com/#q=positional+power+definition

7.   *Sources of Power,* Article by Dr. Terry Stimson. The article identifies five sources of power—legitimate, coercive, and referent. It breaks power into two broad categories – positional and personal. Available from http://www.consultcli.com/Sourcespower.htm   **Page 176**

8.   Blog.gaiam.com, Quotes by Robert Greenleaf, page 1. Available from   **Page 177**

http://blog.gaiam.com/quotes/authors/robert-greenleaf

9.   Blog.gaiam.com, Quotes by Robert Greenleaf, page 1. Available from   **Page 177**

http://blog.gaiam.com/quotes/authors/robert-greenleaf

10.   *Teacher Expectations and Labeling,* Article by Christine Rubie-Davies. Springer International Handbooks of Education, 2009, Volume 21, page 695-707. Available from http://link.springer.com/chapter/10.1007%2F978-0-387-73317-3_43#page-1   **Page 218**

11   *Teachers' Expectations Can Influence How Students Perform,* article by Alix Spiegel, September 17, 2012. Available from   Page 218

http://www.npr.org/blogs/health/2012/09/18/161159263/teachers-expectations-can-influence-how-students-perform

12   *Teachers' Expectations Can Influence How Students Perform,* article by Alix Spiegel, September 17, 2012. Available from   Page 219

http://www.npr.org/blogs/health/2012/09/18/161159263/teachers-expectations-can-influence-how-students-perform

13   *Teacher Expectations and Labeling,* Article by Christine Rubie-Davies. Springer International Handbooks of Education, 2009, Volume 21, page 695-707. Available from   Page 220
http://link.springer.com/chapter/10.1007%2F978-0-387-73317-3_43#page-1

14   Simplypsychology.org, *Skinner – Operant Conditioning,* by Saul McLeod, page 1. Available from http://www.simplypsychology.org/operant-conditioning.html   Page 222

ENDNOTES Part 5

1   Dan Miller, *No More Dreaded Mondays* (New York: Random House, 2009).   Page 252

2   *Module 7: Organizational Direction, Vision, Mission, Goals, Objectives,* McMonkey-Mc-   Page 265
Bean, page 2. Available from http://quizlet.com/11265967/module-7-organizational-direction-vision-mission-goals-objectives-flash-cards

3   Dick Wells, *16 Stones* (Franklin, TN: New Vantage Publishing Partners, 2012).   Page 278

ENDNOTES Appendix

1   Based on experience with a life coaching client – names changed for confidentiality.   Page 313

2   Google.com, Positional Power definition, page 1.   Page 321

Available at https://www.google.com/#q=positional+power+definition

3   Dan Miller, *No More Dreaded Mondays* (New York: Random House, 2009).   Page 343

4   *The Peter Principle,* available from Wikipedia, The Free Encyclopedia. http://en.wikipedia.org/wiki/Peter_Principle   Page 364

5   *The Peter Principle,* available from Wikipedia, The Free Encyclopedia. http://en.wikipedia.org/wiki/Peter_Principle   Page 364

6   Dan Miller, *No More Dreaded Mondays* (New York: Random House, 2009).   Page 365

7   Dr. Spencer Johnson, *Who Moved My Cheese?* (New York: G. P. Putnam's Sons, 1998).   Page 365

Notes

Notes

Notes

Notes

CPSIA information can be obtained at www.ICGtesting.com
Printed in the USA
LVOW02s1019231214

420084LV00001B/1/P